The Courage to Lead

The Courage to Lead

LEADERSHIP IN THE AFRICAN AMERICAN URBAN CHURCH

James Henry Harris

ROWMAN & LITTLEFIELD PUBLISHERS, INC.
Lanham • Boulder • New York • Oxford

ROWMAN & LITTLEFIELD PUBLISHERS, INC.
Published in the United States of America
by Rowman & Littlefield Publishers, Inc.
4720 Boston Way, Lanham, Maryland 20706
www.romanlittlefield.com

12 Hid's Copse Road
Cumnor Hill, Oxford OX2 9JJ, England

British Library Cataloguing in Publication Information available

Library of Congress Cataloging-in-Publication Data
Harris, James H., 1952-
    The courage to lead : leadership in the African American urban church / James Henry Harris
        p.   cm.
    Includes bibliographical references (p.   ) and index.
    ISBN 0-7425-0213-9 (alk. paper)—ISBN 0-7425-0214-7 (pbk. : alk. paper)
    1. African American churches. 2. City churches. 3. Leadership—Religious aspects—Christianity. I. Title.

BR563.N4 H373 2002
253'.089'96073—dc21   2001041691

To my sons, James Corey Alexander Harris and Cameron Christopher David Harris, who have grown up with my encouragement for them to become leaders.

And to

Deacon Leroy Fowler and Deacon Stanley Lucas who have both been mentors to me.

Contents

Tables

Acknowledgments

This book reflects an enduring interest in the issue of leadership, clergy/laity relations and the urban church, social ethics, and the role of the church in public policy issues. I am thankful to Peter Cooper, editor, for his encouragement to revise and reissue *Black Ministers and Laity in the Urban Church* and to Crossroads Monograph Series on Faith and Public Policy for permission to use a significant portion of what I wrote in a debate with Professor Francis J. Beckwith, *Race-Based Affirmative Action: A Debate*.

I am grateful to many teachers, church members, pastors, graduate students, and friends who have helped to refine over the past few years much of what I postulate in this book. I have also been assisted in this project by the insightful comments of the following people who read all or portions of the manuscript: Charlotte McSwine, Christine Fleming, Faith Harris, Sheron Fields, Marla Hawkins, Tira Justice, Bancroft Greene, and Kenneth Willis. Thanks to the following people who provide research assistance: Gardenia Beard, Reggie Williams, and Amin Flowers.

My family has been most cooperative and understanding, providing consistent support of my forays into the intricacies of church and community life. My wife, Demetrius Dianetta, and sons, James Corey Alexander and Cameron Christopher David, have been my perennial inspiration to write in spite of the tremendous responsibilities and demands of teaching in a growing seminary and pastoring a very complex urban church.

My thanks are extended to those in the African American church who have always had confidence in me as a pastor and leader in spite of my frailties and shortcomings. I recognize in this piece brother Leroy Fowler, a former chairperson of the diaconate at

Mount Pleasant Baptist Church in Norfolk, Virginia. Mr. Fowler and his wife, Shirley, helped me to become a pastor and leader during the early days of my ministry through their strong and decisive personalities and their courage to help lead and guide the church's efforts to transform the community. There were many other members who have accompanied me to city hall to demand sidewalks, streets without potholes, and affordable housing for those in our community. Thanks to the many people who have supported me in my efforts to speak on behalf of those who have historically been omitted and treated with indifference and injustice. For ten years, my family and I lived next door to the church, in a parsonage that would be "too close for comfort" for many; however, this living among the people has had a lasting positive effect on my relationship with the ordinary people who support and sustain the church and the hope that God is watching over His people. The spirit of love and help for the poor was also embedded in the life of sister Dorothy Gardner, who lived a block away on Baltimore Street in the north side of Titustown. Sister Gardner always encouraged me to stand up for the less fortunate—those who needed help with food, shelter, rent, or some other difficulty. Joseph R. Brooks Sr. and his wife, Elizabeth, were like parents to me. They always provided me a place to relax, to watch the game, or to retreat from the stress of everyday life in the church and community. Deacon Aaron L. Braxton and his wife, Sarah Lee, took me under their wings and treated me like a son. Deacon Alonza Faison and his wife, Marcella, along with Deacon Roscoe Hatten and his wife, Linda, were always doing something to show their love and support of ministry. Moreover, brother Thomas Campbell and his wife Elsie were some of the kindest Christians I have ever been privileged to meet. They both taught me a lot about the power and love of God.

Part I

Leadership and Church Administration:
New Models and New Practices

· 1 ·

Leadership Matters
in Church and Society

*Be bold and courageous, when you look back on your life, you'll regret the
things you didn't do more than the ones you did.*
—H. Jackson Brown Jr.

*Negroes do not readily follow persons with constructive programs. Almost
any sort of existing appeal or trivial matter may receive immediate attention
. . . and liberal support. . . . Yet the fault here is not inherently in the Negro
but in what he has been taught.*
—Carter G. Woodson, *The Miseducation of the Negro*

ON BEING A LEADER AND A SERVANT

While the Black church is still the best thing African Americans
have going for them in recent years, a generation of people has
popped up among us who do not have a good foundation in the
religious and cultural moorings of the church. This is also the case
for some ministers and even pastors who have only recently been
called to ministry after serving in other careers. This fact does not
obviate the historical and sociocultural reality that the church is
still the most recursive incubator and facilitating center for the
development of responsible African American leaders. This often
begins in childhood, when time and time again one is called upon
to recite a Bible verse or a poem or participate in an Easter play or
Christmas drama. Unfortunately, so many youth and children
today have not had that experience. Many of our children are
growing up outside of the walls of the church, unexposed to the

values, teachings, training, and experience that helped to shape our leaders in almost every phase and area of life.

There is need for a systematic evangelistic effort to form in the people's consciousness a sense of community and a sense of responsibility for the propagation of cultural experiences that are formed and shaped by the practice of religion. In the church I encourage youth to learn about Langston Hughes, Paul Robeson, Richard Wright, Martin Luther King, Sojourner Truth, and Harriet Tubman. Out of the ranks of the local church have come people who have taught school, healed the sick, and led social revolutions, namely, the giant leader of the Civil Rights Movement, Martin Luther King Jr. In the area of education, laudable contributions from Benjamin Mays, Mordecai Johnson, Mary McLeod Bethune, and John Malcus Ellison still provide benchmarks for progress. A Sunday School teacher or auxiliary leader often encouraged self-esteem and instilled the desire to try some project, skit, or public participation that enabled a child or youth to say, "I really can achieve. I can do that!"

In essence, the local church in small cities and towns, large urban areas, and rural hamlets throughout America has nurtured many who were and are leaders today. The courage to lead was instilled in those who participated in the church—those who attended Sunday School, sang in the choir, or simply showed up for church service. As a child, vacation Bible school was a training ground for me. Later, I served as president of the youth group, youth usher, and worship leader, and I sang in the choir. This was the nurturing force in my own Christian journey toward leadership in the church and community. Moreover, I remember being asked from time to time what I wanted to be when I grew up. My answer was always that I wanted to be a leader. Little did I know what that entailed and the constitutive political elements of leadership. Over the years, I have tried to develop as a leader spiritually, intellectually, and managerially. The most difficult element of leadership is indeed the political component, that is, using diplomacy when dealing with the idiosyncratic personalities that are a part of most organizations. Because men and women are political beings, political ingenuity is an absolute necessity to survival, not to mention success. This means that one must often walk a very thin line in order to avoid the bombshells that fall with random precision along the leader's pathway. Political ingenuity is often more critical than management skills; however, both are needed in order to be a successful leader of a nonprofit organization, church, or some other eleemosynary institution.

The inability of the church to operate fully in the realm of peace and in the power of the Holy Spirit is a baffling reality, a weakness of the will to want to do—to practice—what Jesus requires. Too often, in our local churches we see not only the lack of peace among families but a blatant disregard for the presence of peace . . . a careless disinterest in both peace and the Holy Spirit. We have become too combative and confrontational concerning the church and the work of ministry. Although Jesus' original disciples did not practice or display all the characteristics He desired— they were often motivated by humanistic and egoistic ideals and self-interest—they do constantly remind us of what we should be aware of when placed in leadership roles. For example, Simon Peter loved to talk boldly and assert himself, but when it really counted, he conveniently lost his memory; his boldness bade farewell only to be conquered by fear. From Simon Peter to Judas, James, and John . . . time and time again Jesus had to deal with His disciples' deficiencies as well as the destructive outside influences of the community and other traditional religious leaders. His disciples vis-à-vis Scribes and Pharisees provided an antagonistic backdrop for Jesus' ministry (Mark 2-3:6).

Discord is no stranger to the Christian church and the people of God; if we don't get our way or have our say, we know how to start a ruckus and even manufacture rumors that will threaten the cause. Church folk, like political operatives, know how to plant seeds of trust and distrust that can help or damage both the cause and leader. The rise of violence in the Black community spreads decay. Men, women, and children are at risk of survival; leaders are destroyed by either the tongue or the gun. To be effective leaders in this environment, pastors need to form ministry teams.

MINISTRY TEAMS IN THE LOCAL CONGREGATION: PRACTICING DEMOCRACY AND JUSTICE

The pastor is leader of the ministry team in the modern church. As pastor, one becomes accustomed to working with a team of ministers and laity with specific responsibilities and duties that are linked to the vision and mission given by God and the church congregation to minister to the people of God. Moreover, ministers are compelled to work with laity in developing and clarifying the church's vision and mission. Without the critical input of others, the pastor's vision will be an unfulfilled dream. It is imperative that God's given vision for His people become the people's vision as well. Subsequently, it takes every ounce of ingenuity and continuous prayer to clearly articulate one's dream in a way that people can embrace and modify so that they become a part of the vision and can claim it as their own. The team approach to ministry helps keep all participants focused on the mission of the church inherent in the vision for ministry.

It is difficult—virtually impossible—in most congregational churches to operate unilaterally or, as it is more commonly and incorrectly referred to, in a "dictatorship." This term is often a deliberate and politically motivated exaggeration of the leader's role that is used to coerce and foster opposition and suspicion. Terms like this are used strategically to interpret, and often misinterpret, the leader's actions. However, a few pastors do manage to operate in a very authoritative way, and their behavior has negatively affected the entire profession. Most churches have some type of organizational structure already in place before the pastor assumes the leadership position, and if it is not in place, it will be put in place expeditiously. Additionally, in churches where congregational polity is the practice embedded in a church constitution and by-laws, it is an absolute misnomer and calculated piece of propaganda to refer to the pastor as a dictator. When I think of a dictator, I think of one who operates outside the realm of democracy and egalitarian rules and principles. Such an operation brings about issues of social class, social stratification, oppression, and domination.

As a rule, the church is very democratic in its beliefs and practices, and pastors are eager to conform to its norms and traditions. Most young ministers are often so eager to serve in the position of pastor that they will sacrifice or postpone their leadership ability in order to get the position. This becomes an ethical problem that questions the leader's integrity. It is better to stand for something than to fall for anything. For example, when I became pastor of Mount Pleasant Baptist Church in Norfolk in 1976, I was twenty-three years old, just out of seminary. A woman in the congregation had been called to preach, but the church leaders and the former pastors had refused to license her for fear of angering the highly volatile congregation. The issue was grounded in gender politics and oppression. The all-male diaconate was against licensing her because they felt women preachers were unbiblical. The women in the congregation opposed licensing her because they felt that the place for women was prescribed by the tradition and culture of the community. These women had internalized their own oppression and bought into the unjust and unfair practices or the hegemony of the local church. They expected me as the pastor to use their opposition as a justification for maintaining the status quo. Like so many previous pastors and church leaders, I too was expected to reason that since the women were opposed to her ministry, how would I, a man, justify supporting it? Moreover, the local Baptist Ministers Conference was on record opposing the licensing and ordaining of women, and several of its leaders had warned and threatened that if I proceeded with licensing this woman that I would be isolated and put out of the fellowship. As a new pastor in the city, I was very concerned because I wanted to be an active part of the Ministers Conference, but I also wanted to do what was just, fair, and Christlike. Finally, this issue was brought before the congregation, against the advice of the deacons and trustees, and by a narrow margin, the congregation approved the licensure of its first woman minister in 1977, a year after I arrived as pastor.

There are several leadership issues inherent in this experience. Unfortunately, I think I was called to this historic church because I was naive, young, and inexperienced. The leaders of the church had expected me to do as I was advised, so when I indicated that God was a God to all his people, including women, some people were disappointed that I had taken such a radical and contrary political and theological position.

THE ISSUE OF SOCIAL CLASS WITHIN
LOCAL CHURCHES: THIS IS BUSINESS

Because the local church tends to mirror society, many of the middle- and upper-class members of society participate in church as an extension of their civic duty and social status. It is chic to attend church in order to hob-nob with certain people and form a network of like-mindedness, or to extend into the religious realm that which was formed on the job, in the sorority or fraternity, or in some other place of social significance. These members' involvement is often limited to serving in such leadership capacities as president of organizations or boards (which we prefer to call ministries) that have some economic or financial purpose that can readily and easily be discerned or be contrasted with their perception of the spiritual. For example, in many churches, trustees are thought to be businessmen and businesswomen, people who can manage money and material and who have personal assets that they are willing to share with the church in some kind of a financial or fiduciary need or emergency. In addition, trustees are often viewed as small-business owners or entrepreneurs whose mission is to protect the church from the missions-minded members, deacons, and missionaries. So it is not unusual for members of the trustee ministry to be "business-minded" while completely disinterested in the holistic or "spiritual" life of the congregation. The "spiritual" life of the congregation then becomes the focus of the pastor and diaconate only. The practice of a bifurcated religion and ecclesiology is pandemic in church and society. Unfortunately, it accommodates the lack of holistic approaches to life and ministry.

Class distinction is also rampant within local congregations. A particular local church may be sociologically categorized as a mass church; however, the leaders are often the "talented tenth," to coin a term from W. E. B. Du Bois. The people making decisions and formulating policy are often the middle-class members of this mass-oriented congregation. And members of the lower socioeconomic class often entrust their material resources and their guidance to those who are perceived to have some business sense, that is, the ability to detach oneself from those affected by relying on the Orwellian and often unethical language of business. When detached from Christian principles, a "business decision" reflects the indifference and thorough secular interest that pervades the church's operations. The church needs to encourage the development of each person in the community in order to replace the "talented tenth" with the "informed masses." This means that we can no longer develop a few people, but must seek to develop everyone and create parity, justice, and fairness within the church and community. Some may think this is too idealistic; however, when idealism merges with pragmatism, a new reality can unfold. The language "this is business" is a metaphor that in practice means that "this ain't got nothing to do with God, nothing to do with faith and love!" The "this is business" metaphor is a rationalization of behavior that is completely unbecoming of a practicing Christian. It is Christian dualism and the dichotomization of the self, a prevailing archetype of the local church's constituents.

THE BIFURCATED CHURCH VERSUS
THE HOLISTIC CHURCH

The effort to create a holistic ministry within the local congregation is a gigantic, difficult, and often thankless undertaking because of the pervasive practice of a bifurcated religion within the institutional church. Bifurcated religion is the practice of Christianity based on the belief that the church should be divided into two branches, the spiritual and the financial. The two main metaphors representing this reality are the "business meeting" and the "spiritual" leader. The distinct separation of leader and type of meeting signals that one is not a part of the other but rather an intrusion upon the other. To separate the two is a dangerous, albeit pandemic, practice, especially in traditional Baptist and African Methodist Episcopal/Zion congregations. Until we see the "spiritual" as a holistic driving focus for all church functions, we are in opposition to the purpose for which Jesus Christ established His Church. The church of Jesus Christ, as represented by the local congregation, is one that provides wholeness and wellness for all those who come and willingly partake of His goodness. Subsequently, pastors and lay leaders are ambassadors of healing and servant leaders, not managers of specified departments/accounts.

The language and terminology of "business" used by church leaders are designed to inculcate a dialectical tension that never gets resolved or synthesized. For example, I have witnessed people in churches respond to a plea to help someone in need, or to make an exception to a poorly conceived, unclear, and unjust policy, or to lay aside a budget shortfall and take what the philosopher G. E. Lessing called a "leap of faith." This leap cannot be accomplished by stating what has come to represent the embodiment of dialectic or the paradigm of bifurcation in church and in Christian life: "This is business" or "Pastor, I know what you are saying and I believe in God too, but we can't afford to give, to help, to fund, to subsidize, or to pay another blessed cent to feed the poor, empower the disenfranchised, or clothe the homeless. We don't have the income! The money is not coming in! Our budget is already tilting and teetering toward a deficit!" The "this is business syndrome" that permeates the psyche of the church and manifests itself in the practice of Christianity seems to characterize the ways of church folk, especially those lay leaders who feel that it is their God-given duty to serve as keepers of the treasury or gatekeepers for the traditions and practices of a schizophrenic church.

While this bifurcated notion of Christian practice permeates every fiber of the church, the church meeting is its most glaring embodiment. For example, people who do not attend church (public worship, prayer meetings, Bible study, member training, etc.) with any degree of regularity often attend church meetings religiously and sanctimoniously because, in their view, the church meeting is a time for them to be heard, to express their view about whatever the current issues or concerns may be. While their attendance at these meetings is not always or necessarily negative, it tends to shift away from the dominant attitude and personality presented by the same person on Sunday morning or during midweek prayer meeting or at any other time of public worship and praise. Those who consider themselves gatekeepers of the church's organizational integrity and of what they often call the "business side" of things believe this "hell-raising" to be their duty and responsibility. They have rationalized and compartmentalized their schizophrenic approach to the work of the church's ministry.

The church is victimized by the prevailing societal view that hears syncretistically the term "business" as a contradiction to "leadership" or "administration." Peter Drucker is correct when he suggests that when one says management, the hearer internalizes "business management." The word "business" implies profits and losses in reference to capitalism, commodities, rugged individualism, competition, earnings, prices, and a host of other negative and positive terms and connotations associated with the exchange of capital. I believe that when church people say, "This is business" or make a reference to the "business meeting," the church has already internalized certain schizophrenic meanings of this terminology. It reflects a culture more concerned about profit and loss statements, balance sheets, and income and expenditure statements than ministering to the needs of people on the periphery or at the bottom of the social pecking order. These people are disproportionately Black, poor, and undereducated. These functions mentioned earlier are very important in maintaining accountability, but they are not ultimately important to the life and ministry of the local congregation. Unfortunately, they have been elevated to ultimate status—almost God status—or what Paul Tillich referred to as "ultimate concern," thereby replacing virtuous and holistic practices of justice, forgiveness, mercy, love, and fairness—the true attributes of God. If the church allows herself to be engulfed and strangled by the language and practice of division, the quest toward holistic ministry becomes a long, arduous journey leading us away from the promise land to a place of perdition and peril—a place where the church is a clone and puppet of a commodity-based culture. This issue really gets to the heart and soul of the church and the purpose of ministry in a community that is in dire need of help and internal and external transformation.

This metaphor reflects a lack of compassion and spiritual maturity that is indicative of a "smokestack mentality" and a callous disregard for the Word of God and the people of God. This means that not too long ago, before the Internet and e-commerce, before the shift from a manufacturing economy to an information-based economy, business manufacturers like tobacco companies, paper mills, and chemical factories were not extremely concerned about protecting the environment—the lakes and rivers, trees, birds, and the air that people breathed, not to mention African American citizens and communities. It was not unusual to see thick, dark clouds of carcinogenic smoke bellowing from the tops of manufacturing plants throughout the land. This apathy resulted in incidents such as the kepone disaster that polluted the James River in Virginia during the mid-seventies, the nuclear accident at Three Mile Island, and the many toxic waste dump sites that disproportionately and unethically found permanent and dangerous residence in African American communities throughout the nation and especially in the South. There are countless other examples of multinational corporations that have made and continue to make life-and-death decisions based on a model of greed and apathy that is the general thesis of capitalism and American business enterprise. Certainly there are responsible businesses, but the need to make a profit often obviates the ideal desire to be morally and ethically responsible. My first job after high school was at Brown & Williamson Tobacco factory in Petersburg, Virginia. During the summer of 1970, at the age of eighteen, I felt very blessed to have a job that paid more money than I had ever seen. As a child and youth living in rural poverty, we worked in the tobacco fields from sun up to sun down to make ends meet. So when I landed a job at the "factory," my entire nuclear and extended family was very happy because it meant that I could help my father and mother buy groceries and help to support my other nine siblings. I was excited and felt very independent and honored to help my daddy and mother, whom I loved unconditionally. I worked, saved a little money for college, and gave the remainder to my father. I remember that my job in the factory paid more than I ever remember my father earning by working in pulpwood with his brother and several nephews. He was the saw handler, carrying a heavy-duty, fifty-five–pound chainsaw on his shoulder, usually twelve hours a day, five days a week. Cutting and loading pulpwood was no easy task. Having a job at Brown and Williamson was a lot easier than working in the tobacco field, and it paid a hell of a lot more money.

It is a fact that these businesses helped to feed and provide a living for a host of people, but there was and remains a downside. My summer at the tobacco factory in 1970 was instrumental in feeding us as a family, but it also provided the environment to "get hooked" on cigarettes, which we now know is extremely harmful to one's health. The notion of separating "business" from life is a fallacy, whether in the corporate climate or the church. There is no business decision that affects a part of a person—the whole person is affected. When people in church begin to practice their faith every day rather than only on Sundays, they can put to death the "this is business" syndrome that allows confusion and ugliness to pervade the house of God, where it creates a bifurcated rather than a [w]holistic community of faith.

To achieve a holistic church that maintains a multidisciplinary approach to creating awareness and wholeness, I suggest that the following characteristics be embraced:

- Be on the lookout for untapped resources within congregants and put them to good use.
- Facilitate wellness by promoting activities that enhance self-awareness and self-understanding.
- Provide opportunities for congregants to engage in self-development.
- Provide a nurturing environment where lasting relationships can develop.
- Provide wholesome instruction that encourages responsible thinking and behavior.
- Create an atmosphere of "our church" rather than "the church."
- Embrace the "ministries of the church" rather than "church business" mentality.
- Transform church boards into church ministries and extirpate the use of the word *board* from all written and oral communication.
- Focus on doing the will of God for His people and encouraging unity rather than division or bifurcation.

Careful attention to each of the items will create an environment for harmony. Harmony is good soil for growth. We need to remember that the church has no business creating division and separation; its reason for being is to put in practice the teachings of Jesus, not the teachings of Adam Smith.

THE DIACONATE MINISTRY

The diaconate ministry is one where people are chosen to be servants of God and church and helpers in ministry. The diaconate should consist of men and women who will help the undershepherd or pastor render greater service to God. Service, including teaching, evangelizing, fostering unity, assisting in communion and baptism, prayerful leadership in visitation, and generally advancing the Kingdom of God in church and community, is the primary responsibility of the diaconate. In particular, the Bible teaches us the importance of unity (1 Cor. 3:1–23; Eph. 2:1–22, 4:4–6) and service as we seek to emulate Jesus Christ. We are called to serve, and in the book of Romans, Phoebe is described as a deacon who has been of great benefit to Paul. The text states, "I commend to you our sister Phoebe, a deacon of the church at Cenchrea, so you may welcome her in the Lord as is fitting for the saints . . ." (Rom. 16:1–2).

In a diaconate ministry, a church's deacons and deaconesses merge or unify to function as one ministry devoted to service.

The Relationship between Pastor and Diaconate

As a young seminary graduate nearly twenty-five years ago, I was called to a church in Norfolk, Virginia. At the young and tender age of twenty-three, I was thrust into the pastorate of a church that was well over a hundred years old. In its organizing years, it was led by the Reverend Zachariah Hughes, the great–great-grand-father of another prominent preacher, scholar, and teacher, the venerable Samuel DeWitt Proctor. I was honored and awed to follow in the footsteps of people who grounded the community and the church in an unfaltering faith that still resided in the hearts and minds of people who took seriously their role as servants in the local congregation.

When I first preached at the church as a replacement for a more popular and "in demand" preacher, I had no intention of ever returning, much less serving as pastor. I remember when the chairman of deacons, brother Leroy Fowler, asked me if I was interested in applying for the position of pastor, I quickly and emphatically said, "No." I was convinced that my ministry would be something other than serving as pastor of a local church. At the time, I did not know this would be preparation for a life of service to the church and the academy. When I arrived at the church, the first person I met as my new unofficial teacher was deacon Leroy Fowler. The forty-year-old chairman of the deacons ministry at Mount Pleasant Baptist Church, Deacon Fowler greeted me with eagerness and hope, determined to "turn the church over to me," in his words. This was an exciting time. I was twenty-three years old and brother Fowler was the youngest man on the diaconate ministry, although when I arrived he had already served twenty years as a deacon. I now feel that I have been a pastor virtually all of my adult life; he too had been a deacon since he was about twenty years old. Brother Fowler was very devoted to his family, and he and his wife Shirley were serious Christians committed to practicing Christianity in the church and the community. He showed me various parts of the city where our members lived and the locations of the hospitals, nursing homes, funeral parlors, schools, and jails. Deacon Fowler was affectionately known as "Big Lee" by his family and friends in the church and community. I mention him because he nurtured me, advised me, and cautioned and protected me from those who were less caring, less generous, and less interested in the practice of Christianity, although they too were very much a part of the church. I do not want anyone to think, naively so, that brother Fowler and I were always in agreement and that he "was in my pocket" or "one of my boys," to coin some popular phrases so often used to characterize those who vehemently support the pastor's leadership and the church's vision. We often debated and argued lovingly over issues regarding a ministry program and the future of the church; however, brother Fowler had a deep love for ministry and service to God and the community. This brotherly relationship between us was quite commendable and worthy of capturing and emulation by other laypeople in the church.

A pastor's leadership needs to be compassionate, understanding, empathetic, and decisive, but never condescending, vacillating, or waffling. The pastor or the leader of a profit or nonprofit organization must generate and command respect, which is much more important to long-term organization development than the desire to be liked or the desire to control or manipulate people, organizations, or institutions. While leaders crave acceptance and popularity, they must be respected for their ability to envision and plan strategically with others a future for the organization.

MANAGING CONFLICT IN THE CHURCH

Conflict exists where two or more persons disagree. In situations where power is shared, where individuals differ about what actions and behaviors should be taken, and where these differences are of some consequence, the decision-making process often leads to conflict. It does not have to be earth-shattering or serious. In the church, we should be willing to reason together, but there are cases where sound reason fails. The Scriptures indicate that Jesus Christ should be the standard.

Only let your manner of life be worthy of the gospel of Christ, so that whether I come to you or am absent, I may hear of you that you stand firm in one spirit, with one mind striving side by side for the faith of the gospel and not frightened in anything by your opponents. . . . For it has been granted to you that for the sake of Christ you should not only believe in Him but also suffer for His sake, engaged in the same conflict which you saw and now hear to be mine. (Phil. 1:27 ff.)

Because the African American church generally holds the authority of Scripture be above all other authority, the Bible should be the source for resolving conflict in the church. Whenever possible, using Jesus as the model will generally bring about a solution. However, churches often refuse to consult Scripture during heated and difficult conflicts (perhaps because, as people have suggested, and I agree, Jesus is quite unpopular in the church). Caught up in the psychology of the crowd, people become irrational and fail to be guided by the power of reason and the Holy Spirit.

A considerable number of people in the church are not properly discipled. They have not experienced Christ's redemption or been transformed, neither have they been taught the ways of Christ or their responsibilities as Christian leaders in the local congregation. This lack of understanding may lead to conflict. Conflict, however, always has the potential to lead to greater understanding rather than destruction of individuals. To minimize conflict, the church needs to understand the following concepts and practices:

1. The pastor is the chief administrative officer and leader of the congregation, i.e., the "overseer" according to 1 Tim. 3:1–7.
2. The deacons and trustees are not the pastor's boss but his or her helpers, more like his or her assistants who will help encourage and pray for the leader.
3. If the pastor is going to be blamed and/or credited for the church's failure or success as an institution, then he or she must be allowed to lead. However, conflict is inherent to leadership. The pastor's task is to do the will of God and be scripturally sound in his or her efforts. This may not resolve the conflict but will enable the pastor to teach and lead according to the Scriptures, which is the source of authority.
4. Conflict often leads to a greater understanding and appreciation of each other. Unfortunately, it can also lead to bitterness and retributive acts of hate and evil. When the people of God challenge each

other openly and honestly with the intent and hope of doing God's will, conflict among individuals and organizations can be a means of growth and development. Nevertheless, I think that because "trustees" have been given board status without any scriptural foundations for their existence, the churches have secularized their function and given them unbridled power. I believe this is another unnecessary, yet serious, source of conflict in the church.

There is no need for churches to have any boards because the implications of the "board" language presuppose power over some person, group, or organization. In the local church everyone should have equal status; the power comes from below and not from one person or group. This is a true democracy where God rules with justice and mercy. True democracy in the church is theocratically centered in the authority grounded in the will of God. Unfortunately, the church practices a very limited and elitist democracy in which certain individuals or groups tend to control the operations of the entire system, much like American corporations, many of which need serious transformation.

LACK OF RESPECT FOR LEADERSHIP AS THE RESIDUAL AFFECT OF SLAVERY

The African American was enslaved in America for nearly 350 years. During this time, the White slave master systematically taught all of the slaves that they did not ever have to listen to another slave, meaning that no slave was capable of leading another since they all were the property of the owner, the master. This propaganda worked so well that it can still be seen and felt in the twenty-first century. Carter G. Woodson, in his book, *The Miseducation of the Negro*, explains this phenomenon with absolute clarity. He writes,

This refusal of Negroes to take orders from one another is due largely to the fact that slaveholders taught their bondsmen that they were as good as or better than any others and, therefore, should not be subjected to any member of their race. If they were to be subordinated to someone, it should be to the white man of superior culture and social position. This keeps the whole race on a lower level, restricted to the atmosphere of trifles, which do not concern them.

The greater things of life, which can be attained only by wise leadership, then, they have no way to accomplish.[1]

I often lament the growing disrespect for leadership in church and society. In some churches the pastor is expected to play mainly a ceremonial and ornamental role, although a desire may be expressed for something different. People often want leaders whom they can shape and mold rather than leaders who are capable of carving and reshaping the personalities and priorities of those in the church. The pastor as leader probably experiences the greatest level of second-guessing, suspicion, jealousy, and envy because of the job's high visibility. This lack of respect is really a dislike of self. For example, I have heard church folk say, for no apparent reason, that they would not support other African Americans. I remember hearing a lady in church say that she would not patronize a Black doctor when her own Black son was in medical school. This lack of respect for self manifests itself as lack of respect for other African American leaders, particularly church leaders.

THE CHURCH AS A COMPLEX, SOCIAL, AND POLITICAL ORGANIZATION

Every human being is a social and political entity because personalities and behaviors are involved. Politics suffuses every relationship in church and society. For example, in the church, there are people from different and varied families, geographical areas, educational and socioeconomic backgrounds, and likes and dislikes that are shaped by positive and negative experiences. All of these people have come together within the local congregation to form a faith community. However, their understanding of the meaning and practice of faith may be as different as the east is from the west. Even when a church in the African American community is socioeconomically homogeneous, it is still a complex organization. In fact, these organizations often have a very prescribed function and expectation for the leader. For example, the pastor may be expected to be very priestly by praying for and visiting the sick, preaching, administering communion, and counseling members. Providing leadership in other areas such as policy development, budgeting, and personnel management is not as easily welcomed by the pastor, although it may be expressly expected by the laity.

BLACK AND WHITE CHURCHES WORKING TOGETHER FOR SERIOUS SOCIAL CHANGE

The history of Blacks and Whites in America is grounded in conflict and opposition. Because domination and resistance have historically characterized the relationship, two views of humanity have resulted: one characterized by Arthur Jensen as genetic inferiority, and the other insisting on the correctness of a basic biblical anthropology—that we are all created equal in the image of God. The dilemma, however, is further exacerbated by the fact that on the one hand, Blacks want intuitively and moralistically to be loyal to the United States Constitution, which is laden with language of equality and justice. On the other hand, in the practice of law and in the experience of African Americans, the law is another form of institutionalized racism and, like other institutions, functions in opposition to Blacks. So as W. E. B. Du Bois in *The Souls of Black Folk*, or Peter Paris in *The Social Teachings of the Black Churches*, or Cornel West in *Race Matters* and *Keeping Faith* suggest, there is still a "double consciousness" on the part of Black Americans that is reflected in church and the larger society.

Because the White churches often mirrored society in their silence on racial justice and in their practice of racial inequality, the independent Black church movement began. The disassociation of Blacks and Whites in churches is directly related to ecclesiastical authorities' refusal to treat Blacks equally. Nevertheless, Black churches and White churches have worked together and continue to do so on many issues.

In order for social change to take place, however, these churches must become associated again and unite in the cause of justice. Some basic actions can be taken:

1. Whites need to read religious literature written by Black scholars in order to develop a more rounded perspective of the Christian life.
2. Churches and pastors are compelled to develop relationships in communities where honest and sometimes difficult debates on issues of race must be held.
3. Joint worship services, perhaps exchanging services, etc., need to be held.

THE NEW ADMINISTRATION: NO MORE "BOARDS"

If the ministry is to have a new focus in the new millennium, we need to begin developing a new language that extirpates from the vocabulary of the church the term *boards* and replaces it with the terms *ministry* and *service*. There is something about being called "board members" in the church that is unbiblical, unhealthy, and inconsistent with the church's preoccupation with democratic and egalitarian principles. On the one hand, the church wants to guarantee that the pastor operates democratically, and yet wants to retain a board mentality that puts a chosen few above the masses of people. This is a reflection of the embedded and perennial influence of the "this is business" mentality that has permeated and separated the church into boards, that is, managers on the one hand and congregants or layfollowers on the other. This mentality is so pervasive and entrenched that it will take much prayer to be eradicated from the vocabulary and practices of church folk.

To make the church a reflection of the mind of Jesus Christ, we must establish in a Christian manner the importance of order and discipline in church and good up-to-date administrative practices. We have to meet the needs of the whole person, and all leaders must be accountable in their practice of Christian faith. The church is called to be Christian at all times and in whatever situations and places people find themselves, not just on Sunday mornings, but every day of the week. As people work together toward the goals of *church unity* and *spiritual renewal*, they must resolve to be guided by the spirit of Jesus Christ, a spirit of love and peace.

The church should form a commission to promote church unity and to maximize efficient operations and practices through centralized management of the church's resources. This organizational structure will enable the church to fulfill its mission as a community or family of faith.

The commission's goals are:

- To examine the church's current administrative status and recommend in detail how to maximize efficiency and accountability.
- To evaluate the current financial systems in order to develop a unified and centralized system of management and financial accountability.
- To develop a detailed flowchart indicating lines of authority within the church's structure.
- To examine and recommend a policy of stewardship for all members that can be ratified and adopted by the congregation.
- To promote unity and show that no organization, individual, group, or auxiliary operates autonomously and apart from the congregation.

Developing an Organization Structure

Churches want a written constitution, by-laws, and/or administrative procedures. Working together, independently of the current
structure, clergy and laity can develop these tools. The following is
an administrative guide for churches to begin the process of
accountability and administrative efficiency.

Membership in Local Congregations

Complete annual registration to update church records. If a person
does not register, he or should be expunged from the records. No
more "once a member, always a member!"

Multistaff Development

- A Minister of Music, reporting directly to the pastor, should be
  completely responsible for the music of the church.
- A financial secretary will handle the financial reporting and
  record-keeping that concern the church and its membership. The
  financial secretary reports directly to the administrative assistant.
- Establish a volunteer program that provides computer training,
  public relations, and Christian principles to those who will assist
  the church staff for tasks outside of the norm.
- Develop a specific and precise job description for all church positions.
- The pastor shall preside at all staff meetings, joint ministry meetings, and church meetings. The pastor should have veto power.
- An administrative assistant will be completely responsible for the
  pastor's and church's administrative needs. This individual
  should report directly to the church business administrator.
- A church business administrator, who reports directly to the pastor,
  will be responsible for the financial management of the church's
  income, receipts, disbursements, and other resources.

Leadership, Rotation, and Responsibility

- Membership to the diaconate (deacons, deaconesses), Trustee
  Ministry, and Finance Ministry is by recommendation of the pastor. The congregation, in a church meeting or some other forum,
  must approve membership. Recommendation of changes in
  membership in cases of breach of confidentiality, nonparticipation, or noncooperation that caused division among ministry
  participants and/or the pastor will be made to the congregation
  when necessary.

- New deacons, deaconesses, and trustees are to serve for a prescribed term, such as one to two years. Afterwards, they are rotated off the diaconate for one year in order to be eligible to serve again. Reinstatement is not automatic and will depend on faithful adherence to the mission and goals of the church.
- Young people and women who are not wives of deacons should constantly become a part of the diaconate. Recruit junior deacons under eighteen and provide appropriate training for diaconate members during each meeting. Limit meetings to one hour and devote half the time to training and Bible study and the other half to discussing service-related needs of the congregation.
- Leaders of the deacons, trustees, and committees 1) should be appointed by the pastor, 2) should be trained by the pastor, 3) should be chosen based on spiritual maturity, 4) should be queried about his/her development as a potential leader, 5) should open traditionally male-dominated ministries to women, 6) should attend training workshops and seminars, 7) should be honest and committed to stewardship goals, 8) should address parliamentary procedures for conducting group meetings, 9) should possess compassionate leadership ability, understanding, caring, and a serious attitude, and 10) should hold office for a limited one-year term with the possibility for a one-year reelection. Afterwards, the chairperson must rotate out of the position for at least one year to allow others to serve.
- The pastor, in consultation with the chairperson of the Diaconate Ministry, shall be responsible for staff hiring, supervision, evaluation, and termination.
- Establish a Pastor's Advisory Council consisting of the chairpeople of the deacons, trustees, ushers, Ladies' Fellowship, Men's Fellowship, Youth Fellowship, Missionary Society, Christian education, and treasurer. The Joint Ministries shall be called together at the discretion of the pastor.

Other Organizations, Committees, and Auxiliaries

Groups in the church should follow these guidelines to ensure diversity:

- Should elect officers to serve for one year, with no one serving more than two consecutive years as president or chairperson. Rotation is key to growth and transformation in the local church.
- Should be trained continuously by the pastor, who is called to teach the congregation.

- Must elect qualified leaders, such as those born-again, spirit-filled individuals who are committed to love, unity, and peace.
- Should attend training workshops/seminars annually and focus on their purpose and meaning in the life of the congregation.
- Should hold office for a one-year term with the possibility for an additional one-year reelection. Afterwards, the chairperson/president must rotate out of the position for at least one year.
- Overlapping groups should be combined. Other leaders (Board of Christian Education, Sunday School superintendent, treasurer, church clerk) will be appointed by the pastor. 1) The church clerk is a volunteer position responsible for recording, processing, and maintaining records of all church meeting transactions. The clerk is also responsible for all church membership records and communications. The church clerk works closely with the pastor and the administrative assistant.
- Should hold office for the same period as the organization/committee chairperson/presidents.
- Should be trained by the pastor.

CHURCH FINANCES

Stewardship and Tithes

- The pastor of the church, in conjunction with the Minister of Christian Education/Stewardship, must educate the congregation on the meaning, purpose, and practice of stewardship and tithing. Most folk, especially the middle class, don't resist giving time and talents to the Lord, but are more hesitant to give money.
- Programs should be developed to encourage individual tithing in order to phase out group fund-raisers.
- Special churchwide projects should be developed to support various church stewardship goals: 1) mortgage note-burning, 2) giving commensurate with years of membership, 3) sacrificial offerings, and 4) pledges.
- Establish a Stewardship Committee.

Annual Pledges and Regular Offerings

- Membership should make an initial annual pledge, for regular offering, and make a concerted effort to fulfill this obligation.
- Weekly offering envelopes should be designed for better record-keeping. The church envelope should be available to nonmembers and should include one basic category, Tithes and Offerings. Print

other types of envelopes to provide giving opportunities in special categories.

- Purchase computers to facilitate record-keeping.
- To encourage giving, send each member quarterly statements that give the status of member's giving. A letter of thanks and encouragement from the pastor should accompany the statement.

Policy

- Have groups submit annual budgets based on program planning consistent with the mission of the church.
- The annual church budget should be available for each member to see the church's proposed programs and the finances needed to obtain the goal(s).
- The budget should reflect the church's faith and as a rule should increase annually. Ministries should be expanding, not decreasing.

Mission and Church Budget Philosophy: Good Stewardship

The church is a nonprofit religious organization that is at its best when members and officers function in a supportive role to each other and to the pastor, who is the undershepherd and the leader. When the pastor's vision is allowed to flourish and take root in the congregation, the church benefits. The Finance Ministry, like all other church groups and auxiliaries, endeavors to embrace the church's mission as integral to its practice of Christianity. Therefore, every local church needs a mission statement that is clear and concise. For example, the following mission statement reflects the vision of the church:

> The mission of the church is to worship God through Jesus Christ and spread the gospel within our church and community. Moreover, it is to enhance spirituality and faith development through biblical preaching and teaching. We will also seek to embrace, encourage, and equip all who desire to be Christlike by providing *spiritual training, Christian nurturing,* and the environment to transform ourselves and the world.

The budget and the mission are very interrelated such that the church's mission determines its budgetary priorities. The ultimate responsibility for raising the income to meet the budget rests with the tithing membership; however, the membership has entrusted the pastor, as leader, with ensuring that the budget is met and managing the budget with the advice of the trustees and other church leaders, such as the diaconate, internal auditor, and church administrator.

The Finance Ministry is usually a subcommittee of the Trustee Ministry and serves as an advisory group to the pastor. Accordingly, the Finance Ministry generally advises the pastor and other group leaders about the stewardship needs and helps in any way possible to ensure the success of meeting the demands of the budget. This means that they practice and support tithing, offerings, and other agreed-upon methods of making sure the church members fulfill their responsibility as Christians. The Finance Ministry understands that God has blessed them with wisdom and faith and they are to share these gifts with others.

CLERGY AND STAFF COMPENSATION

As a rule, pastors are to be compensated according to their education, experience, and the size and level of stewardship/giving of the congregation. Personnel costs are the major portion of the budget because a church's mission and purpose are directly related to ministry, and professionals need to be compensated adequately. This means in practice that 25 to 30 percent of the budget can be allocated for the pastor's compensation package. This should include but not be limited to base salary, housing allowance, and insurance for major medical, retirement, and death benefit. Other reimbursable expenses include auto allowance or mileage and education, such as workshops, seminars, conventions, social security taxes, and so on.

In addition to the pastor, churches often have other staff members, such as an administrative assistant, youth minister, minister of music, and minister of Christian education. In cases where there is a multistaff, total personnel costs may fall within the range of 50 percent or more of the total budget. It is important to remember that personnel costs and effective ministry are highly correlated.

Finally, pastors are encouraged to seek the advice of an accountant to determine the best way to report income to the Internal Revenue Service. The use of a payroll service responsible for deducting taxes, forwarding taxes to the government, and issuing annual W-2 and 1099 statements can be very cost-effective and can ensure the necessary compliance to the changing rules regarding churches and clergy and their accountability to the Internal Revenue Service.

Investment Teams

Every congregation will be best served by establishing a team of people interested in the financial success and viability of the local congregation. The team should consist of five to seven people who are market-savvy and very well versed in the economy and money management as it relates to service and church. The pastor should look out in the congregation and select a diverse group to constitute the investment team. More than just being strong and dedicated practitioners of stewardship and tithing, these people have to be committed to doing research and analysis. This will help the congregation trust them in the risky enterprise of equity and bond investments. They should be of high moral character and not invest in things that are oppressive and destructive to the environment.

The congregation should agree that it will commit a minimum of 10 percent of its budget to investments other than bank savings accounts. This means investing in individual stocks, stock mutual funds, bonds, land, REITS, etc. This requires faith and the understanding that there is a possibility of losing money, although every precaution will be made to invest wisely.

Church Treasurer Responsibilities

- Promotes good stewardship through the biblical approach to giving, i.e., tithing, offerings, etc.
- Provides assistance to the pastor in the care of the poor, the sick, the distressed.
- Promotes honesty, peace, unity, and purity within the church.
- Promotes brotherhood, fellowship, and loyalty among members of the congregation.
- Explores new areas for Christian service and support.
- Participates regularly in the worship experience of this congregation.
- Maintains financial records of the congregation.
- Receives and disburses all funds.
- Reports on financial activities in appropriate church meetings when called upon.
- Performs risk assessments of internal controls to minimize risk of loss. This is done in conjunction with the Internal Auditing Committee.
- Monitors financial structure and activity.
- Examines supporting documentation of all disbursements and ascertains proper authorization.

- Examines financial statements and monitors deviations in budget amounts compared to actual expenditures.
- Assures funds/cash availability for all signed checks.
- Maintains updated list of all cash handlers for fidelity bond purposes.
- Assists the pastor and/or church administrator in any other ways as requested.

WORSHIP AND CHRISTIAN EDUCATION

There is a continuous need to examine the church's educational needs and responsibility to strengthen the church's community outreach ministry. The staff or a special group should annually assess and evaluate such areas as the Sunday School, public worship, future educational needs and plans, and various areas of ministry as they relate to children, youth, adults (singles, married couples, intergenerational groups), and special people of all ages. The aim of the evaluating group will be to develop people's faith through study, prayer, and other activities and programs. The following mission statement can be used as a guideline:

> The Church's mission is "to respond in faith and obedience," "enter into dialogue with the world," "serve as an instrument of God's gracious activity of reconciling man to God, man to himself, and men to one another," "permeate social structures of the community and world in response to God's redemptive work," and "nurture persons toward maturity in Christ."

The initial task of this evaluating group is to plan a curriculum for the entire ministry. Curriculum in this sense means the overall plan or blueprint of the church. It incorporates and reflects the church's mission statement. Often, plans for worship and educational ministries fail because they are drawn up without a unified goal and are indicative of our bifurcated thinking about ministry planning and program. As stated, curriculum development is done with all ministries in mind. It is far-reaching, it requires vision, and it must be inclusive.

Curriculum and curriculum resources are often used interchangeably in the church, but *curriculum* is the overarching plan and *curriculum resources* are tools used to execute the plan.

Literature, videos, audio materials, artistic materials, and inter-active or experiential learning experiences constitute curriculum resources.

Once the curriculum is developed, individual ministries in turn develop mission statements reflecting the church's mission state-ment. The ministry then operates in accordance with the overarch-ing plan and with its calling to do ministry.

MISSIONS AND SOCIAL CONCERNS

As Christians, we are to tell people about Jesus Christ and His Gospel in order to bring the unsaved to Him. Implicit in speaking the words of the Gospel to the world is the simultaneous responsibility of living the Gospel in relation to fellow Christians and the unsaved. The church is called to demonstrate Christian love. The Word is not being carried exclusively by missions in underdeveloped countries on the other side of the world; the Word is carried when we help someone right in your neighborhood and local community.

The church should perform acts of compassion demonstrating its desire to help others through 1) assistance and service to the membership, 2) assistance to other Christians who are not mem-bers of the church, 3) evangelism, and 4) meeting needs of the unsaved. These activities have been accomplished with the con-scious effort and support of the entire congregation. This can require moderate church financial support of the entire congrega-tion. In fact, a few individuals or groups trying to work within their own resources have accomplished this with moderate church financial support and with limited participation. To accomplish more than a token gesture of assistance requires con-sistent, committed, coordinated workers and financing. This requires the untiring support of the entire congregation through giving of the tithes and offerings and time and talents. All mem-bers of the church are encouraged to get involved in a ministry that seeks to help others within and outside the congregation.

The church should allocate a minimum of 10 percent of its budget for missions and outreach programs. Tithing should be practiced by church organizations as well as individuals.

Basic help programs such as food and clothing programs, coun-seling referrals, and visitations need people and money to be suc-cessful. The following structure provides an organizational nucleus for programs that depend upon volunteer effort.

CHURCH MISSIONARY SOCIETY

Missionary circles can function more effectively with focus, structure, and funding from the church. They can be the nucleus for the church's local mission and outreach programs. The Missionary Society should be combined with other church organizations such as the ushers, choirs, etc., and be given responsibility for specific programs such as the food and clothing programs of the local congregation.

This structure would focus the Missionary Society on a local help ministry, which would be encouraged to support church outreach instead of expending time and effort to raise money for these programs. The Missionary Society should organize additional volunteer support from the general congregation to support the church's help ministry. The direction and focus would come from a coordinating group under the direction of the pastor and/or a designated representative.

The objective of outreach ministries is to provide support for existing services and programs and provide additional services to help close gaps in the social safety net. The programs should be designed to take care of the church's own members and immediate neighborhood. These programs could be expanded in focus as resources increase.

Food and Clothing Provision

Each local congregation needs to develop a ministry to feed and clothe the poor, disenfranchised members of the community. This ministry should provide food for the poor, sick, needy, and children, without charge. It should also provide clothing without fee to those in need. This type of program can be staffed by church volunteers. For example, the ministry could consist of a hot food service, a food pantry, and a food service for those who are shut in. Hot food service and clothing disbursement should operate simultaneously (on the same day and during the same working hours) in order to assist a maximum number of needy people. Initial operation should be one day a week, such as Wednesday, Friday, or Saturday. Food is obtained primarily from food banks and donations, but purchases should supplement donations. Volunteers are needed as servers, set-up and clean-up crews, and food preparation teams.

The clothing distributions require volunteers to screen and sort clothing as well as distribute it. A secure place in the church is needed to store and distribute clothing.

The Food Share Program is designed to assist families, as opposed to individuals. With a Food Share Program, the church gets food and distributes it freely in exchange for community service by recipients.

CONCLUSION

Being a church leader requires diplomacy in dealing with the myriad personalities that exist in a church population. This requires a straight-and-narrow walk among congregants that earns the pastor the needed trust of congregants to lead. Often one's survival as a church leader requires the institution of ministry teams. Ministerial teams enable a congregation to embrace the vision for the church by training the laity in specific responsibilities and duties linked to the mission and vision.

A major concern of the pastoral leader is creating holistic ministries in the presence of a bifurcated church. Many of the problems in the church stem from the dominance of a bifurcated approach to church life and structure. In the bifurcated church, the spiritual is separate from the financial. This endemic practice is paralyzing and destructive to the mission and outreach of the church. In this type of setting, funding for outreach and missions is allocated by a group or committee that doesn't even profess to care about such ministries. There is destruction on both fronts: the group/committee is not aware of or concerned with the mission/outreach required of the church, and those in need are without appropriate help. As a result of such a dilemma, the pastor is compelled to show courage and lead the congregation to new and better ways of practicing ministry in the church and the world.

STEWARDSHIP AND LEADERSHIP

This word stewardship and the essence of its meaning are quite foreign to the practices of the church particularly when it is used as a metaphor for being responsible to God. *Oikononia*, i.e., stewardship, is used by Paul to define his commission as a preacher of the Gospel, a steward of the Gospel, a steward of the grace of God, and a steward of the mysteries of God (Eph. 1:9–10).

Stewardship is being responsible for that which has been entrusted to you. I'd like to focus on two areas of what I'm calling "Pastoral Stewardship," or stewardship and theology, as it relates to preaching.

First, let's look at stewardship of the Word or stewardship of the gospel message. This means that responsible handling of the message, from text to practice is incumbent upon the pastor. The pastor then is compelled to interpret the Word, not only as a reflection of his or her experience but as a reflection of the will of God. Jesus' utmost concern was doing the will of God. The biblical text then becomes the launching pad for our preaching and teaching, our ministry, our practice of Christianity. Too often this is exactly what the church does not want to hear, i.e., the gospel in its bold, rancorous, undistorted, and uncompromising word and practice. Unlike Walter Brueggeman, who suggests in *Finally Comes the Poet* that the community gathers more often to be shaped by the text, I believe that it gathers to be soothed and sanctioned by the text, certainly not challenged and/or confronted. However, pastoral stewardship requires just that. A word that is challenging and confronting is the paradigm of the message of Jesus: "I have not come to bring, peace, but the sword" (Matt 10:34). You have heard it said of old, but I say unto you. . . .

In my book *Pastoral Theology*, I indicate that:

> The preacher is compelled to say something that addresses the needs of the people, directing the message to their hearts and heads . . . They need to hear a word of power and spirit, a word of liberation. Liberation then is a precondition to transformation. This means that before one can actually change his or her life, she or he needs to be free to do so. The process of transformation begins with a new understanding of consciousness, which requires a mental and spiritual transformation.

In order for an individual or society to be liberated and ultimately transformed, that individual or group needs to first understand that liberation means that his or her thoughts and actions are not simply a reflection of the thoughts of others, but rather the ability to think and do for oneself. Our beliefs and practices are shaped too often by television and technology, popular culture and popular religion, rather than a deep sense of moral responsibility and biblical reflection. While liberation is a *sine qua non* to transformation, transformation itself requires a new consciousness and a new mentality. This means that our total awareness and the ability to interpret that awareness must be reflected in our preaching, teaching, leadership, etc. Moreover, too many of those to whom we preach seem to feel a sense of detachment and obliviousness to the gospel—a feeling that "This doesn't apply to me, I am comfortably situated in my own private world." There is a need for a transformation of consciousness on the part of the preacher and the hearer of the gospel. And, as a steward, the pastor must lift up the gospel message, the Good News of Jesus, as the normative method for bringing about community.

Finally, the pastor has been entrusted with a congregation of people, and he or she must take this seriously. These are not people who can be fed anything and treated any old kind of way. They cannot simply be left without teaching, guidance, and nurturing. Moreover, the pastor is called to be leader, and will be held accountable for the growth and development of those whom he or she has been called to lead. Sometimes this will mean confronting personalities, prejudices, practices, and other actions and beliefs of your own congregation. But God has not called us in order that we may reflect the status quo, but that we may reflect the spirit of Jesus Christ. This may require a new boldness and a new sense of responsibility in preaching, teaching, and leading.

· 2 ·

A Philosophy and Theology of Courage and Leadership

Often the test of courage is not to die but to live.
—Vittorio Alfieri, *Orestes*

A man of courage is also full of faith.
—Cicero

The strangest, most generous, and proudest of all virtues is true courage.
—Montaigne

Courage is what it takes to stand up and speak; courage is also what it takes to sit down and listen.
—Anonymous

Without courage, all other virtues lose their meaning.
—Winston Churchill, Herald of Holiness

THE ELECTED/CHOSEN AND REJECTED LEADER IN THE AFRICAN AMERICAN CHURCH TRADITION

Karl Barth argues in *Church Dogmatics, The Doctrine of God*, Vol. 2, that Jesus is the archetype of the elected and rejected man. As the incarnation of God, He is elected, but as sinful man, He is the rejected. In many ways every human being is both elected and rejected; however, I postulate that the leader, pastor, or preacher in the African American community and church best represents this dialectic archetype. However, the preacher or pastor is by no means the only representative of this duality. The "leader" archetype in the history of African American culture may best reflect this reality and this is also represented by people from Scripture and cultural history such as Sojourner Truth and Harriet Tubman.

It is not unusual for the pastor to understand himself or herself as being chosen (or elected by God) to be a preacher in the African American church. This chosenness often leads the leader to mount the pulpit with the assurance that God has given him a message to share with the congregation. This often manifests itself in the preacher uttering before the sermon a prophetic prelude, such as "God has told me to tell you today." The African American preacher has internalized the call to preach as a call to be the voice of God in the church and world. Nevertheless, this elected or chosen one is also the rejected one, just as Jesus has also been both elected and rejected in his humanity. Karl Barth says, concerning "the election of the individual" that

> The man who is isolated over against God is as such rejected by God. But to be this man can only be by the godless man's own choice. The witness of the community of God to every individual man consists in this: that this choice of the godless man is void; that he belongs eternally to Jesus Christ and therefore is not rejected, but elected by God is Jesus Christ; that the rejection which he deserves on account of his perverse choice is borne and cancelled by Jesus Christ. The promise of his election determines that as a member of the community he himself shall be a bearer of its witness to the whole world.[2]

Barth's language, "bearer of its witness to the whole world," suggests proclamation, proclaimer, or preacher, which is also what Jesus embodied and practiced. Jesus was both the object and embodiment of the gospel message. Preaching the gospel is perceived as an awesome, that is, woeful assignment. Thus Paul says, "Woe is me, if I preach not the gospel." Yet people often run or seek to escape from this call or chosenness to preach until there is no longer a place to hide.

I am sure that Barth's discourses had no particular or intended relevance to the African American preacher or to the Black church because the "language of election" seems to be a European–Western philosophical and theological preoccupation. Nevertheless, I am construing election to be tautologous to chosenness or "call-ing" in the tradition of African American Christianity, which is in fact very Jewish. What I mean is that in the practice of the African American church, I have seldom if ever heard any discussion of election per se, but there is a predominant identification with Old Testament characters such as Moses, Abraham, Isaac, and Jacob in relation to Joseph, Job, Jeremiah, Isaiah, and Amos. The African American preacher identifies more readily with the "people of Israel" and their story as found in the Pentateuch and the prophet's verses—a skeptical and more dogmatic approach to the-ology as seen in the Pauline writings. To be elected is to be marked for persecution, or at least lack favor before God and man.

Barth indicates that Jesus Christ is both the elected one and the rejected one. He states, "because this one is the *Elect and the Rejected*, He is—attested by both—the Lord and head of both of the Elect and also of the Rejected."[3] However, he makes a distinction between the elect and the rejected, calling the elect "believers" and the rejected "godless" while simultaneously affirming that the elect and the rejected are two elements of the same person. He states: "That which separates one from the other, and connects them both is properly and primarily realized and revealed, not in two peoples, but where the elect and the rejected face one another in one and the same person—against one another, yet also for one another."[4] Indeed, the African American preacher/pastor is the embodiment of the elected and rejected. He is indeed called to lead, preach, and teach, and yet he is often rejected by the very people—the church and community of faith—who have authenti-cated his call, chosenness, or election. This rejection is not limited to the faith community but is more pronounced and devastating when experienced within the community of faith. For example, Richard Lischer, in his book, *The Preacher King*, indicates that Mar-tin Luther King Jr. was often criticized, albeit rejected, by his own church, Dexter Avenue Baptist Church, because of his involvement in activities of liberation and transformation that affected the nation and the world. The local church wanted him to focus on the needs of the congregation and when his ministry began to expand beyond the parochial interests of the church's lay leadership, they began to reject him out of their *own* feelings of rejection although he was their elected/called leader. This experience is often inter-preted as a rejection by God because the people of God are thought to reflect the will of God in the African American church. It is not unusual for people to say that they are praying that God will send them a leader/pastor. Moreover, when the leader/pastor is "selected" by a particular congregation, he is referred to as the elected or chosen one.

The following discourse explores the concept or doctrine of election as it relates to courageous leadership in its myriad dimensions within the African American church theologically, historically, and philosophically. In the African American church and community, election/chosenness as calling is something less and something more than what is meant by Barth's usage of the terminology.

The Pious Leader—Learning from the Greeks

The chosen, called, or elected leader in the African American church and community can learn a thing or two from the Greeks about the nature of piety, godliness, or holiness by constantly searching for truth. This truth must be told about the self and the community. The leader is responsible for leading and teaching about the moral life and being faithful to the search for truth, justice, and faithfulness. Piety, in essence, is this search for truth and justice, which is often achieved by questioning one's motivation as well as the foundation of one's beliefs. Plato offers some insight into this concept and practice for the leader who believes himself/herself to be chosen by God.

My interest in Plato's *Dialogues* focuses on Euthyphro's dialogue with Socrates about the prosecution of Euthyphro's father for the murder of a man who himself was a murderer. In the dialogue, I find both Euthyphro and Socrates to be quite arrogantly confident in their piety. For me, the issue can be stated rather succinctly: Is Euthyphro's process of interrogation and prosecution pious or impious, or at least as pious as Socrates'? While Socrates seems to think it is impious, Euthyphro is convinced that it is pious. His confidence of the piety of his action makes it impious in Socrates' ethical scheme of reasoning. The notion that Euthyphro's prosecution of his father in court is a form of questioning in search of the ideal—in search of truth and justice. It is not as presumptive as Socrates leads or misleads the reader to think. Euthyphro's knowledge of his father's guilt is preliminary knowledge, that is, knowledge that is not decisive and conclusive but in process. The idea of piety and the process toward attaining it can be achieved not only through the method of questioning that Socrates uses. Euthyphro's intent to take his father to court is indeed a form of questioning and interrogation through reason that is as valid as Socrates' method of teaching the truth. While Socrates is concerned about the difference between the truly wise (pious) and those who think they are wise (impious) but are not, the process of questioning and philosophizing is inherently pious, or at least leads to piety. While he has to learn what Euthyphro sets out to do or claimed to teach, Socrates has learned what Euthyphro was unable to teach him, and this too is pious. When Euthyphro announces that he must go because he is in a hurry, Socrates says sarcastically in his closing statement: "By going you have cast me down from a great hope I had, that I would learn from you the nature of the pious and the impious. . . ."[5]

Finally, if the process of questioning is the means by which justice and piety can be achieved, then Euthyphro will have to actually go to court, which is what he intends to do, in order to display the kind of piety that Socrates seeks. This type of piety is as valid as that which Socrates purports to embrace. If there is a form of piety that constitutes the ideal, then Euthyphro's piety could be a form of the ideal. For he, too, is in search of justice, and the search, the quest, the effort to attain this ideal (in his view) are as pious as Socrates' efforts. In my view, this process is common to both men and Socrates' means of "getting at" piety is no more just or valid than Euthyphro's. Euthyphro states, "I say that the pious is to do what I am doing now, to prosecute the wrong doer, be it about murder or temple robbery or anything else, whether the wrong doer is your father or your mother or anyone else; not to prosecute is impious. . . ."[6]

The emphasis must be on the prosecutorial process as an effort to determine truth and justice, not as a priori knowledge of that which is pious. I submit the contrarian view as an approach to the issue of piety in the dialogue between Socrates and Euthyphro. In other words, Euthyphro was to "cross-examine" his father in court, which is identical to what Socrates does in the public square. Their actions are in essence tautologous. While the federal courts have been more just historically toward African Americans, we do however understand that there is no inherent sacrosanctity to the law or the Constitution. Martin Luther King, Thurgood Marshall, and others realized that the courts could not achieve what love could not do. In other words, the law never has succeeded in changing hateful hearts. It has, however, restrained the practitioners of hate and evil in their overt acts of dehumanization and denial of human dignity. Inasmuch as the African American preacher and leader has sought to bring about justice and social transformation through the legal system designed to foster these ideals, the court of public opinion has also been used to bring about justice and fairness. The television pictures and documentaries of Buchenwald and Auschwitz, vis-à-vis Montgomery and Birmingham, did more to etch these atrocities in the minds of people than any philosophy or theology was able to achieve. Piety is the quest for truth and justice, which I believe the Black preacher/leader has sought since setting foot on American soil.

The Experienced and Skilled Leader—Aristotle

I want to explore what seems to be an unnecessary contradiction in Aristotle's epistemology. I am concerned about what appears to be the prevailing dialectic in Aristotle's thought between knowledge that comes from experience and knowledge and expertise that belong to skill. He sets this up in dialectic fashion as if experience and skill are contraries, or opposites. This boils down to the issue that exists between theory and practice. Is theoretical knowledge more important or valuable than practical knowledge? More precisely, Does skill belong to knowledge and expertise, or does skill come from experience?

Aristotle says that "experience is the knowledge of particulars and skill that of universals, and practical actions, like all occurrences are concerned with particulars."[7] Yet, he holds "that knowledge of universals is somehow higher or more valuable than that of particular things."[8] This seems to be an unnecessary dichotomy between the particular and the universal. I postulate that our understanding of the universal is achieved via particular experience. In other words, skill is not constituted only by knowledge and expertise but also by experience. Experience is to some extent the mother of skill, that is, its nurturer and developer. Knowledge without experience can never be transformed into skill. For example, a surgeon is undoubtedly very knowledgeable about the contours, chemistry, and anatomy of the human body; however, if he never actually operates on a sick body, how can he be said to be a "skilled" surgeon? I propose that in order for one to be considered skilled in any art or science, he or she must be experienced. The fallacy in Aristotle's thought is related to the inherent dialectic that skill and experience are opposites rather than correlates. In my view, only an "experienced" surgeon can be skilled enough, that is, knowledgeable and expert enough to operate on a sick person or to teach others how to operate. The following words of Aristotle represent the source of the issue. He states: "And yet we think that knowledge and expertise belong rather to skill than to experience, and we assume that the skilled are wiser than the experienced, in that it is more in connection with knowledge that wisdom is associated with anything. And the reason for this is that the skilled know the cause, the experienced do not. For the experienced know the 'that' but not the 'because,' whereas the skilled have a grasp of the 'because,' the cause."[9]

In the African American community, wisdom is associated not only with knowledge but with experience. The leader or pastor becomes more skilled with time in the pulpit and in the work of ministry. Experience is indeed the teacher and harbinger of leadership as reflected in the African American pastor.

Courage for the Elected Leader—Paul Tillich

Courage is an essential element of self-understanding and self-actualization, especially if one has been called or elected by God and the faith community to lead. It is the ability and willingness to put one's faith in action, to take risks with what one believes. It is closely akin to faith, but it is not faith. It is best described as faith acted upon, rather than faith itself. Moreover, the foundation of courage is the Holy Spirit, which enables one to embody its essential elements, such as boldness, fortitude, honesty, truth, and justice. This means that courage is the ability to reason and reckon with the important things in one's life, including the frailties and faults of one's *own* life. It takes courage to also face the sins of our parents and children, to come to grips with the salient facts of self-evaluation and honest introspection. Paul Tillich in his book *The Courage to Be*, gives us several perspectives of courage that are worth pondering. He states, "Courage is the affirmation of one's essential nature, one's inner aim or entelechy, but it is an affirmation which has in itself the character of 'in spite of.'"[10] He clarifies this later on by stating that "courage is self-affirmation 'in spite of,' that is in spite of that which tends to prevent the self from affirming itself."[11]

Tillich was discussing courage as it relates to being, nonbeing, fear, and anxiety, but one of the book's great lessons is that self-affirmation is also self-transcending. It is only when the self can be affirmed that it can be transcended and ultimately transformed. "Self-affirmation" in spite of the anxiety of guilt and condemnation presupposes participation in something, which transcends the self.[12] For the believer, this something is really faith in God. The God of the African American church, the God who "makes a way out of no way," the God who "sits high and looks low" is not the same as Aristotle's "Unmoved Mover," but a God who watches over His children, the God who enables us to "wake up clothed in our right mind" in spite of the forces of self-destruction and denial, in the guise of political hatred, that perpetually parade themselves before us. These forces are giants in our paths that have no intention of making life easier or less frightful. In this sense, the courageous leader is indeed the elected or chosen leader who understands that the burden of leadership demands a responsible, self-girded person with integrity and commitment to "do the right thing," in the language of Spike Lee, that is, to serve faithfully, justly, and fairly.

LEADERSHIP REQUIRES COURAGE

When we think of the words *chosen, elected, called,* and *courage,* we think often of people who have exemplified certain distinct and virtuous characteristics in their behavior, attitude, actions, and personality. Courageous, "called" leadership, requires boldness, confidence, fortitude, stamina, fearlessness, and a spirit of adventure and achievement. It takes courage to pursue those qualities that will prepare one to be a leader.

For example, I remember certain details of my initial pastoral experiences. When I arrived in Norfolk, Virginia, nearly twenty-five years ago as the pastor of Mount Pleasant Baptist Church, I knew very little about leadership. However, one thing I did know was that the congregation had elected or chosen me by the will of God to occupy the position of pastor. I was supposed to be ready to fill the position according to my religious experience and academic training. I had studied homiletics, church and business management, theology, church history, and philosophy, but not leadership per se. Yet, I was expected to be the pastoral leader of that congregation at the young age of twenty-three. We know that young preachers can be leaders, however, because one of the great leaders of the twentieth century, Martin Luther King Jr., was in his early twenties when he became pastor of Dexter Avenue Baptist Church in Montgomery and when he led the Montgomery Bus boycott, which led to the Southern Christian Leadership Conference (SCLC), the Civil Rights Act, and the dismantling of segregation in the South. In his book, *The Preacher King,* Richard Lischer talks about how the deacons in that church thought King's efforts to transform the social conscience of the nation kept him away from the congregation too much in the later years. King's courage as a leader did not obviate the local church's tendency toward parochialism or outright rejection. It is not unusual for the leader to feel elected and rejected simultaneously by what Barth calls the "electing God."

Riggins R. Earl Jr., in his book *Dark Symbols, Obscure Signs,* looks at courageous leadership from the slave perspective. In his view, if fear is synonymous with sin, it is the lack of courage to be. Courage, in this instance, is considered to be "God's gift to the fearful."[13] He goes on to say, "God's gift of courage gave the transformed self the sense of being radically free spiritually in the world of bondage."[14] Although this definition refers to those who were in physical bondage during the days of slavery, the author suggests that those who are presently in bondage—economically or psychologically—can be set free through the recovery of this virtue. In the African American tradition, election or chosenness is a manifestation of practical leadership. It is not unusual for people in the church to suggest that "God has called one to preach." Often this "electing God" makes his will known through the people in the pew, who encourage others to acknowledge their call to preach. People are also admonished to understand that they are to be called by God and not man. Because of this, there is an enormous amount of respect accorded to the preacher. Nevertheless, there is a tension in the leader who feels that he is called by God but simultaneously receives his leadership authority from the congregation.

In the foreword of John F. Kennedy's *Profiles in Courage,* he states, "courage . . . is a diamond with many facets, and it owes much to its setting. It is not always a simple trait, for motivations are often complex; and in the rough and tumble of political life, with its heavy pressures, its demands for honest compromise, and its constant presentation of second-best choices, courage can seldom be manifested in simple ways. The right course is not always clear."[15] We will look at one profile from this book later, but this description fits any situation that calls for courageous leadership.

In a discussion on moral values, J. Phillip Wogaman, in his book, *Christian Moral Judgement,* suggests that courage, according to classical ethical literature, is one of three virtues that represent "a habit of the will to overcome a threat to our ultimate good."[16] He further states that "in the case of courage, it was control of fear, so that fear would not immobilize us in the face of physical or social dangers."[17] Along these same ethical lines, Samuel K. Roberts in his book, *In the Path of Virtue,* recognizes courage as one of the four cardinal virtues, and he uses this term synonymously with fortitude. In relation to the African American struggle for justice, he states that "courage, or fortitude, would be understood as a necessary characteristic for anyone involved in the struggle against those who held enormous power."[18] He exclaims that the fortitude or courage of African Americans during this struggle was inspired and strengthened by two different sources. "First, they drew sustained strength from the belief in a moral universe that appeared to support their cause against slavery and oppression."[19] "Second, drew fortitude from the belief that the enlightened and cultivated mind could alter circumstances and the realities around them."[20] It was this virtue of courage that enabled them to endure during the times of struggle.

Courageous Political Leadership among Non–African Americans

Now we turn to some people who exemplified the virtue of courage. The first demonstration of courage is displayed by John Quincy Adams, the son of a former president by the same name and a political figure himself. This former senator from Massachusetts and president of the United States did not make the expected transition from one political post to the other, but rather suffered greatly as a result of his determination to be honorable rather than politically correct or expedient. It is said of this courageous leader that "his frustrations and defeats in political office—as senator and president—were the inevitable result of this intransigence in ignoring the political facts of life."[21] Among his many acts of courage as he sat in the seat of nonpartisanship, he voted in opposition to his Federalist cohorts in the Senate in favor of the Embargo Bill proposed by President Thomas Jefferson. This bill was enacted to shut down international trade with the British in retaliation of their attack and seizure of American ships. The Federalists were not in favor of this bill because the state of Massachusetts received its wealth from British imports. In spite of many threats, Adams courageously stood firm and voted in favor of the bill, taking into consideration the good of the country rather than the wealth of one state that benefited by being "the leading commercial state of the nation."[22] Following his actions, Adams was ousted from both his political and social circles. In fact, "the entire Adams family was damned in the eyes of the ex-president's former supporters by his son's act of courage."[23] In spite of his courageous actions, Adams later succeeded and served a term as president of the United States and was later asked to serve as a representative in Congress for the Plymouth District. Even though Adams insisted on being an independent, he was elected by an overwhelming vote and served in the House until his death.[24]

More recently, presidential candidate Al Gore is said to have made a courageous step in asking Senator Joseph Lieberman to be his running mate. This was the first time a person of Jewish heritage and faith had run for such a high political office in the United States. I agree that this was probably an act of courage, notwithstanding the political calculations of Gore's campaign. An even more courageous act was Gore's determination to count every single vote that was cast in Florida. Gore felt that he had been elected by the people to serve and in talking to African Americans, they believe that something was suspicious about the entire election recount. Unfortunately Gore did not insist on justice and demand that the Florida election debacle be rectified before conceding defeat.

Another intriguing story is about a courageous missionary, Merlin Bishop, who was responsible for guarding the property of an abandoned American university outside a small Chinese village when Japanese troops had taken over that village (*Fellowship*, Jan. 1945, Vol. II, No. 1). During the troop's first attempt to take over the university, Bishop refused to surrender the keys. "He explained that the property belonged to American mission boards, that it had been entrusted to his care, and that he was not at liberty to hand it over to anyone else."[25] After a period of time, being courageously responding in a friendly yet firm manner, the troops finally left him alone. They tried again on several occasions, but eventually gave up until the officer in command of one troop gave Bishop an ultimatum: hand over the keys or be shot. Even when facing the barrel of the rifle pointed at him, he still maintained his demeanor and didn't surrender. When one soldier decided to act on the threat and shoot, Bishop was able to dodge the bullet, grab the rifle, and subdue the man who took the shot. Rather than retaliating with violence, Bishop merely stared the soldier in the eyes and smiled at him, and the soldier ultimately smiled back. The ordeal ended with the troops joining Bishop in his living quarters "to have tea before their tiring journey back to the village."[26]

History is replete with African American courageous leaders worthy of examination. Mark Hyman, in his book *Blacks Who Died for Jesus: A History Book,* tells the story of two courageous Black women named Perpetua and Feliciti. After refusing to deny Jesus and worship Roman gods instead, despite the humiliation and threats bestowed upon them, they were thrown into a den of half-starved lions. The story indicates that "for some strange reason the lions came up to the women and then moved on."[27] In spite of the crowd's demand for the women's freedom, "a Roman tribunal standing inside the gate . . . ordered two gladiators to cut off their heads."[28] Among the many stories of courage in this book is of another Black woman named Crispina, a martyr for Jesus as well. This educated and influential Christian woman was known to be vocal and aggressive about her Christianity. When Anulinius, the Roman pro-consul, received several reports about Crispina, he had her arrested, charging that "she had ignored an imperial command to worship the Roman gods."[29] After much debate, in which Crispina outwitted Anulinius, this Roman official "begged her to reconsider her position and deny Jesus of Nazareth."[30] It goes on to say that "she refused his request by saying: 'If necessary, I will suffer for Jesus. I will sacrifice to the Lord who made heaven and earth, the sea and everything that is in them, but I will never be forced to sacrifice to evil spirits. '"[31] Because of her refusal, she was beheaded. These are just a couple of examples of Black women put to death because of their courage and understanding of their own election and rejection, as seen in their suffering and death. Election, as Peter Ochs says, does not mean favor, but often disfavor and death.

Courageous Leadership and Civil Rights

Black figures, from the Civil Rights Movement exemplified the virtue of courage. Quinton Dixie and Cornel West, in their book, *The Courage to Hope*, indicate that

> in the moments and events that constituted this movement, people cast their activism in terms of responses to God's call to participate; they discovered unknown courage; they exposed the falsity of the seeming normalcy of segregation; they captured the popular imagination and garnered moral capital; they solicited the participation of preexisting institutions to construct the structural base of the movement; and they strategized and dismantled segregation piece by piece.[32]

This "call" to participate in the struggle is what I am referring to as chosenness, or election. Two who served as examples for the faith of this movement during slavery were two brothers named Andrew and Sampson, who were arrested for holding worship services in Savannah, Georgia. Reminiscent of the Apostle Paul in the Bible, "together with about fifty of their followers, they were imprisoned twice and were severely whipped. Andrew told his persecutors that he rejoiced not only to be whipped, but *would freely suffer death for the cause of Jesus Christ.* This is indicative of Black leaders' understanding of their call and is akin to Karl Barth's notion of the elected and the rejected, which is represented in Jesus Christ.

Throughout the South in the mid-1960s, there was pandemic oppression and injustice. For example, in Tuskegee, Alabama, overt discrimination and segregation were obvious. During this time, "a number of Tuskegee Institute students had challenged various forms of overt discrimination which existed in the town."[33] They tried to enter White-only establishments and picketed those that would not hire Blacks, and held rallies. One leader in this movement, named Sammy Younge Jr. was shot and killed by a White man at a gas station when he attempted to use a White-only restroom. These abject acts of injustice and hate were prevalent during this period in history.

The Montgomery bus boycott, the spark that led to the modern Civil Rights Movement, began with the courageous act of a woman by the name of Rosa Parks. It is said that "in the afternoon of Thursday, December 1 [1955], a prominent Black woman named Mrs. Rosa Parks was arrested for refusing to vacate her seat for a white man."[34] This refusal incited the thirteen-month bus boycott. However, it was the efforts of Jo Ann Gibson, in conjunction with the Women's Political Council (WPC), that actually got the boycott off the ground and kept it going for thirteen months. This woman suffered through threats and imprisonment for her efforts, but she tirelessly worked alongside others, such as Dr. Martin L. King Jr., to see through this call to freedom. Unfortunately, Ms. Gibson, a teacher at Alabama State College, was harassed because of her involvement with the boycott, and she eventually "resigned in the summer of 1960 and accepted a teaching position elsewhere."[35]

Of all the courageous figures from the Civil Rights era, Dr. Martin Luther King Jr. is undoubtedly the most well known. Before his life was shortened because of his courageous call to stand for the cause of Civil Rights, he made great strides in this movement. Adam Fairclough, in his book, *Martin Luther King Jr.,* indicates that "King's public career spanned less than thirteen years, but during that time, from 1956 to 1968, he became the most popular and effective leader of the civil rights movement in America, and emerged on the international stage as a forceful and eloquent proponent of nonviolence."[36] He was a significant figure in the Montgomery bus boycott following Rosa Park's courageous refusal to give up her seat to a White man. Serving as the spokesperson for the boycott, he delivered the message to African Americans that it was time to take action. Exemplifying his courage, he emphasized what needed to take place in order to transform the segregated South:

> The time had arrived to protest, King insisted. The right to protest was "the great glory of American democracy," and they would protest with unity and grim determination, in the knowledge that the principles of the Constitution and the declarations of the Supreme Court were theoretically on their side. They would eschew violence, but also accompany their persuasion with coercion. They would undergird their protest with Christian love, but would also insist upon justice, for love and justice went hand in hand.[37]

And his leadership inspired in a whole race of people the courage to stand up for their rights. During the 381 days of this movement, "the city commission embarked on a 'get tough' policy designed to break the boycott."[38] King was harassed, threatened, and imprisoned, and even had his house bombed, but in spite of it all, he remained involved in this movement, emphasizing the practice of nonviolence. Demonstrating his devotion to the cause, he assured people "that even if he were killed, the movement would continue."[39] The movement finally came to its end with the U.S. Supreme Court's affirmation that it was unconstitutional for buses to operate with laws of segregation, and, "on December 21, 1956—the first day of integration—King boarded a bus and took a seat near the front."[40]

Following the Montgomery incident, King continued to work toward Black civil rights and was instrumental in the beginning of the Southern Christian Leadership Conference (SCLC), of which "King was elected president, a position he held until his assassination—the ultimate form of rejection. The SCLC's aim was to build on the success of the Montgomery bus boycott; for the next eleven years it became the vehicle through which King mobilized Black southerners to protest segregation and discrimination. SCLC's motto, 'To Redeem the Soul of America,' reflected both its Christian orientation and its commitment to nonviolence."[41] One of the most courageous participants in this organization was a minister by the name of Reverend Fred L. Shuttlesworth, who fearlessly worked in opposition to Theophilus G. "Bull" Connor, the Commissioner of Public Safety, "a fervent racist [who used] publicity-conscious and high-handed actions to defend segregation."[42] It is said about this man:

> Impulsive, excitable, and egocentric, Shuttlesworth almost single-handedly kept Black protest alive in Birmingham after the suppression of the NAACP in 1956. Intent on integrating the most segregated city in the South, he was blasted out of bed by dynamite, beaten up by white mobs, and repeatedly arrested by Connor's police. The diminutive clergyman displayed a bravado that amused Blacks and caused them to shake their heads in admiration and amazement.[43]

Through times of massive support and lack of support, confrontations with public and political figures (even three presidents), harassment and repeated threats, and numerous imprisonments on trumped-up charges, King continued his mission for racial equality. His persistence persuaded President John F. Kennedy to introduce the Civil Rights Bill to Congress, which "sought more power for the federal government to desegregate southern schools, combat discrimination in employment, and end Black disfranchisement. Above all, he wanted a blanket ban on segregation in public accommodations, including hotels, restaurants, theaters, and shops."[44] King was so influential that he successfully organized the historic March on Washington, "a day-long rally of about 200,000 people, including a large number of whites, in support of the Civil Rights Bill,"[45] where he delivered his famous "I Have A Dream" speech. His life-long mission was carried on until his untimely death, when he was assassinated in Memphis, Tennessee, the evening following what was considered "one of the most powerful speeches of his life."[46] King is the archetype of the modern African American leader, both elected, chosen, and rejected. The elected and rejected are one and the same individual.

Courageous Leaders during Slavery: The Liberators

African Americans identify with Jesus at the intersection of election and rejection, or disfavor. This is where race and ethnicity converge, where nearly 300 years of chattel slavery and the systematic extermination of six million or more Jews came into focus as similar experiences of extermination and annihilation—a type of demoralizing of the soul, an abject violation of another's freedom to be. I am appalled even as I write with Germany's highfalutin and glorious doctrines of God and other grand theological discourses and America's preoccupation with freedom, human rights, and individual liberty and justice—while each produced and nurtured Adolf Hitler and the Holocaust on the one hand and American slavery, with its unknown number of unrecorded lynchings, on the other.

Several courageous leaders bear mentioning in reflecting on the slavery era of our country, such as Frederick Douglass, Harriet Tubman, and Sojourner Truth. These people were the epitome of courageous leadership, called by God to abolish to the best of their ability the institution of slavery. Frederick Augustus Washington Bailey, who later became known as Frederick Douglass, was the son of a Black slave woman and her White slave owner who courageously escaped from slavery and ended up becoming one of history's most notable figures. He was noted for being an "Orator par excellence whose speeches were a rare combination of uncommon courage and brilliant political thought. Founding father of the first Civil Rights and Black Protest Movements, he was the most visible, persuasive, influential African American of the nineteenth century."[47] Once he began reading lessons under the nose of the unsuspecting wife of one of his slave owners, there was no stopping this determined young man. Despite his owner's attempt to prevent him from reading, even to the point of sending him to a vicious slave driver who was known for "[breaking] disobedient slaves with notorious brutality, Douglass remained determined to read."[48] After much abuse Frederick retaliated by defending himself, which eventually ended up in his promise to himself to "never again submit to a whipping—in any form."[49]

Following his escape from slavery, he subscribed to an abolitionist paper called *The Liberator* and joined the American Anti-Slavery Society, mostly made up of Whites, despite the risk. He eventually began to address the atrocities of slavery based on first-hand experience, which led to his career as a "freedom fighter in the cold war against slavery."[50] As he traveled across states in the North, speaking wherever he was permitted to, "he was met with constant hatred and assault. There were 'Kill the nigger!' riots at his speeches. He was thrown from stages, beaten, and pushed down stairs. He was harassed in restaurants, hotels, and railroad cars."[51] Nevertheless, he continued to fight for freedom and even published an autobiography entitled *Narrative of the Life of Frederick Douglass*. Because of that, he fled the country for two years to avoid being recaptured and killed. Once he was invited to participate with John Brown, a fanatical white abolitionist, who was planning a raid on Harpers Ferry, Virginia. However, Douglass "considered the attack on a federal arsenal too provocative and dangerous. So, in this instance, Douglass demonstrated his courageous leadership through *restraint*,"[52] which made him credible even with President Lincoln. As he continued to fight for the abolishment of slavery, he persistently addressed the president on the issue of emancipation. Many Blacks died because of the delay in its issuance. Even after the so-called Emancipation Proclamation was issued, it would be many years before Blacks would begin to see any semblance of equality, which is still not fully actualized to this day. The following was said of Douglass: "His dream of a unified America was, of course, unrealized. But he lived his paramount thought—that human beings must be free and equal—and through his courage in an era of hate and fear, he inspired others to step forward and help their fellowmen get their just due."[53]

Harriet Tubman is truly the epitome of courageous leadership. Along with Frederick Douglass and Sojourner Truth, she too was one who fought for the freedom of slaves. The following description shows her as a living example of courageous leadership:

> Her name (we say it advisedly and without exaggeration) deserves to be handed down to posterity side by side with the names of Joan of Arc, Grace Darling, and Florence Nightingale; for not one of these women has shown more courage and power of enduring and facing danger and death to relieve human suffering, than has this woman in her heroic and successful endeavors to reach and save all whom she might of her oppressed and suffering race, and to pilot them from the land of Bondage to the promised land of Liberty. Well has she been called "Moses," for she has been a leader and deliverer unto hundreds of her people.[54]

Even Frederick Douglass, in a letter to Harriet Tubman, speaks of her courage stating:

> Most that I have done and suffered in the service of our cause has been in public, and I have received much encouragement at every step of the way. You on the other hand have labored in a private way. I have wrought in the day—you in the night. I have had the applause of the crowd and the satisfaction that comes of being approved by the multitude, while the most that you have done has been witnessed by a few trembling, scarred, and foot-sore bondsmen and

women, whom you have led out of the house of bondage, and whose heartfelt *"God bless you"* has been your only reward. The midnight sky and the silent stars have been the witnesses of your devotion to freedom and of your heroism.[55]

From her initial escape from the bondage of slavery until she finally brought her own parents to freedom, Harriet exhibited courage and leadership beyond measure. She worked by day as a free woman, working everywhere from hotels to hospitals, and she even worked for the U.S. Army. But during the night she was known for "her story of going down again and again into the very jaws of slavery to rescue her suffering people, bringing them off through perils and dangers enough to appall the stoutest heart, till she was known among them as 'Moses.'"[56] She had no fear of death in spite of those who had rewards posted for her capture. It is even stated that *"forty thousand dollars* was not too great a reward for the Maryland slaveholders to offer for her."[57] In addition, she did not fear the diseases of those whom she treated at hospitals and for the army. "She had never had these diseases, but she seems to have no more fear of death in one form than another,"[58] trusting the Lord to keep her alive until He was ready to take her home.

Sojourner Truth was another bold, courageous woman in the history of American slavery. Isabella, displayed an independent spirit as soon as she became an adult. She escaped from slavery under the Dumonts's after first being promised her freedom and then denied it, in spite of the fact that there were "only nine months before the law was to free her anyway."[59] Upon leaving a life of bondage in New York, Isabella changed her name to Sojourner Truth. Sojourner was a name that she said the Lord gave her because of her journeying out, and Truth was used because she felt called—chosen or elected—to tell the truth to people as she set out to be a traveling preacher or evangelist. Her courage in this endeavor is obvious, because "for any woman just to wander and speak as the way opened was unusual and even dangerous,"[60] but she was on a mission and was not afraid to carry it out. Once, when she was the only Black attending a camp meeting, rioters invaded the meeting. Fearing death, she initially went into hiding. However, because of her strong convictions, she decided that she would face the rioters and try to calm them down. Although the camp meeting leaders refused to accompany her, she proceeded to ultimately persuade the rioters to leave peacefully. It was during this event that "Truth had developed skill in handling a rough crowd."[61] Sojourner Truth became known as a public speaker for reform in 1850. Her first speech was in October at one of the first national women's rights conventions."The next month, November 1850, when Truth was about fifty-three years old, she gave the first documented antislavery speech."[62] From this point, she became known as a spokesperson for women and Blacks, a preacher, and an author, all of this against the odds of a Black woman being influential in a White man's world. She was truly a courageous woman who helped to lead Black people to freedom.

Biblical Examples of Courageous Leadership

Throughout the Old and New Testaments, the Bible is full of examples of people who exemplify courage, such as Joshua and Esther. Joshua was charged with leading the Israelites into the Promised Land after the death of Moses. In Joshua 1:6, 7, 9, and 18, the Lord instructs Joshua to be "strong and courageous,"[63] which he was from that time until his death. He was most courageous when he led the people of Israel in a military campaign to take over Canaan, starting with sending two spies into Jericho to survey the land. Next, he led the people across the Jordan on dry ground according to the instructions from the Lord, which caused the people to stand "in awe of him, as they had stood in awe of Moses, all the days of his life."[64] At this point, the Lord led Joshua to victory over all of the city-states of Canaan, beginning with the triumph over Jericho on marching around the walls of the city, until the whole land had been taken over with the destruction of the Anakims in the land (11:22). In this instance, the courageous leadership displayed can be equated with obedience to the Lord.

Another courageous biblical figure is Esther, a beautiful Jewish girl who succeeded Vashti as King Ahaserus's queen (Esther 2:16–17). When Esther's cousin, Mordecai, who had exposed two eunuchs who were planning the king's assassination (2:21–23), did not bow down to Haman, the king's head official, Haman plotted the destruction of all the Jews in the kingdom (3:5–6). Hearing of this plan, Mordecai and the other Jews mourned, which got back to Esther. When Mordecai sent word to Esther what she must do to save her people, she decided that she would go and plead for their lives. She courageously and boldly went before the king without being called, and by doing so, she stood the chance of losing her life. For "if any man or woman goes to the king inside the inner court without being called, there is but one law—all alike are to be put to death. Only if the king holds out the golden scepter to someone, may that person live."[65] After a three-day fast along with her people, she did go to the king without being summoned, and not only did he hold out the golden scepter, but he consented to grant her request (5:1–3). By her courageous act, she saved her people from destruction.

The New Testament is also filled with leaders who demonstrated courage. Of them all, Jesus is perceived as the most courageous. Throughout the Gospels, there are several examples of his courageous acts. Such courage was displayed as he faced the devil after fasting for forty days (Matt. 4:1–11; Mark 1:12; Luke 4:1–13). He boldly went about preaching wherever he went, feeding the hungry, healing the sick, casting out demons, and even raising the dead. He associated with undesirables, such as thieves and prostitutes, and even touched with his hands those considered unclean. When the Pharisees confronted him about working on the Sabbath, he responded with a challenge, proceeding to heal a man with a withered hand (Matt. 12:1–14; Mark 2:23–3:6; Luke 6:1–11). Another of Jesus' acts of courageous leadership was his entering the temple in Jerusalem and boldly driving out those buying and selling and overturning tables and chairs, which made the chief priests and scribes reject him (Matt. 21:12–16; Mark 11:15–18; Luke 19:45–48). He showed the ultimate courage when he was tried and sentenced to death and faced death on the cross.

Many others throughout the New Testament demonstrated courageous leadership. The apostles-turned-disciples demonstrated courage as they boldly proclaimed the gospel in spite of the disapproval of the Sadducees and impending danger and martyrdom. Stephen, one of the seven deacons chosen in the book of Acts, was certainly courageous as he boldly proclaimed the gospel in spite of threats and accusations, even to the point of being stoned to death (Acts 6–7). Another example of courageous leadership is seen in the Apostle Paul, who not only formed and led churches, rebuking those guilty of wrongdoing, but he suffered much persecution as well. In 2 Corinthians, he lists the things that happened to him, including numerous imprisonments, countless floggings, beatings with rods, a stoning, a shipwreck, danger of various kinds, hunger, and thirst. Paul's life is another example of the elected, called, chosen leader who is also rejected.

THE COURAGE TO MOVE FROM SIN TO SALVATION

The church is reluctant to talk about her lack of righteousness, about her turning away from God—our wrongness, our unrighteousness. There is a tendency to think of others as sinners but not ourselves. Sin is confined to the terrible acts of the body, a violation of the "Thou shalt nots" and acts of transgression. Sin is, in the church's view, often confined to lying, stealing, and feeling on the buxom body of some beautiful babe or, for the females, some beastly brother. There is a lot in and out of the church, for that matter, which is and should be taboo. The way we act toward one another and the way we talk to and about each other would be prohibited if we could make a law to forbid it. Sin is indeed alienation from God, but it is also exploitation and injustice. Sin is not mainly related to passion and sexuality. It is both individual and collective, personal and societal. As a matter of fact, the collective nature of sin has its genesis in the personal and individual. Adam and Eve's disobedience was personal even though the tendency to disobey God is part of the nature of man.

We have folk in church who think of others as sinners but not themselves. Paul tells us that "Everyone has sinned and is far away from God's saving presence" (Romans 3:23). Sin is both personal and universal. It applies to the Jews and the Gentiles: "All have turned away from God. All have done wrong" (Romans 3:12). This applies to pastors and teachers, choirs and ushers, men and women, the young and old.

Some older folk act as if they never have been estranged, alienated, separated from God. It's alright to give advice, to counsel, to help and guide, as long as it is based on truth and moral integrity. Adults often act shocked by what young people today say and do. No one wants to encourage wrong or condone promiscuity, fornication, violence, or corruption, but neither should church folk act like they have always been who they are today: saved and sanctified, born again, faithful and faultless. There was a time when they too were "foot-loose and fancy-free," "doing everything under the Sun." We all have been deficient, suffered from a spiritual deficit, unable to retrieve ourselves from reckless and riotous living, but God's patience has endured. God also puts us right with Him. Neither law nor the prophets can do it, but God can. God can move us from where we are to where we need to be. God takes us from a place that is possessed and poisoned by fear and enables us to be saved. We can sing with the psalmist: "Even though I walk thru the valley of the shadow of death, I will fear no evil, for thou art with me" (Psalm 23). God moves us from alienation from each other and brings us in fellowship and harmony. God puts us right with God's self in order that we can practice how to treat one another, how to love each other, how to talk to one another, how to be kind and just. God places our sin behind and salvation before us. God transforms us by changing our status from one of sin to salvation through faith in Jesus Christ as Lord and Savior.

God makes us acceptable to Him. He accepts people because they have faith in Jesus Christ. All have sinned and fallen short of God's glory. But God treats us much better than we deserve, and because of Christ Jesus, He freely accepts us and sets us free from our sins. God sent Jesus Christ to be our sacrifice. Christ offered his life's blood, so that by faith in him we could come to God.

Overcoming Hatred and Revenge—Lev. 19:15–18

Hatred and revenge are two attitudes and actions forbidden by law in the Old Testament. How I wish there was a law against them today. From nations and provinces to individuals, families, and communities, we need to eradicate and eliminate the attitudes and practices of hate and revenge. Every day we read and hear of some person who has shot and killed another. We hear of a drive-by shooting, a murder of some sort, or some other atrocity. It's not just killing that results from hatred but also drug-dealing and selling to those already oppressed. One cannot love someone and sell them drugs, knowing that those substances can kill them. This is both hatred of your brother and self-hate. Likewise, in the church, the family, and the community, there should be no hatred in the heart. Hatred in the heart is hatred that is internalized. Hatred that is kept in the heart while the attitude on the outside reflects nothing of what is on the inside. Hatred in the heart leads to deceit and hypocrisy. Hatred in the heart is a masked hatred. It is wearing a mask, concealing the true self. It is fronting! It is acting as if one likes someone but knowing all the time that one hates that individual. Hatred in the heart is also associated with slander, which is telling others about the object of one's hatred behind that person's back. Whenever you say something evil against someone, and at the same time lead them to think that you like them, you are being deceitful and slanderous, and it takes courage to overcome this kind of attitude and action.

THE COURAGE TO CRITIQUE THE SELF

"Let a man examine himself, and so eat of the bread and drink of the cup. For anyone who eats and drinks without discerning the body eats and drinks judgement upon himself. That is why many of you are weak and ill and some have died. But if we judge ourselves truly, we should not be judged. But when the Lord judges us, we are chastened so that we may not be condemned along with the world" (Cor. 11:28–32).

In these directions concerning the Lord's Supper, Paul commends the Corinthians for their remembrance of him and for maintaining the traditions that he shared with them. On the other hand, he offers no words of commendation for some of the things that they were doing when they came to worship. He points out that he had heard about the divisions and factions that existed among them as a church. Evidently, they had turned the Lord's Supper into little separate feasts—cliques whose members were socially compatible, much like the potluck dinners held in churches today. The feast of freedom, the open fellowship, the common meal had turned out to be not a common fellowship, but a misguided exercise in selfishness. Paul encourages a concept of self-examination. In order for us to understand ourselves, we must examine our intentions, our character. Carl Jung, renowned psychoanalyst and author of *The Undiscovered Self*, points out that "We know how to distinguish ourselves from other animals in point of anatomy and physiology, but as conscious, reflecting beings gifted with speech, we lack all criteria for self-judgement." In these times, when the world suffers from moral decay and economic panic, we must begin to look at ourselves in a more holistic and critical way. Self-examination is a look into one's own being and character. It is to seek, to understand the inner recesses of one's life with a purging sense of openness and truth. The psalmist while praying for moral renewal makes it clearer saying, "Behold thou desirest truth in thy inward being; therefore, teach me wisdom in my secret heart. Purge me with hyssop, and I shall be clean" (Ps. 51:6, 7). The individual has to reach the point where she or he can see himself honestly, for only then can there be a change in our lives. Too many resist the power of change, simply because our experiences have been so limited that we are unable to cope with new ideas and new ways of life. Growth is not a static phenomenon; it is achieved through change of lifestyle and spiritual renewal.

The words of Scripture, "Let a man examine himself, and so eat of the bread and drink of the cup," suggest that the self (or individual) is very important to the community. Paul, after hearing about the factions, informs the Corinthians about the Lord's Supper, saying, "For I received from the Lord that which also I delivered unto you, that the Lord Jesus on the night when he was betrayed took bread, and when all of God's children—rich and poor, known and unknown, tutored and untutored shall gather together at the feast of fellowship where everyone shall be fulfilled." Clergy and laity must examine self. If this is done genuinely and honestly, then the hope of redemption can become a reality through Jesus Christ. One should not expect anyone to do for one what one can do for one's self—and when we all have done all that we can, then our hope has substance. It has ground to stand on, and that ground of hope is Jesus Christ.

"If the individual is not truly regenerated in spirit, society cannot be either, for society is the sum total of individuals in need of redemption," says Carl Jung. The church cannot be regenerated or renewed until each individual takes a closer, more serious look at himself or herself. This takes courage! It will serve no purpose to point one's finger unless one points at oneself; it will not do any good to check and see how brother so-and-so is living until one checks out one's self. Nothing is gained by whispering and gossiping about those who should be ashamed of taking communion. Don't worry about so-and-so; he or she may be nothing in your eyesight. He may be a poor sinner, but when he examines himself, he comes to know that he's a sinner—and anyone who knows that he's a sinner is on his way to salvation. We have to recognize ourselves for who we are before there can be any change in us. For self-examination, look to a song that the old folk sang: "It's me, it's me, it's me O Lord, standing in the need of prayer, not my brother, not my sister, but it's me O Lord, standing in the need of prayer."

The great prophet Isaiah, when he saw the Lord, when the foundation of the thresholds shook at the voice of him who called and the house was filled with smoke, Isaiah, said "Woe is me, for I am lost, for I am a man of unclean lips." Likewise, Jesus encouraged others to examine themselves. For example, a woman was brought to him for living a sinful life, but Jesus, instead of condemning her, says, "He who is without sin, cast the first stone." Self-examination is a very important leadership trait for the pastor and anyone else who works with people in church and society, because the perception of self is largely an exercise in fictive reconstruction.

THE COURAGE TO BELIEVE

I can do all things in him who strengthens me.
—Phil. 4:13

In Philippians, a very brief letter, we find some of the greatest discourses on human life ever written. It was a custom of Paul's to close each of his letters with practical applications of what he has previously explained or to refer to his own experience as an example to his readers. This letter is no exception. As a matter of fact, the entire letter is very practical, but in the closing chapters, he shares his experience at Philippi, encouraging readers to think about whatever is true, honorable, just, pure, lovely, and gracious. After the Damascus road experience, his actions have been centered in Jesus Christ, the source of his faith and belief. He had believed that through Jesus Christ, everything and anything worthy was possible. He had learned the secret. He could be content and satisfied. In other words, he had come to the point where he could respond to or accept "whatever" state he was in, saying, "I can do all things in him who strengthens me." This is an expression of the courage to believe.

As a church and as a community, our progress is directly related to our faith and ability to believe. Moreover, as individuals and organizations, our ability to overcome obstacles relates directly to the extent of our belief. Martin Luther, the great reformer who rebelled against the authorities, said, "Here I stand. I can do no other, so help me God." Descartes's maxim, "I think, therefore I am," relates our being to thought, and because God is the alpha and omega—the beginning and the end—our thought and even our very being are related to the Lord, for without Him we would be nothing. But with Him, we have hope because we believe that through Jesus mountains can be overcome and the valleys will not keep us down. We can join Isaiah in his prophecy of the coming of Christ when he says, "Every valley shall be lifted up, and every mountain and hill be made low, the uneven ground shall become level and the rough places a plain. And the glory of the Lord shall be revealed and all flesh shall see it together—for the mouth of the Lord has spoken." Through Jesus, we come to understand the power of believing.

Experiences have a great impact upon one's faith; they indeed teach us well."'For I have learned, in whatever state I am to be content. I know how to be abased, and I know how to abound, in any and all circumstances I have learned the secret of facing plenty and hunger, abundance and want.' In all of the ups and downs of life, he could now find himself equally at home" (Interpreters, Vol. 11, p. 123). Paul had had many experiences—some good, many bad. He knew what it meant to suffer for Christ. He had been imprisoned, beaten, despised as well as comforted, loved, and received. He had been fiercely rejected and also warmly received, so he knew the dialectical nature of life. He could have understood the old Negro spiritual with the words, "Sometimes I'm up, sometimes I'm down, sometimes I'm almost level to the ground—O, yes Lord." He says that he had learned to be content with whatever state he was in, and that's why he proceeds to say, "I know" how to be abased and how to abound. In other words, he knew how to be humble and also how to be haughty. He had known hunger—but also had known abundance. He could deal with the extremes of life.

Often our faith corresponds directly with the good experiences we have had, and too often we forget that each experience in life should contribute to our growth. When we experience hate in society, let that contribute to our appreciation of love. When we experience sorrow, let that increase our appreciation of joy. When we experience pain, let that increase our longing for good health. When we experience abundance, let us not forget the days of poverty and want. Paul had learned because life had been his teacher. He had learned, life had taught him well, and he wanted the church at Philippi to know that although there were feuds and corruption—there were those fighting against each other, there were weak, and there were strong—he, like all of us, was a combination of weakness and strength. He says, "I know how to be abased," that is, how to be degraded and humiliated "and I know how to abound, in any and all circumstances I have learned the secret of facing plenty and hunger, abundance and want. . . . I have learned, in whatever state I am to be content." Paul was sure that through Jesus Christ, everything would be alright. Through Jesus, he didn't have to worry; he could face the joys and the sorrows of life. He could face all or nothing. He could be satisfied no matter what the situation was. When you reach this point, you have already made progress.

Paul says, "I can do all things in him who strengthens me." He was convinced that man by himself can do nothing and is in hopeless bondage to self and the evils of the world. With Christ, we have the power of believing. Young people can believe that they can do without drugs and other synthetic forms of happiness. Our communities can flourish if our faith does not falter. African Americans can lose the chains of oppression if they believe that God sent His son to proclaim deliverance to the oppressed and release to the captives. "I can do all things, not some or a few but all things through Him who strengthens me," says we can get rid of the bad thoughts, we can love each other as we have never loved before. We can pick each other up when the world pushes us down; we can help our churches to be what Christ wants them to be; we can achieve understanding in our personal lives and elsewhere; we can be true disciples and greater stewards if we believe. Our faith has to be like the two blind men in the gospel of Matthew who followed Jesus crying, "Have mercy on us son of David," and then they came to Jesus and he said, "Do you believe that I am able to do this?" And they said, "Yes, Lord." Then he touched their eyes, saying, "According to your faith be it done to you." And their eyes were opened.

There is another incident of faith and courage that gives us insight. A woman who had suffered from continuous bleeding for twelve years saw Jesus in a crowd and made her way up to him. She touched the hem of his garment and said, "If only I touch the hem of his garment, I shall be made well." Jesus turned and saw her, saying, "Take heart daughter, your faith had made you well."

THE COURAGE TO WORSHIP IN SPIRIT AND TRUTH

But be doers of the word, and not hearers only, deceiving yourselves. . . .
If anyone thinks he is religious, and does not bridle his tongue but deceives
his heart, this man's religion is vain. Religion that is pure and undefiled
before God and the Father is this: to visit orphans and widows in their
affliction, and to keep oneself unstained from the world.
—James 1:22–26f

The writer of the book of James expounds on the meaning of true worship by initially saying, "Let every man be quick to hear, slow to speak, slow to anger for the anger of man does not work for righteousness of God . . . put away all filthiness and rank growth of wickedness and receive with meekness the implanted word which is able to save your souls." Salvation is the Word of God—the gospel has saving power.

Some of us don't even want to hear the truth. We want our ignorance and our self-righteousness, our poor attitudes, and our sins to be condoned, but they can't be: "Anyone who puts his hands to the plow and looks back is not fit for the kingdom." Jesus didn't condone sin. Rather, the Scripture says, "The wages of sin is death." "For the measure you give will be the measure you get back."

We need a more concrete understanding of worship. Like all practical theology, worship is fully realized in action, in doing: "But be doers of the word, and not hearers only, deceiving yourselves."

We have heard the idiomatic expression, "Actions speak louder than words," or "show and tell"! Evidently there were people who were to receive this letter who just sat in the temple and listened to the Word without putting it into action. Wickedness must be forsaken and righteousness has to be embraced; otherwise, our worship is in vain. Isaiah makes it clear when he says, "Wash yourselves; make yourselves clean, remove the evil of your doings from before my eyes; cease to do evil, learn to do good; seek justice, correct oppression, defend the fatherless, plead for the widow" (Isa. 1:6–17). There are too many who just hear the Word—but to hear and not to do is self-deception.

The Word of God is a word of peace, unity, love, brotherhood, justice, and compassion. These attributes need to be practiced, not just heard. Too much that is said from those platforms is ignored. The church preaches love, yet some practice hate; the preacher preaches unity and there are those who undermine togetherness with lies and deceit, producing discord and fragmentation. We have heard the gospel; now is the time to act. We have heard, "Love your neighbor as yourself"—so let us begin to practice it. We have heard the gospel—it's high time that we implement it. "For if anyone is a hearer of the Word and not a doer, he is like a man who observes his natural face in a mirror; for he observes himself and goes away and at once forgets what he was like. But he who looks into the perfect law of liberty and preserves, being no hearer that forgets but a doer that acts, he shall be blessed in his doing."

"Religion that is pure and undefiled before God and the Father is this: to visit orphans and widows in their affliction, and to keep oneself unstained from the world" (James 127). Prior to this the author had written, "If anyone thinks he is religious, and does not bridle his tongue but deceives his heart, this man's religion is in vain." In other words, true religion is more than devotional exercises. Evidently, there were those who just went to the temple and participated in devotions and that was the extent of their religion. And there were those who thought that they were religious, yet they did not bridle their tongue. The writer of the book of James knew that the tongue must be controlled:

> So the tongue is a little member and boasts of great things, how great a forest is set ablaze by a small fire! The tongue is a fire. The tongue is an unrighteous world among our members, staining the whole body, setting on fire the cycle of nature . . . with the tongue, we bless the Lord and Father, and with it, we curse men who are

made in the likeness of God. From the same mouth come blessing and cursing. My brethren, this ought not to be so.

Oh, there are those who think they are religious yet their tongue is not controlled. You deceive yourself and religion is vain. An uncontrolled tongue spreads rumors, lies, gossip, and many times garbage. If this applies to us, then our religion is vain. God doesn't require anything except that which is honorable and true. The prophet Micah described true religion when he wrote, "What doth the Lord require of thee, but to do justly and to love mercy and to walk humbly with thy God" (Micah 6:8).

Don't let your mouth destroy you and your relationship with God. Don't waste your time with gossip. Use your tongue, your words to pray and give thanks to God. Paul says we must have the mind of Jesus,

> have this mind among yourselves which is yours in Christ Jesus, who though He was in the form of God, did not count equality with God a thing to be grasped . . . And being found in human form, he humbled himself and became obedient into death, even death on a cross. Therefore God has highly exalted him and bestowed on Him a name which is above every name, that at the name of Jesus every knee should bow, in heaven and on earth and under the earth and every tongue confess that Jesus Christ is Lord. (Cf. Phil. 2:5–11)

The courage to worship is to have discipline and action: Visit the orphans and the widows and do not be stained by the world. Don't turn up your nose at some poor child who may be ragged and hungry, but comfort and feed him. He may be the closest thing to God that you will ever see until that day when the Son of man comes in His glory.

> Before Him will be gathered all the nations and He will separate them one from another, as a shepherd separates the sheep from the goats. And He will place the sheep at His right hand but the goats at His left. Then the King will say to those at His right hand, "Come, O blessed of my Father, inherit the kingdom prepared for you. For I was hungry and you gave me food, I was thirsty and you gave me drink, I was a stranger and you welcomed me, I was naked and you clothed me, I was sick and you visited me, I was in prison and you came to me. Then the righteous will answer Him, "Lord when did we see thee hungry and feed thee or thirst and give thee drink. . . ." And the King

will answer, "Truly I say to you as you did it to one of the least of these my brethren, you did it to me" (Matt. 25:40). Then, he will say to those at his left hand, "Depart from me, you cursed into the eternal fire prepared for the devil and his angels. For I was hungry and you gave me no food, I was thirsty and you gave me no drink. . . ." And they will answer, "Lord when did we see thee hungry or thirsty or a stranger or naked or sick or in prison and did not minister to thee?" And he will answer them, "Truly, I say to you, as you did it not to one of the least of these you did it not to me" (Matt. 25:45).

THE COURAGE TO REJOICE, PRAY, AND GIVE THANKS

Rejoice always, pray constantly, give thanks in all circumstances;
for this is the will of God in Christ Jesus for you.
—Thessa. 5:16–18

The people in the Thessalonian Church were immature. They had little or no leadership. Forces attacked the gospel and questioned Paul's character—accusing him of greed, dishonesty, and other things. Timothy was sent to strengthen and help them to develop their faith. After visiting them, Timothy informed Paul of their faith and loyalty, and in response, Paul writes them this letter explaining how they should act as Christians. He also encourages the Thessalonians to respect their leaders and to think highly of them. Every church needs to respect its leadership if it is to make any substantial progress: "We beseech you brethren, to respect those who labor among you and are over you in the Lord and admonish you, and to esteem them very highly in love because of their work" (1 Thessa 5:12). Too many people love to have good leadership, love to have a dedicated reputable leader, but yet possess no real love for the person, nor his or her labors. So Paul continues encouraging the Thessalonians to be at peace among themselves, to help the weak, and to admonish the idlers.

The words of Scripture are very enlightening: "Rejoice always, pray constantly, give thanks in all circumstances for this is the will of God in Christ Jesus for you" (1 Thessa 5:18). Sometimes these things are hard to do, but the life of the Christian is a life of rejoicing—there's reason to rejoice because Christ has died for our sins and in spite of all else, we can be joyful. Let us consider these words more closely.

To rejoice is to be glad, happy, or delighted. I know that sorrow and agony sometimes weigh heavy upon our hearts and sometimes our own self-pity will drown our joy, and we may really become depressed as church leaders. Sometimes our experiences have been so painful, and our lives have been so marred and wrecked, that we become preoccupied with worry, melancholy, and sadness, but regardless of your situation—in spite of your burdens and heartaches and pain—the Scripture encourages us to rejoice always—rejoice always whether others think you have reason to or not—you can rejoice because only you know what God has done for you. You know what your life has been—you know what your life is today and for many of us there's reason to rejoice. You may not have it any easier—there may still be burdens—your family may be in need of direction, your children that you love so dearly may be gone astray—not living up to the teachings of the family nor the church, nor Jesus Christ, but you can still rejoice always, because although you may have reason to be sad, you may have reason to feel down, you may have reason to be depressed, you have a greater reason to rejoice always because Jesus died for the sins of the world. Rejoice always, because Jesus is the symbol of joy—rejoice because Jesus knows all about us. He knows about our troubles, he knows about our pain or sorrow, our family, and our loved ones, and if we love the Lord, rejoice always. We know that as Jesus journeyed into Jerusalem, the people lined the streets, rejoicing because the King had arrived.

The Scripture says, "As he was drawing near, at the descent of the Mount of Olives, the whole multitude of the disciples began to rejoice and praise God with a loud voice. . . ." We, too, must have a rejoiceful spirit, and Christ gives us that spirit.

Prayer consoles the mind and the spirit. The Thessalonians needed something to aid them in their development and growth, and there is no better consoling element than prayer. Prayer enables the soul to speak to itself—my soul preaches to me through moments of meditation. Our prayers on Sunday morning reflect the constancy of meditation in our lives. How can we pray for the congregation and the community if we don't pray every day? To pray constantly is to recognize that God is with us at all times—God is omnipresent—God never leaves us and our constant prayerful posture is in effect a testimony to the meaning of God in our lives. In the language of the church, "God never slumbers or sleeps." As a child, I was taught to pray, and every night before going to bed, then and now, I pray to God for his continued blessings. The church should embrace a prayerful attitude. Everything that we do should be done after prayer. Sometimes we don't know which way to turn; sometimes we don't know what decisions to make—whether to remain faithful or to go astray. We don't know how to treat our fellow brothers and sisters—sometimes we don't know whether we are doing the right thing. But I believe if we go to our secret closets more often, if we get on our knees more often, if we have a little talk with God more often, he will lead us in the right direction. "Just a little talk with Jesus to tell him all about our struggles, and he'll answer by and by. Just a little talk with Jesus makes it right." Talk to him about your family—tell him that you need the help of the spirit. Talk to Jesus about your pain, about your sorrows, and about your fear. He understands. When everyone else is unable to comfort you, call on God. Jesus had to pray as he began to face the agony of the cross. Hezekiah prayed as death was about to look him in the face. Paul and Silas prayed as they were held captive in prison, but as Wordsworth says, "Stone walls do not a prison make," especially when Jesus is in your heart. Martin Luther King and many others who were incarcerated unjustly were able to endure because God heard their cries. He hears our prayerful cries. He has heard you and me. I have prayed constantly that the church, would come to be an example of God's people that was true and faithful. I have prayed constantly that the church, would realize that God does answer prayer and we can do anything worthwhile if we believe that God is able. I have prayed constantly that the church would learn to work together, in unity and in love. I have prayed, you have prayed, my grandmother prayed, my family has prayed, those who love me have prayed that my life will make a difference, that Jesus will use me to glorify his name and I'm so glad. I'm glad that I know prayer changes things. It changes hate into love, it changes broken families into loving relationships, it changes churches from cold, empty buildings to warm, loving fellowships. Pray constantly.

Moreover, "give thanks in all circumstances for this is the will of God in Christ Jesus for you"(1 Thessa 5:18). Thankfulness is a part of a Christian's posture, not just in times of joy, but in all times. It's difficult to be thankful in times of grief and sorrow, but it is in these moments that we really have reason to thank God. The older people thank God that "while they slumbered and slept last night, the hands of death did not snatch them from this life." Whatever circumstances we find ourselves in, we need to be thankful. Thank God in all circumstances, for this is the will of God.

Part II

Working Together:
Black Ministers and Laity
in the Urban Church

· 3 ·

The Urban Church:
Leadership among Clergy
and Laity

Except the Lord keep the city, the watchman waketh but in vain.
—Ps. 127:16

Behold, how good and pleasant it is when brethren work together in unity.
—Ps. 133:1

HISTORICAL OVERVIEW

The African American church began in the hearts and souls of Afro-American slaves who had been uprooted and transported to the United States to be auctioned to the highest bidder. As chattel for 250 years, these Black people had been legally and socially violated to the extent that their ontological status was essentially denied by the wielders of power. Their humanness was rejected by the nature and spirit of law and social structure. This was indeed the most serious effect of slavery, because as an institution, slavery tended to negate not only Descartes's existentialist maxim, *cogito ergo sum*, but, more importantly, God's will to freedom. However, this attempt at total emasculation—a deliberate effort to strip the African American of any vestige of honor and respect, failed from the beginning. Much of this failure can be attributed to the inner ability of Blacks to survive in the midst of extremely difficult situations. The journey to America aboard the slave ships was a cruel odyssey to a land where oppression would be perpetuated and commodified. Nevertheless, those who survived had to have been physically tough and spiritually determined to defy and even obviate the odds. Defiance was a necessary ingredient in the personalities of those who survived. The

Black church was born out of defiance and a determination to be free.

So the slaves' inner strength and stamina, along with the Quakers' teaching and evangelization efforts, helped enable the Black church to begin. Carter G. Woodson states that:

> The real interest in the evangelization of the Negroes in the English Colonies . . . was manifested by the Quakers. . . . In accepting these persons of color on a basis of religious equality and denouncing the nakedness of the religions of the other colonists at the same time, the Quakers alienated their affection and easily brought down upon them the wrath of the public functionaries in these plantations.[1]

The White slaveholders did not want the slaves to read, write, or be taught the ways of self-determination because they felt "nonbeings" should not be accorded such rights. Moreover, education would become a route to freedom. In spite of this, "George Fox was advocating the instruction of Negroes in 1672 and in 1679 boldly entreating his coworkers to instruct and teach the Indians and Negroes how 'Christ by the grace of God has tasted death for every man.'"[2] The Quakers' evangelization effort provided the foundation for the slaves to assert their own humanity in later years. Moreover, as time elapsed and Christianity became more understood, slaves began to draw inferences and make deductions from their experiences. Religious equality advocated by the Quakers was not compatible with social, economic, political, and humanitarian inequality advocated and perpetuated by law and public policy. The slaves recognized and were repelled by this contradiction as they witnessed America's resolve to be free from the oppressive power of England while her citizenry simultaneously subjugated them and violated their human rights. According to Albert J. Raboteau, "As early as 1774 American slaves were declaring publicly and politically that they thought Christianity and slavery were incompatible."[3] The Black church was born in the midst of this political and social struggle. Whites were struggling for their freedom from their mother country and Blacks were enslaved and struggling to be free in America. This paradox represented the embodiment of racism, contradiction, and oppression. During these early years the African American church was formed and shaped by the experience of degradation, despair, and disgrace coupled with a desire to be free. Leroy Fitts indicates that:

During the formative period of Black church life, the Black Baptist Preachers, more specifically had to come to grips with the pragmatic situation of life in America. They had to relate a relevant theology to slavery in the South and White racism throughout the nation. They had to keep in tune with the heartbeats of their brothers in Black.[4]

The minister and laity have historically reflected each other; however, the minister's commitment to preaching the Gospel required a level of boldness that all did not possess. As a preacher, the minister was a leader who enabled others to understand the sociopolitical and theological dimensions of life. "The Black Baptist Preachers were, in a real sense, the political and social philosophers of the race. They were able and fearless advocates of truth, justice, and equal rights for an oppressed people."[5]

THE STRENGTH OF THE LAITY

The Black church was born during slavery and continued to grow and thrive throughout each phase of American history. Today, it is a strong and viable institution, consisting of several national conventions and millions of constituents. The laity in these churches possess a strong numerical presence and power capable of changing the face of urban America if this power can be harnessed and directed toward transforming our society. The Black church is a social institution, as Kenneth Clark and others have described; however, it is also the harborer of tremendous political strength that is becoming more apparent via the laity. The laity have become more educated and economically stable; however, they have not capitalized on the economic boom that characterized the 1990s in the same way as the Whites. Their ranks include professionals from every major field of expertise, such as medicine, law, business, humanities, social science, and engineering. The constituents of the Black urban church have survived many hardships and difficulties, and these experiences have contributed to their stamina and strength.

Much research and analysis reveal that the Black laity constitute a relatively stable, captive audience that can influence the political and socioeconomic agenda of the pastoral leader/minister if he or she is aware of their expectations. This is not to suggest that ministers will or should adhere to the political wishes and wants of the laity, but suggests that there is a great strength ready to be used for agreed-upon purposes. Who constitutes the Black laity, and what expectations do they have for Black ministers' involvement in political and socioeconomic issues? More specifically, we explored whether people who attend the Black church expect the minister to deal with socioeconomic and political problems. What particular urban problems do they expect him or her to offer leadership in facing or solving? Are people who attend church interested in spiritual growth of some sort, and what more do the Black laity expect other than spiritual leadership from the minister?

Distinction is often made between types of churches because the cities have sufficient numbers of Black Protestant denominations as well as other forms of Christian churches to merit a meaningful contrast in points of view regarding their expectations. However, here the term Black urban church laity refers to all of those denominations or sects that constitute organized Black religious bodies.

The minister and laity are inextricably tied. Their relationship is akin to a doctor's relationship to patients or a teacher's relationship to students. More precisely, there is a mutual relationship—each group needs the other in order to function as an effective group. Simultaneously, there is a chasm between the two as implied by the perceived dichotomy of classification.

The laity are an important, powerful group representing the essence of power in congregational churches as well as a growing force in the hierarchical churches. In autonomous churches, or churches with congregational polity, the laity are the ultimate decision-making body. Almost every recommendation, policy, procedure, or action that commits the church has to be approved by the church's laity. Congregants' expectations of the minister in dealing with the community and world's political and social problems provide the minister with some guidance in meeting the needs of his/her congregation and the larger urban community.

The laity's expectations of the minister's involvement in political and socioeconomic leadership issues in the urban community may help to develop a mechanism for addressing some of the prevailing urban issues and problems. The a priori assumption is that as responsible social and political beings, ministers will often seek to adapt to the laity's level of expectations if these expectations do not morally and ethically diminish his or her character or negatively affect one's leadership. This adaptation is a positive sign of the minister's flexibility in situations that demand pliability rather than embracing an excessive dogmatism.

The Black church is an intricate part of the urban community in America. Moreover, it is also the most independent, self-determining institution in the Black community. Each person who participates in the church, however marginally, and is not a licensed or ordained minister constitutes the laity. Much has been written about the Black church as a forerunner in developing leaders, especially clergy. Conversely, very few have focused mainly upon the laity's expectations of the leaders. There is a paucity of data on laity expectations that focus extensively on the Black minister as a leader in an urban setting. Dubose writes,

> As Blacks became urbanized, they became better educated. They produced outstanding leaders. Out of Black ghettos of America have come some of the leading citizens in education, politics, sports, and entertainment. The church has been prominent in developing these leaders. The Black pastor today still enjoys a much higher community status than his White counterpart.[6]

Because the Black minister serves a people who have historically been victimized by institutional oppression, injustice, and racism, it is important to understand the expectations of the laity in urban areas in order to chart the future directions of the minister as he or she serves the urban community. The laity are a critical segment of the population, with the potential to help shape the agenda and political involvement of the minister. The urban minister and laity are surrounded by a variety of political and social conditions of poverty, racism, injustice, and oppression endemic to their existential situation. The laity's expectations can foster a more active role in effectuating change or at least confronting the problems of the urban community.

Clergy already occupy political positions or are involved in attempts to eradicate social and political dimensions of the urban milieu. People such as Nat Turner and Gabriel Prosser, whose names are "buried forever under the debris of the citadel of slavery," as well as modern leaders such as Adam Clayton Powell, Malcolm X, Martin Luther King Jr., Leon Sullivan, and Walter Fauntleroy have exemplified the fact that Black ministers are involved in the political and social life of urban America.[7] The extent to which Black urban laity expect such involvement is largely the focus of this part of the book.

THE ROLE OF THE BLACK MINISTER AND LAITY

The minister is like no other professional. He is preacher, teacher, administrator, encourager, counselor, leader, and friend to all types of individuals. In the book, *Ten Faces of Ministry*, Milo Brekke, Merton Strommen, and Dorothy Williams describe the minister quite thoroughly. They state,

> Ministers occupy a peculiar and sensitive position; they are people both more powerful and less powerful than others with similar education and social status. People feel free to admire them extravagantly and criticize them severely. A minister occupies a very public position, yet often shares people's most private thoughts and concerns.[7]

The minister is expected to be a leader with the attendant administrative responsibilities in the church, but his or her role extends beyond church responsibilities into the wider community. Moreover, there are those within the local church who feel that the minister should devote his or her time and energy to evangelistic goals and that the gospel be propagated and reflected in his activities. Other laity want the minister to be actively involved in the dismantling of oppressive social, economic, and political barriers. The minister understands that laity have mixed feelings about his active involvement in what is considered politics, but it is good to remember that few institutions are more political than the church itself. The church, both Black and White, is laden with elements of the political—from the selection of the pastoral leader to selection of committee members.

Historically, the Black minister has had to play numerous roles in the urban community because he was more insulated from the power of retribution wielded by Whites who vehemently disagreed with efforts to liberate oppressed people. The autonomy of the African American church, especially the Baptist Church, remains one of its most powerful tools. Because the church to a large extent operates independent of the White power structure, it is uniquely and strategically capable of positively affecting the urban condition.

The condition of Black America demands that the urban minister give direction to the empowerment of a people who have been victims of the abuse of power in American society. This empowerment can be achieved by educating African Americans about the serious need to develop a strong nuclear and extended family structure, a strong and viable local church, and a pool of economic and political analysts to develop the most viable methods of enhancing the position of African Americans.

The minister and the church are critical to the development of a just and fair society. Certainly, the gospel must be preached, but the minister is also responsible for helping to liberate people from the forces of oppression that pervade the cities and towns of this nation. The harnessing of the strengths of the minister and laity will take ingenuity, creativity, and commitment to the cause of freedom and justice.

THE BLACK CHURCH DURING AND SINCE E. FRANKLIN FRAZIER AND C. ERIC LINCOLN

The Christian church occupied by those of African descent has undergone a transformation from being a Negro church as described by E. Franklin Frazier to the Black church as described by C. Eric Lincoln. For Frazier, the Negro church represented an acculturated entity devoid of any African influences. However, Frazier's study is important more for what it postulates about the power of the church—whether Negro or Black. The Negro church as the forerunner of the Black church created a social system that gave order and meaning to Black life. Frazier describes the Negro church as a "nation within a nation," which I believe has been weakened if not destroyed by integration and other semblances of equality and justice. In many ways the Negro church was much more powerful and central to Black life than the so-called Black church.

The Negro church was born out of the merger of the "invisible institution" and the institutional church. This merger created a more structured and organized life for Black people. Frazier asserts, "The merger resulted in the structuring or organization of Negro life to an extent that had not existed."[8]

Frazier indicates that slavery and the plantation economy had prevented any efforts to organize and create a viable social system, i.e., family or religious development. However, after emancipation this changed. Frazier argues forthrightly stating:

This all changed when the Negro became free, and it is our purpose here to show how an organized religious life became the chief means by which a structured or organized social life came into existence among the Negro masses. The process by which the invisible institution of the slaves merged with the institutional churches built by the free Negroes had to overcome many difficulties. These difficulties arose chiefly from the fact that there were among the free Negroes many mulattos and that they, as well as the unmixed Negroes, represented a higher degree of assimilation of white or European culture.[9]

To some extent there remain vestiges of this differentiation in churches today. Some Black churches continue to be characterized by a worship style more indicative of European influences than what might be termed "Africanisms, or influences from Africa. Overall, the Negro church became an amalgamation of African and American influences."

There is a tension that continues to exist within particular congregants and therefore within local congregations. Frazier argues that this merged church, now the Negro church, became an agency of social control, a promoter of economic cooperation and educational development, an arena of political life, and a refuge in a hostile white world. By social control he means a regulator of sexual activities and a formulator of marriage and family values reflective of the public behaviors of whites in the United States. The values and morals of white folk as expressed in their documents and laws do not necessarily mean that this is what they practiced. Black folk have always known that the ways of White folk represented their true values and morals, rather than idealistic written documents, e.g., the constitution or the Declaration of Independence.

The fact that Negroes learned to pool their money for the express purpose of buying land and building their own churches, as well as to mutually aid one another during time of sickness and death is a testament to the spirit of unity and love that permeated Black ontology and ecclesiology. This obviates, to some extent, the belief in popular culture that Black folk are like crabs—always pulling each other down out of self-centeredness and self-interest. The Negro church did work together for the betterment of Black people.

The role of the church and the Negro preacher in establishing educational institutions cannot be overemphasized because religious training was of paramount importance. Moreover, as Frazier says, "The Negro preacher who was often the best educated man in the community took the initiative in establishing schools."[10]

Additionally, the church was the place that developed and encouraged preachers and others to become political leaders. People, such as Bishop Henry McNeil Turner, were probably the first Blacks to serve in the Georgia State Legislature during Reconstruction. Also, Bishop James W. Hood was elected president of the first convention of Negroes in North Carolina and served as the Assistant Superintendent of Public Instruction for the State of North Carolina. Frazier points out that "These ministers who became the political leaders of Negroes were all Republicans and shared on the whole the conservative political philosophy of the party."[12]

Frazier's perspective, unlike Melville Herskovits, can be capsulized in the following words from the conclusion of his book *The Negro Church in America:*

> The Negroes were practically stripped of their social heritage and their traditional social organization was destroyed as the result of the manner in which they were enslaved and became the labor force in the plantation economy. They did not possess a historical tradition and whatever memories of their African culture were preserved through oral transmission lost their meaning when there was no longer a social organization to sustain them.[13]

I believe that this conclusion does not logically follow from the earlier assertions made about the Negro church and the slaves that helped to bring this institution into existence. In this sense, Frazier's conclusion is a non sequitur. The very fact that the Negro church became a critical religious and social force in the life of African Americans (Negroes) implies that there were memories and practices sublimated by the chains and whips of White oppression—but not annihilated or destroyed. For Frazier to assert that "They did not possess a historical tradition" and their memories of Africa were lost is not a valid conclusion based upon the reality of Black religious and social life. Du Bois, Herskovits, Levine, Sobel, and others have suggested otherwise. Du Bois particularly suggests in *The Souls of Black Folk* that the slave preacher represented a continuous line of influence of Africa on American soil. In many ways Frazier makes the same point, but concludes something entirely different. Frazier seems to vacillate between accepting and not accepting the role of Africa in the religious and social life of the development of the Negro church in America.

C. Eric Lincoln argues that the Negro church has been transformed into the Black church where there is a new life created by a new radical consciousness. The Negro church died and the Black church was born. This new church took pride in its Blackness, no longer ambivalent about its ontology or its role in the freedom struggle. Lincoln makes a pointed statement about the church Union efforts of the sixties and suggests why Black denominations never had a serious interest in Committee on Church Union (COCU).

> Black Christians have had a bitter experience with religion in the White Man's church and that experience transcended slavery and freedom alike. Wherever White Christians and Black Christians had come in contact with each other in America, Black Christians had been demeaned by the White Man's presumption of social superiority.[14]

Clearly, the Black church represented a new understanding of God and the existential situation in which Blacks found themselves. The fact that White folk had been constructing theologies and philosophies that were grounded in exclusionary dogmas and practices gave birth to the movements of persons like Martin Luther King Jr. and Malcolm X as well as to a constructive Black theology—a theology of liberation. Moreover, the Black church since Frazier was a church with a new language, a more radical theology, and a church that took seriously the words of singer James Brown, "I'm Black and I'm Proud." The Black Power movement helped to focus the Black church on issues of racial pride, justice, and freedom.

The next three chapters explore the relationship between ministers and laity and determine more clearly why neither can afford to be passive in a society that is actively trying to exacerbate the inequities and unfairness endemic to life in urban America. The leadership of the pastor in the local churches, both large and small, will be necessary to foster individual and societal transformation. As a general practitioner in the ministry, the pastor is expected to provide leadership in a host of areas that include faith development, social and political policy development, education and training of children, youth, and adults within the local congregation, and a host of other practical and theological areas.

· 4 ·

We Hold These Truths:
What the Laity Expect
of the Minister

To ascertain the Black church laity's expectations of clergy in urban areas, specifically related to social and political issues, a survey consisting of sixty-three questions and statements was used to determine if the laity expect the minister to deal with socio-economic and political problems in urban areas, and if so, which particular problems. This chapter focuses on statements that constitute three categories, or clusters. These clusters—Aggressive Political Leadership, Active Concern for the Oppressed, and Precedence of Evangelistic Goals—reveal the contrast between the ministry's social and political sphere and its traditional sphere. After the statements were determined to constitute the said subgroups, each cluster were formed using the social science cluster analysis technique. Both the clusters and individual statements constituting the clusters were provided by the national study conducted by the Association of Theological Schools in America and Canada that culminated in the book *Ministry in America*. Because this writer does not utilize the complex statistical technique called analysis of variance, the emphasis here is placed on the uniqueness of each individual statement within each cluster. Chiefly concerned with the social and political expectations of laity regarding clergy, this study does not attempt to duplicate, to any degree, the national study mentioned earlier. This chapter provides an explanation of the responses to each statement that constitute the clusters.

Statistically significant relationships between specific variables measured at the .05 level are discussed in order to test the hypothesis. The chi-square statistic was used to determine if there was a significant relationship between denomination affiliation and each of the items in the core clusters that constitute independent variables. Moreover, chi-square also was used to determine if the respondent's socioeconomic status (income, education, and occupation) was statistically significant relative to the individual items that constitute the relevant clusters.

CHARACTERISTICS OF RESPONDENTS

The survey utilized ten urban churches representing seven denominations. There was a total of 338 respondents. Of those who responded, 240 were females (71.3%) and 97 were males (28.7%). The two largest percentages of respondents were Baptists, who made up 36.1 percent of the total sample, and the Church of God in Christ, which was 19.8 percent of the sample. The fact that the urban church constituents are mostly female and Baptist is no surprise. This suggests that the sample is representative and, therefore, represents a microcosm of the African American church today. While a negligible percentage of other races were represented, 95.9 percent of the respondents were Black. Also, 28.4 percent of the respondents had attended college; 21.3 percent had attended high school or trade school. College graduates totaled 15.7 percent (table 4.1).

These statistics indicate that the Black urban church laity are becoming more educated—an indication that corresponds with the general increase in the number and percentage of Blacks matriculating and graduating from colleges in the past twenty years or more.

A study by the Center for the Study of Social Policy found that: Between 1960 and 1981 Black males made a gain of 4.4 years of schooling on the average, compared with 1.9 years for White males. By 1981, the median level of schooling for Black males and females was above 12 years, and the difference between White and Black years of schooling was only half a year.[1]

Although the percentage of Black college graduates has increased over the past fifteen years, it is much less than the 15.7 percent found in this study's sample.

Census Bureau data show that in 1967, the year before a big push for education began, 6.8 percent of White adults and 2.6 percent of

TABLE 4.1 Demographic Characteristics of the Respondents

	Number of Respondents	Percentage*
Denomination		
African Methodist Episcopal (Zion)	32	9.5
Baptist	122	36.1
Church of God in Christ	67	19.8
Episcopal	33	9.8
Presbyterian	18	5.3
Lutheran	23	6.8
Disciples of Christ	43	12.7
Total	**338**	**100.0**
Sex		
Male	97	28.7
Female	241	71.3
Total	**338**	**100.0**
Education		
Eighth grade or less	8	2.4
Some high school or trade school	36	10.7
High school or trade school graduate	72	21.3
Some college	96	28.4
College graduate	53	15.7
Some graduate or professional	31	9.2
Seminary graduate	1	0.3
Master's	20	5.9
Master's plus	14	4.1
Doctorate	7	2.1
Total	**338**	**100.0**
Income		
Under $3,000	20	5.9
$3,000–$5,999	9	2.7
$6,000–$8,999	15	4.4
$9,000–$11,999	23	6.8
$12,000–$14,999	38	11.2
$15,000–$17,999	31	9.2
$18,000–$20,999	30	8.9
$21,000–$23,999	31	9.2
$24,000–$26,999	29	8.6
$27,000–and above	112	33.1
Total	**338**	**100.0**

*Percentages in some of the following tables do not add up to exactly 100 due to rounding.

Black adults had graduated from college. In 1983, the figures rose to 11 percent of White adults and 5.7 percent of Black adults.[2]

The percentage of college graduates was almost three times larger than the percentage of Black graduates in the general population. These have changed dramatically in the last ten years.

Moreover, 33.1 percent of the respondents earned $27,000 or more, while 11.2 percent earned $12,000 to $14,999. These data suggest that the sample was more economically advantaged than the general Black population. Although the economic boom of the nineties has helped to boost the economic condition of more African Americans, the rate of poverty among Blacks in the South and the nation is increasing at an alarming rate. In December of 1984, Steve Suitts prepared a report for the Southern Regional Council which stated

> Some groups have been particularly affected by the steady increases in the poverty rate in both the South and the nation since 1979. Including more than 1 in 3 Blacks, the nation's poverty rate of 35.7 percent for all Black persons rose in the last four years from 31 percent in 1979. Not since 1968 has the poverty rate for Blacks reached such a high level. While the exact statistical rate is not available, poverty among Blacks in the eleven southern states has probably risen to 39 percent rate, which now makes almost 2 out of every 5 Blacks below poverty.[3]

In a June 1995 report written by Leatha Lamison-White of the Economics and Statistics Administration, U.S. Department of Commerce, statistics showed that, in 1990, more than 1 in 5 Americans—or 52 million—lived in a "poverty area." Poverty areas are census tracts or block numbering areas (BNAs), where at least 20 percent of residents were poor in 1989. Just over two-thirds of poverty area residents lived in a metropolitan area. In some of these areas, poverty was especially widespread, as 40 percent or more of residents were poor. About 1 in 25 Americans lived in such a tract, or BNA, known as an "extreme poverty area."

Most residents of poverty areas were not poor. Poverty areas have high concentrations of poor persons, but that doesn't mean that everyone living in them is poor. In fact, the majority of the nation's poverty area residents (69%) were above the poverty line in 1989.

Poverty areas had a different racial and ethnic makeup than the rest of the United States. Whites made up more than half of the population living in poverty areas. However, they comprised a higher proportion of those living outside such areas. This was not the case for Blacks and Hispanics. Four times as many Blacks and three times as many Hispanics lived in poverty areas than lived outside them.

In poverty areas, earnings were lower. Workers living in poverty areas earned an average of $15,521 during 1989, much less than the $23,122 earned by those living outside such areas. At the same time, persons in poverty areas were more than three times more likely than nonpoverty area adults to have received public assistance income that year (10% compared with 3%).

In poverty areas, unemployment was more than twice as high as in nonpoverty areas (12% versus 5%). In addition, those in poverty areas were more likely not to have worked at all in 1989 (38% compared with 27%). Conversely, persons in nonpoverty areas were more apt to have worked year-round, full-time (43% versus 30%).

Families maintained by women with no husband present were more prevalent in poverty areas. Families in poverty areas were nearly twice as likely as those elsewhere to have a female householder (29% versus 13%) and less likely to be maintained by a married couple (65% compared with 83%).

Very large families were also prevalent. One in twenty-five poverty area families consisted of seven or more persons. In nonpoverty areas, only about 1 in 75 families were that large.

Poverty area householders were less educated. For 29 percent of poverty area householders, high school was the highest level of education completed; the same was true of a similar proportion of their counterparts who lived outside poverty areas. But poverty area householders were less apt to have furthered their education. For instance:

- Fifteen percent had attended college without obtaining a degree.
- Ten percent more had a bachelor's as their highest degree earned.

The corresponding proportions for householders residing outside poverty areas were higher: 21 and 25 percent, respectively.

Self-care and mobility limitations were more common in poverty areas. Eleven percent of persons in poverty areas had a self-care or mobility limitation. In other words, they had been suffering from a health condition for at least the last 6 months, which made it difficult for them to take care of personal needs (such as bathing or dressing) or go outside the home alone. The corresponding rate in nonpoverty areas was 6 percent.

Poor homeowners, rather scarce outside poverty areas (where they made up about 5% of all homeowners), were considerably more prevalent inside poverty areas, where they comprised 15 percent.

For many in poverty areas, rent took a real bite out of income. Almost 1 in every 4 renters living in poverty areas spent at least half their 1989 household income on gross rent (contract rent plus the cost of utilities) in comparison to only 16 percent elsewhere.

Nearly half the nation's poverty area population lived in the South. The South, home to 34 percent of the nation's total population, contained 48 percent of its poverty area residents. This was because 30 percent of southerners lived in poverty areas—the highest percentage of any region. The corresponding rate was 19 percent in the West, 17 percent in the Midwest, and 15 percent in the Northeast. (U.S. Dept. of Commerce)

The income of the respondents in this study was almost the exact opposite of the general population of Blacks in southern states. Whereas 39 percent of Blacks in southern states are living in poverty, 33.1 percent of the respondents in this study made $27,000 or more. The income of the laity in this study suggests that Black urban church members are economically stable in a time when a growing number of African Americans are in poverty. Moreover, there seems to be a positive correlation between church attendance and participation and escaping from the grips of abject poverty. Most people in church not only look like they are doing well, but are in fact doing better than the general population. There is something about being connected with the African American church that tends to moderate one's poverty status.

Examination of the Data

Tables 4.2 and 4.3 contain two of the most important core clusters to this study, Aggressive Political Leadership and Active Concern for the Oppressed.

Aggressive Political Leadership is characterized by working actively to protest and change social wrongs. Active Concern for the Oppressed is characterized by knowledgeably and earnestly working on behalf of minority and oppressed people.[4]

TABLE 4.2 Aggressive Political Leadership

1. Participates in an effort to remove an incompetent or ineffective official from school, church, union, or government
2. Speaks from the pulpit about political issues
3. Uses principles and methods of social organization for political change
4. Organizes groups to change civil laws that seem in light of Scripture to be morally wrong
5. Encourages nonunion laborers to organize
6. Is willing to risk arrest to protest social wrongs
7. Works to make sure that all people are free to buy property in areas of their choice
8. Pressures public officials on behalf of the oppressed
9. Organizes action groups in the congregation to accomplish directly some political or social goal
10. Organizes study groups in congregations or community to discuss public affairs
11. Declares a willingness to run for public office in the community (school board, city council, etc.)
12. Takes an informed position on controversial community issues

TABLE 4.3 Active Concern for the Oppressed

1. Works toward racial integration in the community
2. Uses authoritative information and facts to meet racism and prejudice in the congregation and community
3. Works to integrate people of varying educational, ethnic, and cultural backgrounds into the congregation
4. Acquaints self with the history and aspirations of minority groups and other oppressed people
5. Makes individuals aware of their possible part in causing world poverty
6. Recommends that the parish cut off financial support for institutions (hospitals, missions, etc.) that discriminate against minorities

These two core clusters contain eighteen statements that are more perceived to be political and/or social than religious. Conversely, there is within the questionnaire items that emphasize the religious more than the political. These items have been core-clustered to form Precedence of Evangelistic Goals (table 4.4), which indicates that there is an overwhelming belief that the process of creating a better society is not as important (comparatively) as the evangelization of humanity.[5] Four items form this cluster; an explanation of each item is provided near the end of this chapter.

TABLE 4.4 Precedence of Evangelistic Goals

1. Holds that the church's task of proclaiming the gospel by preaching and teaching overshadows in importance the task of helping to eliminate physical sufferings of people
2. Frequently approaches strangers to ask about the condition of their soul
3. Priorities in use of time and the belief that the one and only way to build an ideal world society is to convert everyone to Christianity
4. Insists that clergy should stick to religion and not concern themselves with social, economic, and political questions

Survey respondents rated statements that constituted the dependent variables. The relationship between the independent variables (i.e., denomination, income, education, and occupation) and the dependent variables is analyzed using the chi-square statistic. For descriptive purposes, responses to each of the items that constitute the three core clusters already mentioned will be reviewed and analyzed. Moreover, for this discussion, the original seven category labels were reduced to three categories in order to handle the results more concisely and to reduce the possible perception of redundancy.[6] Nevertheless, tables used in this chapter reflect the actual responses.

AGGRESSIVE POLITICAL LEADERSHIP AND THE PETER PRINCIPLE

This cluster, Aggressive Political Leadership, contains twelve statements that describe its content. Each of these statements is discussed relative to the respondents' expectations of the minister. A summary of this cluster follows the explication of the last statement.

Participates in an Effort to Remove an Incompetent or Ineffective Official from School, Church, Union, or Government

According to the data, there was no statistically significant relationship between occupation, education, and denomination when these variables were cross-tabulated with responses to the statement, "participates in an effort to remove an incompetent or ineffective official from school, church, union, or government." In effect, one's response to this item was not significantly affected by the type of church he/she attended or by one's socioeconomic status. This suggests that the respondents were more willing to tolerate the effect of the Peter Principle than to forge the idea of eradicating perceived incompetence in officials of school, church, union, and government. Moreover, because the issue is incompetence or ineffectiveness and not the institution where it occurs, it would be impossible to determine if one's effort to remove an incompetent from one institution would differ from one's effort to remove an incompetent from another institution. The Peter Principle suggests that individuals tend to rise to their level of incompetence:

> Occupational incompetence is everywhere. . . . We see indecisive politicians posing as resolute statesmen. . . . Limitless are the public servants who are indolent and insolent; military commanders whose behavioral timidity belies their dread-naught rhetoric, and governors whose innate servility prevents their actually governing. In our sophistication, we virtually shrug aside the immoral cleric, corrupt judge, incoherent attorney, author who cannot write and English teachers who cannot spell.[7]

In general, respondents indicated that this item was important; 61.2 percent rated it as important and 28.7 percent said it was undesirable, while 10.0 percent had no opinion (see table 4.5).

Speaks from the Pulpit about Political Issues

Basically, three-fourths of the respondents indicated that they expected the minister to speak from the pulpit about political issues. African Americans know that the church has been historically the place where people learned about voting and working together for the cause of freedom. Moreover, one who has worked

TABLE 4.5 Participates in an Effort to Remove an Incompetent or Ineffective Official from School, Church, Union, or Government

Responses	Number of Respondents	Percentage
Highly important	88	26.0
Quite important	45	13.3
Somewhat important	74	21.9
Undesirable	22	6.5
Detrimental	75	22.2
Reject item	20	5.9
Does not apply	14	4.1
Total	**338**	**99.9**

intimately in church is well schooled in the political nature of leadership because the church is very political in all aspects. An overwhelming 74.5 percent rated this item important; 18.0 percent felt it was undesirable, while 7.4 percent had no opinion. Responses to this item suggest that the laity expect the clergy to use the pulpit as a forum for addressing political issues. Adam Clayton Powell, Jesse Jackson, Martin Luther King Jr., and many others have done this quite effectively. Table 4.6 describes the responses.

It is important to note that of the total sample of 338 respondents, the largest single category of respondents who felt that this item was important were people with some college education. This suggests a positive correlation between college education and expectations of the laity relative to the minister's use of the pulpit to address political issues. The relationship is not *statistically* significant, yet it may have *practical* significance because more and more people are getting involved in church for reasons they describe as "networking." Networking by its very nature is a political activity, whether it's done in church or on the golf course. And, since more African Americans attend church than play golf, the church has become the natural place to rub shoulders and hob-nob with those who are seeking their Christian growth.

Uses Principles and Methods of Social Organization for Political Change

Two-thirds of the respondents to the statement, "Uses Principles and Methods of Social Organization for Political Change" indicated that it was important to them; 21.9 percent felt that it was undesir-

TABLE 4.6 Speaks from the Pulpit about Political Issues

Responses	Number of Respondents	Percentage
Highly important	94	27.8
Quite important	83	24.5
Somewhat important	75	22.2
Undesirable	37	10.9
Detrimental	24	7.1
Reject item	12	3.6
Does not apply	13	3.8
Total	**338**	**99.9**

able. This clearly suggests that the majority of people in the urban church expect the minister to effect political change by using social organization. This strategy demands creativity and imagination to effectively bring about political change. The minister's understanding of the principles and methods of social organization will strengthen his or her ability to usher in political change, as long as he or she is able to adapt these methods to the particular problem and to convince constituents of the usefulness of this approach. In practice, this may mean establishing focus groups in the church to determine the feasibility of a certain course of action, as well as, sampling organizations/age groups to determine the likelihood that certain changes can be effectuated without destroying the organization. Table 4.7 describes the frequency of responses to this item.

Organizes Groups to Change Civil Laws That Seem in Light of Scripture to Be Morally Wrong

Creating effective methods to change civil laws, such as organizing groups, is a clear departure from traditional clergy roles. In response to this item, the laity believe that injustice as manifested in civil laws should be confronted by the Black minister. More precisely, an overwhelming 62.5 percent of the respondents felt that it was important to organize groups devoted to changing unjust civil laws to conform with the spirit of the Scripture. A meager 23.3 percent felt that this was undesirable, and 14.2 percent had no opinion.

The organization of groups to advocate change in civil laws that are perceived to be biblically and morally wrong is conceptually and practically a real part of the Black minister's experience. For

TABLE 4.7 Uses Principles and Methods of Social Organization for Political Change

Responses	Number of Respondents	Percentage
Highly important	63	18.6
Quite important	96	28.4
Somewhat important	67	19.8
Undesirable	54	16.0
Detrimental	20	5.9
Reject item	16	4.7
Does not apply	22	6.5
Total	**338**	**99.9**

TABLE 4.8 Organizes Groups to Change Civil Laws That Seem in Light
of Scripture to Be Morally Wrong

Responses	Number of Respondents	Percentage
Highly important	106	31.4
Quite important	12	3.6
Somewhat important	93	27.5
Undesirable	13	3.8
Detrimental	66	19.5
Reject item	16	4.7
Does not apply	32	9.5
Total	**338**	**100.0**

example, the Southern Christian Leadership Conference was the
result of a minister's ability to organize regional and national support for changing unjust laws that were first repelled by Rosa
Parks. The Montgomery Bus Boycott represented the embryonic
stages of a massive movement that revealed the Black minister's
ability to organize and mobilize. In the new millennium, there is a
need to remind some Blacks who have migrated to the predominately White church that racism is still alive and kicking although
it is not as blatant and boisterous as it has been. The Black church
was born out of protest against racial injustice and more indifference. Those who are comfortable in the White church need to be
reminded that Blacks have been forced out of the White church
before because of issues of race and class. Let's not forget Richard
Allen and Absolom Jones.

Encourages Nonunion Laborers to Organize

Interestingly, less than half of the respondents expected the minister to encourage nonunion laborers to organize. Actually, 47.3 percent indicated that it was important and 31.7 felt that it was
undesirable, while 21 percent had no opinion (see table 4.9).

On this particular item, the laity had no definite expectations of
the clergy. Yet, from a historical perspective, urban ministers played
a key role in the organized labor strike of the garbagemen of Local
1733 of the American Federation of State, County, and Municipal
Employees (AFSCME) of the AFL-CIO in Memphis, Tennessee,[8] in
the sixties. The respondents to this question may be influenced by
the gradual but persistent effort of the business community, with
the cooperation of the government, to limit the power of unions to
influence policy issues and therefore bring about change.

TABLE 4.9 Encourages Nonunion Laborers to Organize

Responses	Number of Respondents	Percentage
Highly important	38	11.2
Quite important	51	15.1
Somewhat important	71	21.0
Undesirable	81	24.0
Detrimental	26	7.7
Reject item	28	8.3
Does not apply	43	12.7
Total	**338**	**100.0**

Is Willing to Risk Arrest to Protest Social Wrongs

The majority of the sample, 61.9 percent, indicated that this was an important expectation of the minister, while 24.3 percent thought it was undesirable.

This item reflects the degree to which oppressed people would go to convince the larger society of the reality of inequity and injustice. Historically, Black ministers have been arrested when protesting segregation and Jim Crow laws. In this connection, explaining why he was in Birmingham in 1966, Martin Luther King Jr. wrote from his jail cell:

I am in Birmingham because injustice is here. . . . Moreover, I am cognizant of the interrelatedness of all communities and states. I cannot sit idly by in Atlanta and not be concerned about what happens in Birmingham. Injustice anywhere is a threat to justice everywhere. We are caught in an inescapable network of mutuality, tied in a single garment of destiny. Whatever affects one directly, affects all indirectly. Never again can we afford to live with the narrow, provincial "outside agitator" idea. Anyone who lives inside the United States can never be considered an outsider anywhere within its bounds.[9]

It was in this spirit that clergymen Walter Fauntroy, Joseph Lowry, and other civil rights advocates were arrested in the fall of 1984 for staging anti-apartheid sit-ins at the South African embassy in Washington, D.C. More recently clergy such as Al Sharpton and Jesse Jackson were arrested for protesting America's use of the Puerto Rican island of Vieques for military bombing practices.

Risking arrest to protest social wrongs has been the tradition of Black religious leaders, and the laity continue to consider this an important part of the urban minister's responsibility to help bring about a just and equitable society (see table 4.10).

Works to Make Sure That All People Are Free to Buy Property in Areas of Their Choice

In responding to this item, 69.2 percent indicated that it was important and 16.8 felt it was not important. Table 4.11 describes the frequency of responses to this item.

Urban Housing

The law forbids racial discrimination in housing. Yet racial steering and other methods are sometimes used to ensure that people do not always buy the property they want. Changing the rules and

TABLE 4.10 Is Willing to Risk Arrest to Protest Social Wrongs

Responses	Number of Respondents	Percentage
Highly important	72	21.3
Quite important	60	17.8
Somewhat important	77	22.8
Undesirable	59	17.5
Detrimental	23	6.8
Reject item	23	6.8
Does not apply	24	7.1
Total	**338**	**100.1**

TABLE 4.11 Works to Make Sure That All People Are Free to Buy Property in Areas of Their Choice

Responses	Number of Respondents	Percentage
Highly important	78	23.1
Quite important	66	19.5
Somewhat important	90	26.6
Undesirable	39	11.5
Detrimental	18	5.3
Reject item	22	6.5
Does not apply	25	7.4
Total	**338**	**99.9**

practices, rather than the actual laws, is responsible for maintaining limited numbers of African Americans in predominately White neighborhoods. This same process which is used to maintain or foster racial homogeneity in some neighborhoods perpetuates a neighborhood's transition from White to Black in others.

Moreover, residential housing patterns and their racial composition are intricately connected to many facets of urban life. There are many auxiliary effects of housing patterns, and the history of neighborhood change reflects the degree to which neighborhoods are homogeneous. Homogeneity can be racial, economic, or social, but the degree of homogeneity and diversity within the larger urban environment helps to balance tension in urban communities. Katherine Bradbury et al., state,

> This tension is often partly resolved by two types of spatial separation. One is the separation of residencies from most production activities. . . . The other is the maintenance of separate neighborhoods for different ethnic, social or economic groups—especially those with significantly different values.[10]

There is a clear relationship between housing, schools, police protection, and a host of other social realities. In urban America, one's address is almost as telling as one's social security number!

Pressures Public Officials on Behalf of the Oppressed

This is one of the most significant questions in the study because the real-life situation of minorities and poor people in urban areas is one of oppression in several respects. Oppression often manifests itself in discrimination in employment, underemployment, inadequate housing, education policy, and other areas. Moreover, a disproportionate number of those out of work are Black, and often the working poor are also African American. The effects of this tragedy are manifested in disease and depression, suicide, and a disbelief in the so-called Protestant work ethic.

> Minority young people between the ages of 15 and 26 years have the highest suicide rate in the country according to U.S. National Center for Health Statistics. Numerous studies have established the connection between unemployment and deterioration in general health and emotional well being, stress, crime and family violence.[11]

Most Black men and women want to work because working is a form of freedom which fosters self-respect.

Because the effects of oppression have immeasurable conse-
quences, it was not surprising that 71.8 percent thought the statement, "Pressures public officials on behalf of the oppressed" was
important, while 18.3 percent thought it was not important. If
institutions such as the Black church don't speak up and fight
against the status quo, then no one else will, because so many are
easily co-opted by Big Brother.

Organizes Action Groups in the Congregation to Accomplish Directly Some Political or Social Goal

A decisive majority of the respondents indicated that this item was
important (72.2%), while less than 20 percent (19.8%) felt it was not
important. A meager 8 percent had no opinion regarding this item
(see table 4.13).

TABLE 4.12 Pressures Public Officials on Behalf of the Oppressed

Responses	Number of Respondents	Percentage
Highly important	89	26.3
Quite important	63	18.6
Somewhat important	91	26.9
Undesirable	44	13.0
Detrimental	18	5.3
Reject item	16	4.7
Does not apply	17	5.0
Total	**338**	**99.8**

TABLE 4.13 Organizes Action Groups in the Congregation to Accomplish
Directly Some Political or Social Goal

Responses	Number of Respondents	Percentage
Highly important	74	21.9
Quite important	68	20.1
Somewhat important	102	30.2
Undesirable	47	13.9
Detrimental	20	5.9
Reject item	15	4.4
Does not apply	12	3.6
Total	**338**	**100.0**

Organizes Study Groups in Congregations or Community to Discuss Public Affairs

Just over two-thirds (69.2%) of the sample indicated that this statement was important, 18.9 percent felt it was undesirable, and 11.8 percent had no opinion (table 4.14).

Policy Analysis

The organization of study groups to discuss public affairs is the beginning of the process of policy analysis. It takes an organized effort to have a meaningful impact on urban policy; therefore, the high percentage of laity who felt that this was important suggests considerable support for such practices. Study groups would determine priority items that should be analyzed. This is the beginning of political activity that will inevitably escalate. Yet, there are limitations.

> The factors that limit political activity are of cardinal importance in understanding public affairs. Activity is costly. It eats up time and energy. . . . One must attend meetings, listen to or participate in discussion, write letters, attempt to persuade (or be persuaded by) others, and engage in other such time-consuming labors. This means devoting less time to the job, to the children and to hobbies. Yet these private activities are the primary interest of most people, and so the cost of participation in public affairs seems greater than the return.[12]

Study group members should be aware of the limits and constraints of participating in this process so that the discussion of

TABLE 4.14 Organizes Study Groups in Congregations or Community to Discuss Public Affairs

Responses	Number of Respondents	Percentage
Highly important	73	21.6
Quite important	72	21.3
Somewhat important	89	26.3
Undesirable	49	14.5
Detrimental	15	4.4
Reject item	18	5.3
Does not apply	22	6.5
Total	**338**	**99.9**

public affairs will not be the banal exercise in polemics that often-times characterizes such discussions, but rather a creative and pragmatic experience for understanding the serious effects of public policy on the oppressed.

The minister who organizes such groups and focuses on the issues that are important to the advancement of an equitable and just urban environment will meet the expressed need of his/her constituents by facilitating their interests and in effect nurturing community power. There is no reason why the African American church can't have her own in-house policy analysts to advise the pastor and write position papers and letters to newspapers on everything from standards of learning in public education to investing in the equity and bond markets.

Declares a Willingness to Run for Public Office in the Community (School Board, City Council, etc.)

A clear majority of respondents indicated that this item was important. Yet there was no overwhelming expectation from a comparative perspective. Exactly 63 percent felt that this item was important, while 26.6 percent felt it was not important and 10.3 percent had no opinion (table 4.15).

Inasmuch as a majority of the sample did indicate that this was important, the urban minister who is seeking public office or occupies public office has the support of the laity. More precisely, the majority of people who attend the urban church expect the minister to be willing to run for political office. However, a willingness to run for office is not the same as actually running for office. Although the laity may expect the minister to declare a

TABLE 4.15 Declares a Willingness to Run for Public Office in the Community (School Board, City Council, etc.)

Responses	Number of Respondents	Percentage
Highly important	69	20.4
Quite important	65	19.2
Somewhat important	79	23.4
Undesirable	61	18.0
Detrimental	29	8.6
Reject item	14	4.1
Does not apply	21	6.2
Total	**338**	**99.9**

willingness to run for office, this does not mean that he or she will necessarily be supported by all of them. In fact, the 26.6 percent who felt it was not important may actually be *opposed* to the minister running for office. In this case, the minister would have a very difficult time balancing the support and the opposition. The fact remains that a majority of the urban church laity want the minister to seek public office, but from a practical perspective, a few people can make it difficult for the minister to effectively balance the responsibilities of the church and the demands of a political office. In cases where ministers have won political appointments or elected office, they need to have additional administrative staff support and, if possible, an assistant pastor to perform some of the ministry tasks.

Takes an Informed Position on Controversial Community Issues

Almost 80 percent of the respondents expected the minister to take an informed position on controversial community issues. This suggests that the urban laity want to be well represented by African American clergy who speak on their behalf. It also indicates that controversial issues should be studied and approached analytically and from a substantive perspective—not in an impetuous and emotive fashion. The laity expect an ability to utilize the cognitive and affective approach in explicating controversial community issues. The rule is to begin somewhere and keep at it. Few issues cannot be mastered.[13]

Furthermore, the data indicated that 11.6 percent of the respondents felt that taking an informed position was not important and 9.7 percent had no opinion (see table 4.16).

TABLE 4.16 Takes an Informed Position on Controversial Community Issues

Responses	Number of Respondents	Percentage
Highly important	99	29.3
Quite important	89	26.3
Somewhat important	78	23.1
Undesirable	28	8.3
Detrimental	11	3.3
Reject item	15	4.4
Does not apply	18	5.3
Total	**338**	**100.0**

Summary and Conclusions of Aggressive Political Leadership

A majority of the respondents rated each of the statements that constituted the cluster Aggressive Political Leadership as important. The items covered a wide range of political activities and the respondents indicated that they expected the African American urban minister to provide aggressive political leadership for these problems. This indicates, as some instinctively felt, that the suffering and oppression of people in urban communities cannot be eradicated by passive and detached acknowledgment of the problem, nor by sterile homilies on hunger or recondite discourses on church dogmatics. The urban church laity expect the minister to provide aggressive political leadership on the problems of incompetent or ineffective school, church, or government officials, perhaps by organizing groups to change civil laws and lobby on behalf of the oppressed. The laity do not dichotomize the responsibilities of the preacher; rather, they expect a synchronization of the social and political with the pastoral and priestly.

The mean level of importance for all of the statements that constituted this cluster, Aggressive Political Leadership, was 68.5 percent. This indicates that nearly seven of every ten respondents to these statements rated them as important expectations of an urban minister. This clearly suggests that the constituents of the African American urban church expect the minister not only to provide spiritual leadership but aggressive political leadership as well.

ACTIVE CONCERN FOR THE OPPRESSED

This cluster, Active Concern for the Oppressed, consists of six statements that effectively describe its content. These statements are discussed individually in order to provide a description of the respondents' expectation of the Black urban minister.

Works toward Racial Integration in the Community

In 1977, Alan Pifer, president of the Carnegie Corporation, wrote, "At least 80 percent of all American families today live in segregated neighborhoods, White or Black. Defacto, the United States is still two nations."[14] This indicting characterization of America by the president of one of this country's leading philanthropic foundations indicates the magnitude of the chasm between the races that has resulted in a dichotomous system of housing accommodation, education facilities, etc. This clearly suggests that de jure efforts to dismantle the reality of segregation have not manifested any cataclysmic changes. In effect the law has created more subtle and ingenious ways to circumvent its mandates and preclude most forms of substantive sharing of power and property, including integration.

Inasmuch as racial integration is not a fact in spite of all the civil rights, anti-discrimination, and fair housing laws, the Black church laity expect the minister to help bring about a more balanced and equitable system. Toward this end, an overwhelming 81.7 percent of the respondents indicated that they expected the minister to work toward racial integration in the community. This reflects near unanimity among the Black urban church laity regarding this issue: Only 9.8 percent felt it was not important (table 4.17).

The Black urban laity clearly express the desire for racial integration in the community. These church members know that segregation is not an imagined phenomenon, but real and concrete as evidenced by the facts. Moreover, it suggests that in spite of the law and rhetoric of equality, there is still a need for real integration.

> In fact, real integration is still very much more a hope (or fear) than a reality in most areas of the country because of the almost irresistible impact of residential segregation. We simply do not know, therefore, what the effects of true integration practiced over several generations would be. . . .[15]

Ironically, the chance for thorough integration of public schools is continually decreasing because of the large numbers of people who refuse to accept the equality of all people. Though our society is pluralistic, it continues to treat non-Whites with discrimination

TABLE 4.17 Works toward Racial Integration in the Community

Responses	Number of Respondents	Percentage
Highly important	163	48.2
Quite important	55	16.3
Somewhat important	58	17.2
Undesirable	22	6.5
Detrimental	11	3.3
Reject item	16	4.7
Does not apply	13	3.8
Total	338	100.0

and inequality. Racial integration continues to be a future goal—
not a present reality.

Uses Authoritative Information and Facts to Meet Racism and Prejudice in the Congregation and Community

In response to this item, 73.1 percent of the respondents indicated
that it was important to discuss racism and prejudice with facts
and authoritative information (table 4.18). This suggests that the
laity are concerned with documented facts rather than conjecture.
Because of the emotional and oftentimes irrational approach used
in confronting racism and prejudice, it is important to gather the
facts in order to effectively address the problem.

These tables represent authoritative information compiled by
the U.S. Census Bureau, the U.S. Department of Commerce, and
research organizations. These facts have been collected and published by the Council on Interracial Books for Children under the
title, *Fact Sheets on Institutional Racism*. The information contained
in these tables represents statistical facts on income earned by
Whites and Blacks and unemployment rates by race, sex, age, and
education. Additionally, the types of jobs held by minorities suggest that discrimination and racism may be factors contributing to
a minuscule percentage of minorities in managerial positions,
while a disproportionate percentage occupy positions as laborers
and service workers. The use of authoritative information and
facts to combat racism and prejudice was very important to the
respondents in this study.

Though statistical facts on income, education, unemployment,
and the types of jobs held by minorities are difficult to challenge, the

TABLE 4.18 Uses Authoritative Information and Facts to Meet Racism
and Prejudice in the Congregation and Community

Responses	Number of Respondents	Percentage
Highly important	105	31.1
Quite important	74	21.9
Somewhat important	68	20.1
Undesirable	35	10.4
Detrimental	20	5.9
Reject item	19	5.6
Does not apply	17	5.0
Total	**338**	**100.0**

interpretation of these facts differs considerably. Neoconservatives are less likely to attribute large discrepancies in income and education between Blacks and Whites to racism and prejudice. Therefore, the victims of these statistics are left to explain why they have failed to succeed in a system that offers "equal opportunity" to all.

Edward Banfield, in *The Unheavenly City,* and George Gilder, in *Wealth and Poverty,* suggest that racism and prejudice in today's society is more myth than reality. These writers represent an increasing cadre of scholars who argue that reasons other than racism and prejudice account for Blacks' and minorities' disproportionate unemployment and low-level jobs. Indeed, they offer an alternative interpretation of the figures in *Ministry of America.*

In response to this item, 16.3 percent indicated that it was not important, while 10.6 percent had no opinion (see table 4.18).

Works to Integrate People of Varying Educational, Ethnic, and Cultural Backgrounds into the Congregation

One major criticism of the Black church has been that it remains a basically segregated institution twenty years after other institutions have become partially integrated or desegregated. It is also argued that the Black minister—a key factor in effectuating change in other segments of society—has failed to coalesce the races in the practice of religion. While it is a fact that Black churches remain basically Black, the reasons cannot necessarily be attributed to the minister's lack of encouragement, nor to the laity's passivity. Inasmuch as integration has been a painful process in the public sector, accomplished only by legal duress, it is too simplistic to suggest that only a few reasons are responsible for the present racial status of the Black church. Nevertheless, the data in this study indicate that an overwhelming 82 percent of the respondents felt it was important for the minister to work to integrate the congregation ethnically, culturally, and educationally. Again, the laity are suggesting that the Black urban minister create a heterogeneous congregation, comprised of members not just different racially, but multiculturally, socially, and economically. Less than 10 percent of the respondents felt this item was not important and 8.3 percent had no opinion (table 4.19). There is a growing number of educated and middle-class Blacks who are attending churches where the leadership is White. I cannot explain this new phenomenon that began in the last decade of the twentieth century and continues today.

TABLE 4.19 Works to Integrate People of Varying Educational, Ethnic, and Cultural Backgrounds into the Congregation

Responses	Number of Respondents	Percentage
Highly important	150	44.4
Quite important	71	21.0
Somewhat important	56	16.6
Undesirable	16	4.7
Detrimental	17	5.0
Reject item	10	3.0
Does not apply	18	5.3
Total	**338**	**100.0**

Acquaints Self with the History and Aspirations of Minority Groups and Other Oppressed People

In response to this item, approximately 80 percent of the respondents indicated that it was important, while 13.7 percent felt it was not important.

The importance of this item to the urban laity suggests that they expect the minister to be broad-minded and empathetic. Moreover, the minister is better able to understand and evaluate his own predicament if he is familiar with the history and hopes of others who have had similar political, legal, economic, and social experiences. Understanding the forces of oppression that impinge on other minorities, regardless of their nomenclature, creates a necessary sensitivity to the condition of others who suffer from kindred forms of inhuman treatment and oppression (see table 4.20).

Makes Individuals Aware of Their Possible Part in Causing World Poverty

World poverty is a growing catastrophe in spite of the fact that millions of pounds of food are discarded every day. Less-developed countries (LDCs) in Africa and South America have not reaped the benefits of the new international economic order. There, poverty has not been alleviated, much less eradicated. The United Nations Development Program (UNDP) has been charged with perpetuating self-sufficiency on the part of the LDCs. The definitive yardstick of the UNDP's capabilities is its ability to diminish world poverty and expand the frontiers of human and economic opportunity throughout the developing world. For example, the state of poverty and hunger in places like Ethiopia gained worldwide

TABLE 4.20 Acquaints Self with the History and Aspirations of Minority
Groups and Other Oppressed People

Responses	Number of Respondents	Percentage
Highly important	120	35.5
Quite important	82	24.3
Somewhat important	61	18.0
Undesirable	34	10.1
Detrimental	12	3.6
Reject item	16	4.7
Does not apply	13	3.8
Total	**338**	**100.0**

attention because it represented the dehumanizing effects of these conditions wherever they are found.

Poverty is not simply a distant reality. It exists in the urban centers of the United States. Every day many churches feed people who are hungry and homeless. Over the past thirty years, the hunger problem has continued to grow. In the midst of posh and plenty, millions are hungry.

> The working poor are not an isolated few. In 1985, 2 million adults —50 percent more than in 1978—worked full time through-out the year, yet they and their families remained in poverty. Another 7.1 million poor worked either in full-time jobs for part of the year or in part-time jobs.[16]

In response to this item, 75.1 percent of the respondents indicated that it was important for the minister to make people aware of their part in causing world poverty, while 16.9 percent indicated that it was not important (table 4.21).

Recommends That the Parish Cut Off Financial Support for Institutions (Hospitals, Missions, etc.) That Discriminate Against Minorities

Invidious discrimination, as well as discrimination based on national origin, age, and sex, is illegal and too blatant to be practiced overtly. Because most American institutions believe in the sacrosanctity of the concept of law, any blatant violation of the law is meticulously avoided. Interestingly, the results of discrimination are often more obvious than their cause, because the results can be documented in quantitative terms.

In response to this item, 52.9 percent of the respondents indicated that they expected the minister to recommend that the church cease providing financial support to institutions that discriminate against minorities. This is not an overwhelming majority. In fact, an impressive 25.2 percent indicated that it was undesirable to cut off financial support (table 4.22). This suggests that the urban laity are not overwhelmingly unified on this particular item. This can be attributed to several factors. First, the laity may be reluctant to believe that eleemosynary institutions would discriminate against minorities. Second, some may believe that discrimination is nonexistent or is a myth. From this perspective, George Gilder states,

TABLE 4.21 Makes Individuals Aware of Their Possible Part in Causing World Poverty

Responses	Number of Respondents	Percentage
Highly important	97	28.7
Quite important	72	21.3
Somewhat important	85	25.1
Undesirable	45	13.3
Detrimental	12	3.6
Reject item	13	3.8
Does not apply	14	4.1
Total	**338**	**99.9**

TABLE 4.22 Recommends That the Parish Cut Off Financial Support for Institutions (Hospitals, Missions, etc.) That Discriminate Against Minorities

Responses	Number of Respondents	Percentage
Highly important	86	25.4
Quite important	42	12.4
Somewhat important	51	15.1
Undesirable	57	16.9
Detrimental	28	8.3
Reject item	34	10.1
Does not apply	40	11.8
Total	**338**	**100.0**

One of the problems in dealing with the expanding array of claims of discrimination—reaching far beyond the obvious and paramount victims in American history, the Blacks—is that anyone looking for bias can find it. . . . The last thirty years in America, however, have seen a relentless and thoroughly successful advance against old prejudices to the point that it is now virtually impossible to find in a position of power a serious racist. Gaps in income between truly comparable Blacks and Whites have nearly closed. Problems remain, but it would seem genuinely difficult to sustain the idea that America is still oppressive and discriminatory.[17]

Discrimination can be demythologized only by first recognizing its existence. Clearly, a majority of the Black church laity expect the minister to respond to discrimination against minorities by withholding economic support. While George Gilder makes a valid point, the fact is that during the 2000 political campaign, issues of race and discrimination were center-stage in the Republican primary between George Bush and John McCain. The myriad acts of violence against Blacks by police in New York and Los Angeles strongly suggest that racial discrimination is alive and well.

Summary and Conclusions of Active Concern for the Oppressed

The statements that made up this cluster demanded that the urban minister be involved in the actual dismantling of the mechanisms that sustain racism, prejudice, segregation, and discrimination. The oppressed are victims of these mechanisms that have been sewn into the structure of society. Active Concern for the Oppressed is characterized by working toward racial integration, using authoritative facts to combat racism and prejudice, and acquainting oneself with the history and aspirations of minorities. The majority of the respondents indicated that the items in the cluster were important expectations of the minister.

The mean level of importance for all the statements that constituted this cluster, Active Concern for the Oppressed, was 78 percent. Approximately eight of every ten respondents to the statements comprising this cluster felt that it was important for the Black urban minister to be actively concerned for the oppressed. This suggests that the Black urban church laity expect the minister to be more than a traditional spiritual leader. They expect him to help bring about a just and equitable society by helping those who are oppressed.

PRECEDENCE OF EVANGELISTIC GOALS

This core cluster, Precedence of Evangelistic Goals, contains four statements that describe its content. Each of these statements is explained relative to the respondents' expectations of the Black urban minister. Statements in the cluster provide a traditional description of expectations of the minister.

Holds That the Church's Task of Proclaiming the Gospel by Preaching and Teaching Overshadows in Importance the Task of Helping to Eliminate Physical Sufferings of People

This item reflects the traditional role and expectation of the minister, which is proclamation of the gospel. In response to this item, 52.9 percent indicated that it was important, while 25.2 percent felt it was not important (table 4.23).

This item creates a dichotomy between preaching and teaching and helping to eliminate the physical suffering of people. In actuality, there is a nexus between the two. According to Luke's gospel, Jesus said, "I have come to set at liberty those who are oppressed."[18] This statement is the archetype of liberation theology from a christological perspective. It expresses the goal and aim of the preaching and teaching ministry of Jesus.

The chi-square statistic indicated that the difference in assessment by denomination was statistically significant (P = .0056). The findings also indicated that the difference in education, congregation size, and income was not statistically significant.

TABLE 4.23 Holds That the Church's Task of Proclaiming the Gospel by Preaching and Teaching Overshadows in Importance the Task of Helping to Eliminate Physical Sufferings of People

Responses	Number of Respondents	Percentage
Highly important	86	25.4
Quite important	42	12.4
Somewhat important	51	15.1
Undesirable	57	16.9
Detrimental	28	8.3
Reject item	34	10.1
Does not apply	40	11.8
Total	**338**	**100.0**

Responses to this item suggest that the African American urban laity continue to respect and hold in high esteem the preaching of the gospel. Preaching and teaching are very important in the life of the church. The spiritual power inherent in preaching and teaching helps the believer to deal with the eradication of physical suffering. The healing power of the gospel is real to the believer.

Frequently Approaches Strangers to Ask about the Condition of Their Soul

This item represents an often practiced—albeit simplistic—method of traditional evangelism. Questions regarding the soul of man have occupied such great religious philosophers as Aristotle, Eckhart, Kant, Plato, and Plotinus,[19] and the condition of one's soul is a concern in the practice of religious evangelism.

This method of evangelism leaves a lot to be desired, but it continues to be a popular practice in the church. People want to feel that the church has not become an isolated institution, practicing its rituals and worship only among its own members. There are strangers within the church and in the community who need to be approached, consoled, and helped. Although there is a growing risk in approaching strangers, it remains a viable method of contributing to church growth and practicing the faith.

In response to this item, 60.7 percent of the respondents indicated that it was important, and 28.7 percent felt it was not important. An additional 10.7 percent had no opinion (see table 4.24).

Priorities in Use of Time and the Belief That the One and Only Way to Build an Ideal World Society Is to Convert Everyone to Christianity

In response to this item, 72.5 percent of people responding to the survey indicated that this was important; 16.9 percent indicated it was not important and 10.6 had no opinion (see table 4.25).

This item clearly reflects a belief in the Christian evangelization of humanity; an overwhelming percentage of the respondents expect the minister to prioritize his or her time accordingly. Responses to this particular item also indicated that the laity expect the Black urban minister to be a religious and political leader. While the practice of Christianity is important, I believe that we learn from all the religions of the world, and African Americans are especially fond of Islam and its emphasis on family unity and brotherly love.

TABLE 4.24 Frequently Approaches Strangers to Ask about the Condition of Their Soul

Responses	Number of Respondents	Percentage
Highly important	73	21.6
Quite important	50	14.8
Somewhat important	82	24.3
Undesirable	69	20.4
Detrimental	28	8.3
Reject item	10	3.0
Does not apply	26	7.7
Total	338	100.1

TABLE 4.25 Priorities in Use of Time and the Belief That the One and Only Way to Build an Ideal World Society Is to Convert Everyone to Christianity

Responses	Number of Respondents	Percentage
Highly important	99	29.3
Quite important	74	21.9
Somewhat important	72	21.3
Undesirable	31	9.2
Detrimental	26	7.7
Reject item	18	5.3
Does not apply	18	5.3
Total	338	100.0

Insists That Clergy Should Stick to Religion and Not Concern Themselves with Social, Economic, and Political Questions

This is the most prototypical statement in this cluster to characterize a preference of concern for evangelistic goals. In response to this item, 46.8 percent of the sample said it was important. This suggests that less than half of the laity felt that the minister should stick to religion and not be concerned with social, economic, and political questions (see table 4.26).

This percentage is the lowest of any "important" responses in all categories or clusters, suggesting that the urban clergy are expected to remain focused on the congregants' real-life situation, the urban environment. Moreover, it suggests that there must be a balance between the traditionally religious and eschatological

TABLE 4.26 Insists That Clergy Should Stick to Religion and Not Concern
Themselves with Social, Economic, and Political Questions

Responses	Number of Respondents	Percentage
Highly important	60	17.8
Quite important	42	12.4
Somewhat important	56	16.6
Undesirable	79	23.4
Detrimental	45	13.3
Reject item	29	8.6
Does not apply	27	8.0
Total	338	100.1

focus of the church and the social and political focus. In this connection, 36.7 percent of the respondents indicated that it was not
important for the minister to stick only to religion, and 16.6 percent
had no opinion.

The chi-square statistic indicated that the difference in denomination, income, education, and congregation size was not significant. This means Baptists, Methodists, and Pentecostals—middle
class or poor—all felt that the preacher has to be able to synthesize
the social and political with the religious.

Summary and Conclusions of Precedence of Evangelistic Goals

This particular cluster of statements was used to represent the
opposite emphasis of the other two clusters. Precedence of Evangelistic Goals focuses on the traditional understanding of ministry with emphasis on proclaiming the gospel by preaching and
teaching, asking strangers about the condition of their souls,
proselytizing, and insisting that clergy should focus on religion
exclusively. These evangelistic or relatively traditional religious
statements clearly contrast with the statements found in the other
two clusters.

The mean level of importance for all of the statements that constituted this cluster, Precedence of Evangelistic Goals, was 60.25
percent. This was the lowest of the three clusters, which indicates
that fewer respondents felt that the evangelization of society was
as important as providing strong political leadership and expressing concern for the oppressed. Nevertheless, the fact that 60.25 percent of the respondents indicated that they expect the minister to

focus on evangelistic goals does suggest that there is no absolute dichotomy in the laity's expectations of the clergy. There is a both/and phenomenon at work here that seems to indicate that the Black church laity expect the minister to be priest as well as social and political leader.

OVERALL SUMMARY OF THE CORE CLUSTER RESPONSES

The aggregate data indicated that the mean levels of importance for each of the core clusters were 68.5, 78.0, and 60.25 percent, respectively. This suggests that there is no true dichotomy in laity expectations of clergy relative to the religious and sociopolitical. Yet, the category Active Concern for the Oppressed has the highest combined percentage of important responses.

The statements in each of the clusters were important to a large percentage of the respondents. This suggests a nexus between the sociopolitical and the religious that may be unique to the Black urban church laity because of their experience in the church and society.

Results of the Hypothesis

Laity in Different Denominations Have Different Expectations of the Minister's Active Involvement in Social and Political Ministries in Urban Areas

There was not an overwhelming statistically significant relationship between the independent variable, denomination, and a majority of the dependent variables in the survey. Nevertheless, the chi-square statistic indicated that the difference in denomination was statistically significant regarding each of these three variables:

1. Organizes groups to change civil laws that seem in light of Scripture to be morally wrong.
2. Works to integrate people of varying educational, ethnic, and cultural backgrounds into the congregation.
3. Holds that the church's task of proclaiming the gospel by preaching and teaching overshadows in importance the task of helping to eliminate physical sufferings of people.

An in-depth analysis of the data indicates that a majority of the respondents from different denominations rated the aforesaid items "important." While there is a statistical significance, an analysis does not support the existence of a substantive significance. Therefore, there seems to be no practical significance to the statistical difference because a large majority of each congregation rated these items "important."

Each of these variables relates to ecclesiology in some way, however small. More precisely, each of the variables is less oriented toward discerning social and political involvement than many of the others. Moreover, there was no statistically significant difference between denomination and the majority of the dependent variables. Taken as a whole, the null hypothesis is true. When viewed individually, there is a statistically significant difference between denomination and the three dependent variables discussed.

Laity with High Socioeconomic Status (as Measured by Income and Education) Have Higher Expectations in Terms of Social and Political Involvement Than Laity of Low Socioeconomic Status

There was a statistically significant difference, according to the chi-square statistic, regarding the education and income of the respondent and his/her response to the item:

1. Priorities in use of time and the belief that the one and only way to build an ideal world society is to convert everyone to Christianity.

This was the only dependent variable that had a statistically significant chi-square when cross-tabulated with education. Moreover, the statement addresses the traditional perception of the minister and confirms a dichotomy in the laity's expectations of the minister. While the majority of the people who attend the Black urban church expect the minister to be involved in social and political activities, they also expect him or her to use time to proselytize others to the Christian religion. This is not a contradiction because the church is still foremost a religious institution. Moreover, there is an interrelationship between the religious and the political in the African American community, as discussed earlier.

Second, the chi-square statistic indicated that there was a statistically significant difference ($P = .0467$) in the respondent's income and his/her response to "Priorities in use of time indicate the belief that the one and only way to build an ideal world society is to convert everyone to Christianity." The chi-square statistic also indicated a significant difference (P = .0230) and (P = .0410) in the respondent's occupation and his/her response to these items:

1. Works to integrate people of varying educational, ethnic, and cultural backgrounds into the congregation.
2. Acquaints self with the history and aspirations of minority groups and other oppressed people.

SUMMARY OF THE FINDINGS

The majority of the statements that constituted each of the three core clusters—Aggressive Political Leadership, Active Concern for the Oppressed, and Precedence of Evangelistic Goals—were rated as important by the respondents. Of the three core clusters, Active Concern for the Oppressed received the highest percentage of "important" responses from the laity. An impressive 78 percent of the respondents felt that the statements in this cluster confirmed important expectations of the minister. This cluster was followed by Aggressive Political Leadership, with a mean level of importance of 68.5 percent, and Precedence of Evangelistic Goals, with a mean level of importance of 60.25 percent.

The findings suggest that the Black urban church laity expect the minister to be not only a spiritual leader but a social and political leader—one who seeks to transform the social and political order.

A macrocosmic analysis of the results suggests that neither socioeconomic status nor denominational affiliation was a statistically significant factor in the responses to the questionnaire. Conversely, from a microcosmic perspective, the respondents' denomination made a statistically significant difference in the these three variables:

1. Organizes groups to change civil laws that seem in light of Scripture to be morally wrong.
2. Works to integrate people of varying educational, ethnic, and cultural backgrounds into the congregation.
3. Holds that the church's task of proclaiming the gospel by preaching and teaching overshadows in importance the task of helping to eliminate physical sufferings of people.

Because denominational differences affected responses to only three dependent variables and because these variables were in three different core clusters, the writer accepts the null hypothesis that there is no relationship between denominational affiliation and African American urban church laity expectations of the ministers' social and political involvement.

Socioeconomic status, as measured by education and income, is statistically related in the respondents' answers to these statements:

1. Works to integrate people of varying educational, ethnic, and cultural backgrounds into the congregation.
2. Acquaints self with the history and aspirations of minority groups and other oppressed people.

Again, because socioeconomic status was statistically significant for such a miniscule number of variables, we conclude that there was no difference between the social and political expectations of laity with high socioeconomic status and those with low socioeconomic status. Regardless of how much money they make and no matter their level of education, Black folk expect the minister in the urban church to get down in the trenches and fight for the freedom of those who are poor, needy, and disenfranchised. Unfortunately, all of these expectations may not have noble origins. Some folk do not want to take on this kind of unpopular advocacy work because it is often payless and thankless. There are others who are afraid to stick their necks out for others because their own income and employment may be threatened. This leaves the minister, the pastor, the clergy who are often less concerned about their own well-being or personal gain and more concerned about the plight of a people, a community, a cause such as justice and righteousness!

. 5 .

Ambivalence among Minister Leaders and Followers

The African American urban minister and laity are a part of the church and the world. Their existential reality is conducive to feelings of polarity and tension. Inasmuch as evangelistic goals characterize the priestly role of the minister, and the activist role is characterized by active concern for the oppressed and aggressive political leadership, clergy and laity are caught between these two relatively contrary phenomena. Evangelism and politicism, though not mutually exclusive, generally have different goals. However, the condition of African American life in urban America allows neither the minister nor laity the luxury of dichotomizing these concepts. As an instrument for socioeconomic improvement in the city, evangelism cannot succeed. Inadequate housing, unemployment, discrimination, and other social and economic atrocities continue to pervade urban America. These conditions contribute to the ambivalence of the minister and laity because the Black church and the larger urban community must coexist. This coexistence of institutions with contrary feelings, goals, and interests produces ambivalent attitudes and subsequent behavior. The majority of people in the Black urban church expect the minister to be socially and politically active by providing aggressive political leadership and active concern for the oppressed; however, the same group wants evangelistic goals to have precedence in the minister's life. This paradox and the laity's inability to prioritize their expectations of the minister suggest a level of unsurety that is puzzling. The lack of unanimity inherent in the laity's expectations may be more accurately described as internal conflict or ambivalence.

Because of the Black church's historical relationship with the White church, historian and theologian Gayraud Wilmore says, "Black religion has always been something more and something less than traditional European religion."[1] Nevertheless, the nexus between Black and White religion, however different, continues to exist. The contact between Black slaves and their White masters was bound to leave an indelible imprint on both groups. Historically, African Americans have been ambivalent about the relationship—vacillating between levels of caring and not caring, trust and distrust. Additionally, the formal worship of Blacks was often held in the presence of Whites, in their church building or with Blacks as congregants and a White man as minister. The religious situation was the epitome of paradox because the White preacher represented the oppressor as well as the bearer of a message of the gospel. He was both prophet and propagator of the status quo. This dualism, represented by word and deed, clearly characterized the master/slave relationship. Moreover, because Black religion combines African and European traditions, the Black laity represent an amalgamation of the elements that constitute both heritages. This makes the Black laity and clergy unique: They harbor vestiges of both cultures, which manifest themselves in a tension that suggests inherent ambivalence. Moreover, the issue of race cannot be completely extirpated from the practice of religion in America because the independent Black church began as a protest movement against the racism inherent in the White church and in society in general. The White slave master and his wife could by law and custom sexually abuse the Black male and female.

This chapter examines several reasons for the ambivalent attitudes of the laity relative to their expectations of the minister. The basic reasons expounded on are selfishness, narcissism, fear of discrimination in employment, and the fear of physical harm or death.

SELFISHNESS: AN INHERENT ELEMENT IN THE LAITY'S AMBIVALENCE

The minister's social and political involvement in the community helps legitimize the interests, frustrations, and complaints voiced by those who are essentially powerless to effectuate positive change. However, the Black church laity are reluctant to fully endorse the minister's involvement for fear that his participation in so-called outside activities will leave less time to pursue evangelistic goals, such as visiting the unchurched, encouraging church members, and preaching the gospel. Because evangelism, in its many forms, still represents the prototype of traditional ministry, social and political efforts—however progressive and humanitarian—appear to be viewed with a degree of skepticism. The skeptics are not without understanding; indeed, they fully understand the needs of the community and the necessity for the minister to become involved in the social and political process that will address the urban situation of distress and despair. However, the laity are also motivated by a natural, seemingly inherent selfishness that is mostly innocent. They simply want their minister for themselves almost as if he or she were a commodity, and some pastors tend to accept that "selfishness" as an expression of love and overwhelming interest in his or her well-being. However, genuine Christian love is selfless and understanding, always focusing upon the needs of others." In the letter to the Corinthians, Paul writes, "Love is patient, love is kind, and is not jealous; love does not brag and is not arrogant, does not act unbecomingly; it does not seek its own, is not provoked, does not take into account a wrong suffered. . . ."[2]

The minister must be adept at balancing the needs of the local church laity with the needs of the larger community. In a way, the laity constitute both the church and the community. The laity do not exist in isolation and the church is not immune to the problems that plague urban America. As a result, there is some tension and ambivalence regarding the minister's active involvement in the community because Black pastors, educators, and political leaders have failed to develop the proper linkages between the church and public policy (which will be dealt with in Part III). The fact that the Black church laity feel ambivalent or unsure about their expectations of the minister—whether he or she should be either "priest" or "politician"—suggests that pastors must teach their urban laity to recognize the interrelationship between the church and the urban community. The ambivalence is based on a type of subliminal desire to keep the church out of the political sphere of society, although the local church is laden with its own politics. Some of the greatest White proponents of the separation of church and state are probably in church on Sunday and working in the U.S. Department of State and other areas of government on Monday. Their churches' views often become an extension of the corporation or government philosophy and vice versa. The Black church laity should understand that they are potentially the most powerful reservoir of political and social strength in urban America. If organized, taught, and encouraged properly, this group of people could prompt a cataclysmic change in the nature of the urban milieu and create an entirely new landscape as we embark on the new millennium.

The parochial, rather boxed-in, view of the minister embraced by many in the church will have to be overcome. Indeed, too many laypeople perceive the world in a narrow and confining way. This means that the community is perceived and discussed in limited geographic, social, and political terms. Instead of viewing the entire city as the community, the laity have parochialized the city and helped to establish a limited view of neighborhoods. This is not their fault, however. They have only been affected by the need to create words and other geopolitical categories. Black laity must not allow spatial distances—geographical or social—to circumvent the belief that unity and not fragmentation will bring meaningful social, political, and economic change. Where African Americans live within the city, especially if it is in a middle-class community, must not cause them to lose focus of the residential status of most of their brothers and sisters. It is understood that where one lives is a measure of social status such that differences in people, at least socially, are readily presumed. However, residential segregation tends to make these differences more easily discernible.

> An address is far more than a convenient way of organizing the supply of public services or of locating an individual in physical space. It also locates him in social space. The address of a person immediately identifies him as a member of a particular social group. . . . So pervasive is this effect that residential location has frequently been used as one of the measures in an individual's position in local prestige hierarchy.[3]

NARCISSISM, ANXIETY, AND AMBIVALENCE

Since the fervent 1960s, with their social and political emphasis on justice and equality for all, interest has been growing in personal achievement and the attainment of individual goals. The spirit of acquisition and self-satisfaction has engulfed the church and society to the extent that the laity are stridently pursuing that which is personal and economic, i.e., education, houses, cars, etc. Christopher Lasch, in the preface to his book, *The Culture of Narcissism*, states that:

After the political turmoil of the sixties, Americans have retreated to purely personal preoccupations. Having no hope of improving their lives in any of the ways that matter, people have convinced themselves that what matters is psychic self-improvement, getting in touch with their feelings, eating healthy food, taking lessons in ballet or belly-dancing, immersing themselves in the wisdom of the East, jogging, learning how to "relate," overcoming the "fear of pleasure." Harmless in themselves, these pursuits, elevated to a program and unwrapped in the rhetoric of authenticity and awareness, signify a retreat from politics and a repudiation of the recent past.[4]

This concentrated effort upon "self" has also created an anxiety that manifests itself in an inability to clearly discern what the church expects of the pastor or minister. "The new narcissist is haunted not by guilt but by anxiety," says Lasch.[5] The anxiety is a product of man's inherent dichotomy. In this vein Reinhold Niebuhr argues that anxiety is a part of the nature of man. He quotes Soren Kierkegaard by stating,

Anxiety is the inevitable concomitant of the paradox of freedom and finiteness in which man is involved. Anxiety is the internal precondition of sin. It is the inevitable spiritual state of man, standing in the paradoxical situation of freedom and finiteness.[6]

St. Augustine, John Calvin, and Martin Luther were proponents of the view that sin was essentially pride—a view consistent with Pauline theology, but a view that African Americans have not embraced. Paul felt that anxiety, tension, and ambivalence within him was a war between good and evil. This is akin to the tension, or anxiety, that manifests itself in the laity. If anxiety is the permanent or inevitable concomitant of freedom, and the laity are free to participate in the social, political, and economic sphere of society, then that freedom to participate is also the source of their bondage to indecision. This bondage precludes the laity from expressing absolute certainty about their expectations; however, they are as certain as their freedom will allow them to be. The laity are often reluctant to jeopardize their freedom, their positions of comfort, their job security, and the general feeling of success by tampering with controversial social and political issues. More important, they love themselves more than they love others. This narcissistic practice is partly responsible for the ambivalence that the laity feel about the pastor. Niebuhr captures the spirit of this love of self when he says that ". . . all human life is involved in the sin of seeking security at the expense of other life."[7] Security for oneself is quite natural and expected. However, maintaining a certain level of security may affect the urban laity's inability to decisively and overwhelmingly indicate what they expect of the pastor in Black urban churches regarding social and political issues. This becomes more important because the minister's increased social and political involvement may force the laity to proceed cautiously and indecisively because of their dependence on other institutions, such as business, government, or industry, for a livelihood. Theoretically, they must want to be involved; however, their ambivalence is the product of their own self-interest rather than interest in the larger community.

This personal and existential dilemma has ontological significance simply because it takes *courage* to be able to do at least that which we expect of others. The laity have not come to grips with the relationship between expectations of the pastor and the pastor's participation with equal vigor and commitment. This type of committed participation requires courage. "Courage is self-affirmation 'in spite of' that which tends to prevent the self from affirming itself."[8] However, ambivalence is a cross between courage and fear. According to Paul Tillich "Fear . . . has a definite object, which can be faced, analyzed, attacked, endured."[9] Consequently, the African American church laity are ambivalent about the social and political expectations of the minister mainly because they fear that somehow his activism may be traced back to their encouragement and support. This will make them quasi-activists, and they may be viewed negatively by their employers and clients. Caution and fear are the essence of narcissism because they are the tools for survival in a politically conservative society. Additionally, the laity may feel very uneasy about being identified with anyone who has waged an overt effort to eradicate some of the inequities that their companies or employers have perpetuated.

Racial Discrimination in Employment as a Source of Ambivalence

An urban pastor becomes socially and politically involved when he or she encounters ambivalence first-hand. There exists an intricate connection between what individuals are willing to say and do publicly and the perceived impact of their stance on the ability to keep their job and gain promotions. This is crucial because one's employment status has ontological and psychological significance;

that is, one's employment status determines how involved in controversial social and political issues one becomes. Because African Americans exhibit little economic power, their leverage is usually grounded in political prowess. Often, the most potent element that African Americans bring to the bargaining table is the ability to rally the troops in support of a cause that negatively affects the majority of urban citizens.

The relatively high median income and educational level of the Black church laity provide an economic stability that sharply contrasts the increasing poverty of people throughout the South and the nation. This difference may account for much of the ambivalence. People who are poor, jobless, and clearly oppressed are less likely to be ambivalent about their expectations of ministers or their personal involvement because they simply have little or nothing to lose. Conversely, the largest percentage of people used in this work was clearly Black urban professionals (buppies) who earned significantly more than the national average. Their ambivalence is connected to their economic survivability, which directly results from their dependent employment status. These individuals understand the subtleties and the magnitude of racism and discrimination in employment. Additionally, they understand that the likely victims of discrimination are usually Black; therefore, understanding the reality and fear of racial discrimination in employment is one of the reasons for the ambivalence of the laity.

Unemployment and its auxiliary effects are by-products of discrimination. If pressed to its logical conclusion, discrimination in employment and the reality of unemployment are so intricately interdependent that the alpha point is impossible to determine. The fact is that a disproportionate number of those out of work are Black. The effects of this tragedy are manifested in depression, suicide, and a rejection of the belief that we live in a fair and color-blind society. The full effects of the lack of employment, especially among Black men, have not been completely determined. However, we suspect that joblessness caused by some form of racial profiling and discrimination accounts for a large percentage of those African Americans who are unsuccessful in finding work even during the greatest economic expansion in United States history.

Covert mechanisms of discrimination are responsible for the overrepresentative number of African Americans who are unemployed. Every reputable company today claims to be committed to equal opportunity and affirmative action. Yet, the people behind the unemployment statistics are disproportionately Black. The new means of discrimination are more subtle and covert than the blatant acts of invidious discrimination practiced in the past.[10]

Discrimination in employment is as real as the existence of minorities. It cannot be adequately remedied unless it is first recognized as a reality. Invidious discrimination is hailed as a thing of the past; however, the facts indicate that people who are not White are systematically underpaid, underemployed, disproportionately unemployed, subject to racial slurs when employed, etc.

Discrimination can be based on a potpourri of characteristics, such as sex, age, religion, and handicaps. There is a fear, too, of being discriminated against for being active socially and politically. Discrimination in employment is a phenomenon that must be reckoned with during times of economic austerity and prosperity because African Americans are the first to feel the crunch. The new rising tide of conservatism, which is evidently committed to totally dismantling any vestiges of the Great Society programs, has a profound impact on the employment status of African Americans who can barely survive the practices of discrimination in employment during a booming economy. The latitude given employers in the past must be rejected and consciously opposed by those who are suspicious of the system. Additionally, the general social milieu that exists throughout the country today does not look promising for Blacks and minorities in any area. In an article on the future of Blacks in urban management, Lenneal Henderson Jr. explains, "Economic recession, expanding unemployment and underemployment, tax and expenditure limitations and a public opinion backlash against affirmative action cloud the future of minorities in urban management."[11]

Even after the Civil Rights movement, only forty-two of 3,000 city managers were Black. Surely the present and future look better for Blacks and minorities in top management positions in the public sector. The scarcity of minorities in upper-level positions will increase, according to some, because the conservative city councils are unwilling to risk employing minorities because of a perceived political liability. Henderson writes,

> The penetration of the city management profession by Blacks continues to be difficult. Joining traditional political and administrative

resistance to affirmative action programs . . . are the politics of increasingly conservative city councils and the economics of increasingly tight budgets. Some city councils consider even the best-qualified Black management prospects a political liability and a management risk. This is particularly true in cities with less than 50 percent Black population.[12]

Discrimination in employment continues to be too pervasive to ignore and too endemic and malignant to overcome in a short period of time. There is still hope that the poor will be fed and those who have succumbed to the sickness of despair will find the strength to have hope. Racial discrimination is a vicious monster that is genocidal. People sensitive to oppression on any level because of their own situation must be aware of racial discrimination in employment, and all African Americans must resolve to seriously address its causes.

The fear of discrimination felt and understood by minorities continues to plague people who feel compelled to fight for social and economic equity through political activism. These people are ambivalent because they understand the subtleties of the employment market, the necessity to provide for one's family, and the need for fairness and equality for all people. The process of deciding to become involved in something that may cause one to suffer discrimination in employment creates ambivalence.

THE FEAR OF PHYSICAL HARM AND DEATH AS A SOURCE OF AMBIVALENCE

The African American urban minister is the symbol of leadership authority and confidence in the church. While his or her position may be more symbolic than real, his responsibility is varied and comprehensive—ranging from performing perfunctory activities such as marriages and baby dedications to critical activities such as preaching, teaching, and participating in the eradication of social ills. The minister is often a father figure in the church, a role model for many people who are victims of poverty, discrimination, and a host of social and economic problems. For the most part, the Black laity love the minister; however, their love and care breed the fear of losing him or her to the whimsical and aberrant behavior of those who wish to physically harm him. Most of the time, this is an external threat, but sometimes it may come from within. Laity ambivalence (and clergy ambivalence) is caused by the fear of losing the minister's leadership skills to some other church or organization or, more importantly, permanently losing him because he may be physically harmed or killed. This separation anxiety is similar to the way a child feels when her parents leave, or plan to leave, her alone for an extended period of time. The child is afraid that the parent will not return and feels a sense of abandonment. This is not to suggest that the laity are like children, but rather to indicate that emotional and spiritual attachment to the minister often runs deep.

History has proven that this fear of physical harm and death is justified when a minister is trying to change the status quo by becoming a politically active advocate of justice and fairness. For example, Nat Turner met his demise because of his efforts to destroy the source of oppression and slavery in Southampton County, Virginia, in 1831. As a minister, his actions were certainly not evangelistic; instead, they embodied social radicalism. More recent history shows that Black ministers and laity who have led the effort for social reform, however nonviolent their methods, have encountered the violent wrath of the oppressor. Martin Luther King Jr. was killed because of his social activism. His efforts to bring about a color-blind society with "liberty and justice for all" were despised by many and viewed with suspicion by others. Medgar Evers, Emmet Till, Malcolm X, and a host of other Black activists who cannot be accounted for met their deaths through mysterious disappearances or blatant murder. These facts are not easily forgotten. The laity and clergy personally remember these violent incidents and are reminded of them through historical documentation. Many African Americans vividly remember the evening of Dr. King's assassination, because he was the paradigm of struggle, hope, determination, and commitment to righting the social, political, and economic ills of a society that was in complicity with sin and the evil of injustice. Dr. King's effort to correct these pathological social problems was contrary to the view of the establishment. This made him a target for those who advocated racism and perpetrated injustice. The Black clergy and laity continue to live with this painful history and recognize that social and political activism may bring physical harm to the minister and his family. Moreover, 300 years of American slavery cannot be easily forgotten. These experiences are etched in our DNA and embedded forever in our psyche.

The historical reality of lynchings, accidental deaths, and malicious murder of ministers and other social activists causes some laity to feel serious ambivalence about their pastor's interest in political office or participation in other processes of social change. They understand that if their leader is killed, their loss is not only emotional and psychological but also political and strategic. They realize that the development of committed clergy takes a long time, and it is not easy to overcome the loss of one being taken from this world by the hands of hate crime. Those who remain fear that the next leader will be equally subject to being violated. The pain and loss are so real that the laity do not want to risk this excruciating pain as a necessary by-product of active social and political involvement. This fear of physical harm is one reason why so many laity and clergy are burdened with feelings of ambivalence.

The ambivalence of the Black clergy and laity has its roots in the history of African people in America. The reality of slavery as a substantial part of the Black man's and woman's history cannot be dismissed as a past inequity that has ceased to affect the present. In the language of W. E. B. Du Bois, Blacks possess a "double consciousness" because of the double standard that they have experienced throughout history. He describes it by saying,

After the Egyptian and Indian, the Greek and Roman, the Teuton and Mongolian, the Negro is a sort of seventh son, born with a veil, and gifted with second-sight in this American World, a world which yields him no true self-consciousness but only lets him see himself through the revelation of the other world. It is a peculiar sensation, this double consciousness, this sense of always looking at one's self through the eyes of others, of measuring one's soul by the tape of a world that looks on in amused contempt and pity. One even feels his twoness—an American, a Negro; two souls, two thoughts, two unreconciled strivings; two warring ideals in one dark body, whose dogged strength alone keeps it from being torn asunder.[13]

These words, originally from *The Souls of Black Folk*, clearly describe the nature of the present African American clergy and laity in urban America. This ambivalence is a pathological phenomenon that has followed the Black American from the slave era of the sixteenth and seventeenth centuries to the present time—the new millennium.

. 6 .

Leadership in the Urban Church: Implications of the Laity's Expectations

Although much has been written about the Black church and the Black minister, few studies, if any, have focused exclusively on the urban laity's expectations of the minister's social and political leadership. For this reason, this work was designed to determine if people who attend the Black church expect the minister to deal with socioeconomic and political problems that are part of the urban condition. It determined that African American church laity do expect the minister to be both priestly and activist/political. They expect the minister to accommodate a confluence of expectations arising from a people whose real-life situation represents the prototype of polarity and complexity. This partially explains why 78 percent of the respondents expected the minister to be actively concerned for the oppressed, 68.5 percent expected him or her to be an aggressive political leader, and 60.5 percent expected him or her to give priority to the evangelization of society. Accordingly, these findings suggest that the expectations of the laity are multidimensional and cannot be neatly or easily systematized into dichotomous or mutually exclusive categories.

Each of the items (dependent variables) that truly represented social and political statements was interpreted and discussed relative to the responses. The chi-square statistic indicated a statistically significant difference in respondents' denomination, income, and education and their response to several items. Additionally, most responses were favorable, and a majority indicated that they expected the minister to be an active social and political leader. Because the African American minister as well as the laity are a part of the same urban environment, the urban minister is not afforded the luxury of insouciant passivity because urban problems can be addressed only by understanding their impact on human lives. Compassion for the oppressed is a prerequisite to addressing and eradicating the insidious nature of many social and political problems. Therefore, the laity expect the minister to address areas of inequality, injustice, and poverty.

In 1983 the threshold for poverty for a family of four was $10,178. According to the standards of the U.S. Bureau of Census, "Since the standard was originally defined, it has been increased yearly in order to allow for inflation."[1]

The Black urban minister has the responsibility of not only preaching justice and freedom but participating in the process of transforming these virtuous concepts into actuality. The urban church must object to jails and prisons overflowing with young Black males. It must actively support political movements and politicians that are not only sympathetic to the plight of African Americans but willing to implement programs that will alter the historical status of Blacks in the system. Joseph R. Washington states,

> The moral and theological basis for the Negro church's involvement in politics is not . . . in conflict with or in contradiction to the function of the church. Together with the moral requirement to meet the needs of Negroes through a positive acceptance of the masses and their capacity to engage in the challenge of change, the theoretical, theological, moral, and political groundwork is unmistakable.[2]

The church has always been the largest Black-owned institution in the urban community. It has served historically as a meeting place for strategic planning and distributing information to the masses. Furthermore, it is compelled to institute educational programs that will help obliterate apathy over public policy and the urban condition. In order to destroy this apathy, the Black church needs to listen to the voice of the laity—a voice calling for the engagement of the pastor and the church in social and political activities.

Direct engagement of the Negro church in politics will result not only in a broad base but the much needed injection into the movement of Black politics, the hope based upon the Kingdom of God which cannot be shaken by despair. Despair is the inevitable result of hope based on human beings and institutions. Based on the brotherhood of man demands, Black politics will be informed by a faith more sustaining, if not more instrumental, than an ideology.[3]

The liberation theology of some progressive leaders in the Black church must be a practical theology that seeks to change the conditions that exist in the community. It can reemphasize some of the attributes that have sustained African Americans, such as self-help, self-determination, freedom, justice, morality, and community. This expands the church from being a community of faith to a conglomerate community concerned not only with faith but with politics, development, and the total plight of Black people. The laity expect the pastor to be a holistic leader—a community leader as well as spiritual leader. Yet, the minister has to internalize these expectations and decide to what extent his or her social and political leadership will be determined by these expectations. It is one thing to know what is expected; however, the difficulty lies in deciding whether one wants to actually conform to the expectations.

In comparing this study with the national study, it should be noted that the national study by Schuller, Strommen, and Brekke, although comprehensive, did not really address the African American urban minister—nor the laity's expectations of him or her—from a social and political perspective. The national study focused on clergy and laity expectations of beginning ministers, while this work focused on laity expectations of clergy in the Black urban community's social and political arena. The national study established the categories or areas of ministry and the core clusters that this study used extensively. Use of one of its major themes, Ministry to Community and World, was limited in this study. Additionally, the scope of the national study was so extensive—and this study's scope was so narrow—that comparing them would be like comparing apples and oranges. Moreover, this field research study was limited in its focus as well as its sample because it aimed to deal only with laity's expectations of the African American urban minister regarding a specific and focused area of ministry—the social and political. The national study developed the usage of the nomenclature as well as the taxonomy for the areas of ministry, core clusters, and the individual items constituting the core clusters. This study is very indebted to the Schuller, Strommen, and Brekke study for use of one of the eleven areas of ministry—Ministry to Community and World—and three of the core clusters and the items that made up these clusters. Yet, the results of the national study and the results of this study are basically incompatible because of the aforesaid reasons. Additionally, the majority of respondents in this study were National Baptist, American Baptist, or affiliated with the Church of God in Christ; therefore, they had little or no association with the denominational affiliation of the respondents in the national study.

SOME CONCLUSIONS

1. Denomination made a statistically significant difference in the laity's expectations of clergy on the following variables:
    a. Organizes groups to change civil laws that seem in light of Scripture to be morally wrong.
    b. Works to integrate people of varying educational, ethnic, and cultural backgrounds into the congregation.
    c. Holds that the church's task of proclaiming the gospel by preaching and teaching overshadows in importance the task of helping to eliminate physical sufferings of people.
2. Education and income made a statistically significant difference in the laity's expectations of clergy on the variable. Priorities in use of time indicate the belief that the one and only way to build an ideal world society is to convert everyone to Christianity.
3. Occupation made a statistically significant difference in the laity's expectations of the Black urban minister on the variables:
    a. Acquaints self with the history and aspirations of minority groups and other oppressed people, and
    b. Works to integrate people of varying educational, ethnic, and cultural backgrounds into the congregation.
4. Denomination did not make a statistically significant difference in the laity's overall social and political expectations of the Black urban minister.
5. Socioeconomic status did not make a statistically significant difference in the laity's overall social and political expectation of the Black urban minister.
6. A majority of respondents had income over $21,000. Moreover, the largest percentage of respondents, 33.1 percent, had an income of $27,000 and above.
7. The majority of the respondents in this study had attended college, and 15.7 percent were college graduates.
8. The highest percentage of the respondents were Baptist and female—36.1 percent and 71.3 percent, respectively.

The conclusions of this study suggest that the African American urban minister has a constituency in the church that will support his or her active involvement on behalf of the oppressed as well as aggressive political leadership in the urban community. Moreover, Black laity seem to be quite homogeneous in the expectations of the minister such that denomination and socioeconomic status do not affect the overall expectations of the Black church constituency.

SOME LIMITATIONS

This study was limited to 338 respondents in one southeastern Virginia city. It was also confined to Black church laity who were basically unassociated with the Association of Theological Schools. This contributed to its uniqueness while simultaneously disenabling any substantive comparison with the national study.

This section of the book resulted from a survey developed by the Association of Theological Schools to gather information nationally from its affiliated schools and churches in order to determine clergy and laity expectations of beginning ministers. A portion of that survey was used in this study to determine laity expectations of clergy. While the validity of the survey is not questioned, the use of only a segment of it was a limitation of this study from a comparative perspective.

Moreover, because the permission of several ministers could not be secured in order to administer the survey in their churches, other churches whose pastors were more cooperative had to be chosen. This limitation, as well as some people's refusal to participate, even though they were present at the churches during the administration of the survey, was expected and could not be avoided. Overall, this study proceeded according to plan.

IMPLICATIONS

Because the African American church and its constituents are a major part of the urban environment, many implications for urban ministry management can be made from this study. "City governments today stand amidst a host of pressures and conflicts and successful urban managers must develop an understanding of these myriad external forces."[4] The local church is one of many external forces that characterize urban America. Moreover, the Black church is such an integral part of the urban milieu by coalescing the somewhat latent force inherent in its numerical and political strength, the Black church laity have the potential ability to change the face of urban America.

> Since the turmoil of the sixties, however, city governments have found it necessary to shift their attention from physical and technical concerns to human problems. In particular, urban public leadership increasingly has been called on to provide justice and services for those whose needs are greatest—the poor, the old and handicapped and the subjects of ethnic and racial discrimination.[5]

Our research found that the laity expected the minister to be actively concerned about the plight of the oppressed and to provide political and social leadership in the community; therefore, specific implications of our research have been divided into three areas—ministerial, laity, and church/state.

1. African American ministers in urban areas are expected to actively seek political office. This will enable them to actively participate in the political process and to contribute to the transformation of society.
2. Black ministers also need to value the opinions of their constituents, the laity. This means that after the minister attains a political position, he should use that position to advance the plight of the poor and minorities. He should risk becoming a gadfly in the Socratic sense in order that the voice "from down under" will be heard. Too often leaders become a reflection of the majority once they take office and forget why they were put in these positions.
3. The laity clearly expect the minister to be socially and politically active. This demands time and other resources that few ministers have. In fact, many already have second jobs. What are the laity willing to do in order to accommodate their own expectations of the minister? Are people who expect the minister to be both socially and politically active, as well as evangelistic, willing to support an increase in the church's staff so that the minister can meet more expectations?
4. If the urban laity expect the minister to be socially and politically active in the community, will there be a corresponding level of activity on their part? If the expectations of the laity reflect their inherent interest to augment or complement the efforts of the minister, then a collaborative effort by both groups has the potential to transform the urban community.

5. The national issue of separating church and state, or politics and religion, is nebulous to African Americans because they expect the minister to synchronize these two concepts, so that the problems of oppression and injustice in the urban milieu will be addressed from a political and religious perspective. For the Black laity, there is no absolute polarity or bifurcation between the pragmatic use of politics and religion. The church laity understand that the church and the state are already intimately aligned. For example, Protestant marriages are performed by clergy after the state grants a license to the parties involved. Is marriage a church or state function? This example suggests that the dichotomy between church and state or politics and religion is more perceived than real—more ideal than practical. Historically, the Black laity understand that slavery was not simply a state institution sanctioned by law—the church (religion) corroborated its intent and collaborated in maintaining its sacrosanctity by biblically substantiating its virtues. The eradication of oppression and injustice, however biblically based, presents society with a political dilemma.

6. Some questions have been raised by this study. Some of them are:

a. Would this study have been more compatible with the national study had it sought to determine laity and clergy expectations of ministers using all of the core clusters constituting Ministry to Community and World?

b. Would a larger sample of the Black church laity (maybe fifty large cities) have yielded the same results?

c. What types of people did not complete the survey? Was the population of the churches, on the particular Sunday of the survey, representative of the normal attendance of these churches?

d. How are expectations of laity conveyed to the minister? And, once expectations are known, how do they correlate with actual performance?

SUGGESTIONS FOR FUTURE RESEARCH

Future research could focus on some of the following:

1. A comparison of White and Black expectations of the urban minister regarding social and political issues would clearly establish the similarities and differences between these two races. This study could focus on a particular urban area or region.

2. The national study conducted by the Association of Theological Schools in America and Canada should be duplicated in the Black urban church in America to determine differences between clergy and laity expectations of beginning ministers.

3. What is the Black urban church's impact on the stability of the nuclear family? Inasmuch as the church is a staple of the Black community, this research will determine how it (the church) positively affects the Black family as a social unit.

Part III

Speaking the Truth to Power: Social Ethics, Church Leadership, and Social Policy

. 7 .

Church Leadership
and the Race Issue

Some African American church folk are mad because they feel the pain of injustice and the stress of living in a world obsessed with skin color and color prejudice. Anger was the reaction to such high-profile cases as that of the four White policemen exonerated in the Amodou Diallo case. In 2000, Mr. Diallo, an African immigrant, was shot to death on his own front porch in the Bronx because the four policemen thought or suspected that his wallet was a gun. African Americans are angry because of the callous and indifferent attitudes of Whites toward their plight of poverty and pain. Unfortunately, some others are too anesthetized by drugs to be angry or effective. They are being controlled by substances that create illusions and unreality that conceal the true degree of rage and disappointment churning in the hearts and souls of Black Americans."Getting high" is a symptom of repressed rage; however, as long as one is "high," the problem cannot be solved and maybe not even addressed. White folk, I suspect, are mad, too, because they think Blacks are getting too many economic and social opportunities to achieve and progress toward parity. They often feel that because they didn't have anything personally to do with slavery, segregation, discrimination, etc., and they are not the cause of the former or current problem, they should bear no burden or responsibility for its searing residual effects. The race issue must concern the African American church and her pastoral and lay leaders as we move into a new century because it continues to infiltrate every fiber of American life. It will not go away with the with start of the new millennium, as history attests. From the beginning race has affected religion and the African American church.

America is so divided along race and class lines that I am appalled by a continuing debate on Affirmative Action, which at its best is a minuscule and quasi-effective way of remedying the pandemic presence of invidious discrimination. There is also indeed a high correlation between race and class. One's skin color is often a good indicator of socioeconomic class, and one's address is likewise an indicator of both race and class. I reiterate, quite forthrightly, that Affirmative Action, as a form of government coercion urging the nation to practice some semblance of fairness, remains a very narrow method for dealing with an endemic and pathological problem that permeates the fabric of American society. De facto Affirmative Action, or action that in fact affirmed the superiority of Whites, has been a staple of the American social, economic, and political system from the time that Columbus "discovered" America. This racist presumption, which ignored the ontology of the native inhabitants, has saturated every nook and cranny of America's consciousness. Jonathan Kozol, in his book, *Savage Inequalities*, describes the educational and economic differences between America's richest (White) and poorest (Black) school districts. These inequalities are embedded in the lives of children and follow them to college and the workplace. To expect them to be equal when they sit down to take tests such as the SAT, LSAT, or GMAT is a gross exercise in reverse logic. Moreover, Andrew Hacker, in his book, *Two Nations: Black, White, Separate, Hostile, Unequal*, argues that America practices her own form of apartheid obsessed with race and the effects of race on education, housing, economics, and politics. We indeed live in two nations: I remember growing up in the 1960s in rural poverty without running water or electricity in our house; however, directly across the road was a White family with every conceivable amenity—even sharecroppers and chauffeurs. As a Black person, this is not an academic exercise or a theoretical enterprise for me. The fact that I have two earned doctorates and am an ordained minister and a tenured professor means absolutely nothing to the young White bank teller, the store clerk, the White policeman, or the New York City cab driver who refuses to stop because he sees only a Black man's face, a media-concocted metaphor for a violent criminal concocted by the news media to suggest in the Diallo and the Louima cases during the past year. Diallo and Louima are metaphors for every African American male!

I remember a few years ago, several people from my church and community were attending a convention in Nashville, Tennessee.

During our free time, we decided to visit the Opryland theme park. As we went into one of the souvenir shops, an elderly African American gentleman and his wife, who were with me and some youth, opened and held the door for all of us. To our surprise, a White man and his wife jumped in front of us, and as they went through the door, the White man said, "Thank you, boy." Before I realized that the degrading and derogatory remark was directed toward one of us, this couple had disappeared into the crowd. This was long after slavery, after Reconstruction, after the Civil Rights Act, after the Great Society, after school desegregation, and after the long, arduous battles and marches for freedom and justice led by Martin Luther King Jr. and a host of others.

Langston Hughes's unpublished poem, "Dream of Freedom," captures the natural yearning for freedom and justice regardless of race or class.[1] Like so many of his poems, it speaks to the oppressed and the poor by nurturing a deep-seated hope for freedom.

In the poem's discussion of equality, justice, and fairness, Langston Hughes seeks the eradication of the racial caste system that too often traps African Americans in their pursuit of the dream. "Affirmative action is about this dream with its back against the wall."[2] It encompasses legal principles and principles of equality, fairness, and justice. It is an effort to eliminate a pervasive racial caste system of inequality. "We are compelled to erase the very obstacle of race . . . which has been engineered . . . to prevent future equality for all people within this country."[3]

The controversy over affirmative action is a controversy over equality, fairness and justice, and because Black people are disproportionately affected by the lack of equality and justice, this naturally becomes an issue of race and class. After several hundred years, we are still dreaming of equality, but the stark reality is that the goal of eliminating the effects of over two hundred years of slavery, segregation, and inequality still eludes us not withstanding the enactment of laws (Affirmative Action programs) to eradicate long-standing patterns of racial discrimination.[4]

The principles of justice and equality are embedded not only in the United States Constitution but more basically in the Bible. For example, the great prophet Isaiah says, "The Lord, says to his people, 'Do what is just and right, for soon I will save you (Isa. 56:1).[5] Even a cursory reading of the Bible, especially the prophets and the Gospels, reveals the concept of justice to be embedded in Judeo-Christian ideals and practices. Affirmative Action based on race or class exemplifies America's quest to obtain justice and righteousness for those who are victims of the nation's disinterest in redistributing its wealth. Affirmative Action is morally right, mandated by a need to address the inequities of both the past and present. Discrimination and racism are abominations of God and man. The history of Africans in America reveals an unending, yet unfulfilled quest for justice and equality of opportunity and, more important, equality of results. Affirmative Action has proven to be a marginal means for Black America to achieve some semblance of fairness, justice, and righteousness. Without Affirmative Action, the blatant mendacity of America's power brokers would simply maintain the status quo that favors Whites, both males and females.

JUSTICE AND RIGHTEOUSNESS: BIBLICAL BASIS FOR AFFIRMATIVE ACTION

"God through his Word commands mankind to do justice and be righteous."[6] A review of the Scriptures illustrates that Affirmative Action programs represent an effort to do justice. God defines God's self as a defender of the poor, loyal to those in need of fair treatment (Mic. 2).[7] Moreover, the prophet Micah explains that Yahweh requires justice, love, and humility from the people of God. As long as America feels that she is chosen and blessed by God to be a Christian nation whose sovereignty includes subjugation and oppression of lesser developed countries, as well as Blacks and Native Americans within her own gates, the practice of freedom and justice continues to elude her. The Lord tells us what is required of us ". . . to do what is just, to show constant love, and to live in humble fellowship with God" (Mic. 6:8).[8] Jesus also reveals our duty to others and justice. In quoting the prophet Isaiah, Jesus said, "The Spirit of the Lord is upon me, because he has chosen me to bring the good news to the poor. He has sent me to proclaim liberty to the captives . . . to set free the oppressed and announce that the time when the Lord will save his people" (Luke 4:18–19).[9]

In Proverbs 21:3, we are compelled to "do what is right and fair."[10] Moreover, Proverbs 8:1–20 tells us that we are wise if we walk in the way of righteousness and . . . follow the paths of justice.[11] And finally, in Philippians 2:1–8, Paul tells us that Jesus was unselfish and gave himself for us. Moreover, as Christians we have a responsibility to look out for the welfare of others.[12] Paul Spickard acknowledges this in his article, "Why I Believe in Affirmative Action." Just as he received the benefit of his Mayflower ancestors' profits from the slave trade through an inheritance, he feels that he must support Affirmative Action even if it costs him something (a job opportunity as a White male). He concludes that Affirmative Action may not always be fair, but it is just.[13] Likewise, we are called to pursue that which is just and righteous. Accordingly, we must commit ourselves to justice as it is achieved through Affirmative Action even if it costs something to those who have benefited from slavery, institutionalized racism, and invidious discrimination.

THE CONDITION OF BLACK AMERICA AND THE QUEST FOR JUSTICE AND RIGHTEOUSNESS

Even as the Founding Fathers declared freedom and equality for all, they were devising a means of ensuring a cheap labor force and oppressing the Black brethren.[14] White Americans, from George Washington and Thomas Jefferson to Richard Nixon and Ronald Reagan, claimed justice and righteousness for themselves but sought to oppress and make captive America's Black citizens. From the 1640s to 1865, most Black people were slaves by law.[15] In 1837, the decision in the case of *Dred Scott* v. *Sanford* 60 U.S. (19 How.) 393 (1857) relegated Blacks to the status of chattel.[16] They were less than human and as such had no rights that could or should be respected by Whites. There was no pretense of justice or righteousness for Blacks. It took a Civil War and constitutional amendments to alter the law, but Blacks continued to be treated like animals as justice continued to elude them.[17] Unfortunately, many southern cities and towns, such as Richmond, Virginia, are still fighting the Civil War in their hearts.

A host of laws passed during Reconstruction provided race-conscious relief to eradicate the vestiges of White supremacy from the law of the land.[18] Some of these laws promised justice and righteousness for all. For example, the Civil Rights Act of 1875 declared all people to be entitled to full and equal employment, applicable alike to citizens of every race and color, regardless of any previous condition of servitude.[19]

The promise was once again broken. Within forty years, the Civil War amendments could not fulfill their designed objective.[20] First, the federal government failed to enforce these.[21] Second, the slave chains of the law were replaced by the slave chains of peonage, disenfranchisement, segregation, and cultural domination.[22]

The case of *Plessy* v. *Ferguson* validated the enslaving doctrine of "separate but equal."[23] Most states passed additional laws or Black codes depriving Blacks of the rights previously conferred under the constitutional amendments and the Civil Rights Acts.[24] Blacks were once again relegated to quasi-slave status. In 1890, for example, a generation after slavery was outlawed, seven out of every eight Black workers were still harvesting in plantation settings or performing domestic work in urban settings.[25] And, today, one of my thirty-two-year-old assistants, a native of Greenwood, Mississippi, documents the fact that she grew up on a plantation where de facto segregation, oppression, and injustice remained the order of the day.

From 1945 until 1964, a congressional bill to outlaw discrimination in employment was introduced but continuously rejected.[26] In 1957, the idea that primary educational institutions could be "separate but equal" was declared illegal in *Brown* v. *Board of Education*.[27] By 1964, Senator Hubert Humphrey noted that Negroes were the principal victim of discrimination. They represented 22 percent of the population and 25 percent of the unemployed.[28]

In a speech given at Howard University the same year, President Lyndon B. Johnson noted that "The great majority of Negro Americans—the poor, the unemployed, the uprooted, and the dispossessed—are another nation. Despite the laws, court order and legislative victories, the walls are rising and the gulf is rising."[29] The unemployment of Blacks had doubled since 1940 compared to Whites, the income had decreased compared to Whites, and the number of Blacks relegated to poverty status had increased.[30]

AFFIRMATIVE ACTION BASED ON RACE

Affirmative Action was established to eliminate the blatant and insidious inequalities grounded in law and custom and forged by over 200 years of slavery and a well-established, century-old system of overt and covert institutionalized racism. The legal foundation for Affirmative Action traditionally includes the Equal Protection Clause of the Fourteenth Amendment, Title VII of the Civil Rights Act of 1964, Executive Order #1123 from President Lyndon B. Johnson, and several other ensuing Civil Rights Acts and executive orders.[31] This legislation was the product of the many years of struggle and resistance of Blacks from the time of slavery in the antebellum South to the political and social agitation of the late 1950s and early 1960s. Black church progressives, the student Civil Rights Movement's demands for freedom and empowerment, and the courtroom challenges to segregation and Jim Crow also made the legislation possible.[32]

Title VII of the Civil Rights Act in 1964 prohibited discrimination based on race, color, national origin, and religion in the areas of employment, labor organizations, and training programs.[33] Executive Order #11246, issued in 1965 by President Johnson, prohibited discrimination in government employment and required federal contractors to submit written Affirmative Action plans to the government.[34]

Affirmative Action programs have helped Blacks achieve a greater level of equality and justice in America. For example, Bernard Anderson, Assistant Secretary of Labor for employment standards, indicates that a forthcoming study on Affirmative Action programs will show that programs administered under the Office of Federal Contract Compliance Program (OFCCP), which implemented Executive Order #11246, have greatly expanded employment opportunities for women and minorities and should be continued. As of 1993, 17,200 corporations and universities, with a total of 92,500 sites and 25 million employees, and an additional 100,000 construction establishments were required to comply with OFCCP's requirements as established by Executive Order #11246.[35]

Significant improvement has occurred in the economic status of Black men. In 1940, Black men earned around $4,500; by 1980, a similarly employed Black male earned $19,000. Black men still earn less than their White counterparts. In 1940, only one in twelve Black men earned an income larger than the average White male. By 1980, 29 percent of working Black men had incomes above that of the median income of White males. Two dimensions of education helped close the economic gap: the narrowing of educational disparities between Blacks and Whites and improving the economic return of schooling. Even with the passage of Civil Rights legislation and the implementation of Affirmative Action programs in education, educational differences still persist but are less pronounced than in the past. In 1989, most Black males had a year and a half less schooling than Whites; however, a majority of Blacks had completed high school. Between 1940 and 1980, 60 percent of the gap in education between Blacks and Whites had been filled.[36]

Even with the enactment of Affirmative Action, equality and justice are still a dream unfulfilled. Justice Thurgood Marshall observed in *Regents of the University of California* v. *Bakke*, 438 U.S. 265, 395–97 (1978) (footnotes omitted), in 1978:

> The position of the Negro today in America is the tragic but inevitable consequence of centuries of unequal treatment. Measured by any benchmark of comfort or achievement, meaningful equality means a distant dream for the Negro. The percentage of Negroes who live in families with incomes below the poverty line is nearly four times greater than that of whites. The relationship between those figures and the history of unequal treatment afforded to the Negro cannot be denied. At every point from birth to death the impact of the past is reflected in the still disfavored position of the Negro.[37]

Black unemployment had worsened by 1964. Family poverty for Blacks was triple that of whites; Black families earned 59.5 percent of a White family's earnings of 1964. And in 1985, a Black family earned 57.5 percent of a White family's earnings.[38] More recently, a report by the Glass Ceiling Commission shows that women and minorities are still underrepresented in top-level corporate jobs.[39] Even with laws and programs designed to mandate justice and equity, Blacks in America are still lagging behind because of the presence and subtleties of racism and the ways people justify it.

Equality has not and probably will never be fully achieved through Affirmative Action. According to Shirley Wilcher, Assistant Secretary of Labor, "Discrimination is alive and well in America, and Affirmative Action is still needed to combat ongoing discrimination."[40] Even with the recent protests in Florida and the backlash of minorities, many policy-makers and governments are still trying to take away the crumbs that Affirmative Action provides.

Where Do We Go From Here?

History teaches us that power yields only to power. Many people will not voluntarily do what is right and just, and Americans are no exception. The Constitution and its history demand that the federal government enforce the rights guaranteed by the Thirteenth, Fourteenth, and Fifteenth Amendments, which marked the end to Reconstruction and relegated Blacks to quasi-slave status. Neither the states nor the American people voluntarily complied with the equal protection laws of the Fourteenth Amendment then or now.[41] Much of the Affirmative Action legislation recognized that America would not voluntarily render justice and equality to Blacks after a century or more of making such promises. For example, after his experience with the President's Commission on Equal Employment Opportunity, President Johnson issued Executive Order #11246 because he realized that there was a need to require Affirmative Action, rather than just negotiate with contractors.[42]

A draft report, referring to the mission of the Labor Department's office of Federal Contract Compliance Programs, corroborated this.

Past efforts to improve employment opportunities for minorities, through voluntary action without government enforcement, have left no residue of success. When the threat of enforcement is not real, the contract compliance program ceases to have a demonstrable or lasting positive effect on minority or female employment.[43]

When controls are eliminated, we witness a return to pre-Affirmative Action, according to Rev. Jesse Jackson. Slavery lasted for another eighty years and White supremacy, according to Cornel West in his book *Race Matters*, continues to be a pervasive ideology. With the courts' restrictive interpretations of the legality of Affirmative Action programs, cries of reverse discrimination, and mistaken assertions that Civil Rights have been substantially accomplished during the 1980s and 1990s, we must question whether we are returning to a retrenchment similar to the post-Reconstruction era.[44]

IN SEARCH OF JUSTICE AND MORALITY

I turn now to Blacks' effort to achieve what seems to be illusive—justice. This is something that Martin Luther King Jr., like Sojourner Truth and Richard Allen before him, yearned for. The complexity of the term and idea of *justice* have not fostered a more faithful carriage of justice, but instead have created an atmosphere where justice is called injustice and continued injustice is claimed as true justice.

Glenn R. Negley, in *Collier's Encyclopedia* (Vol. 13), indicates that there are two meanings of justice. The first, "procedural" justice, refers to the outcome of a decision arrived at by the proper functioning of the machinery of the law. The application of existing and accepted law, whether it be a statutory code or common law, by the processes of the judicial system in a particular set of circumstances is said to have as its purpose the achievement of justice.[45] Procedural justice then has to do with the legal system and its working, the carrying out of the duties of the established law as well as its mechanics and administration. This justice operates as a self-propelled entity. "The second sense or meaning of justice involves reference to some criterion or set of values which is presumed to be higher than and superior to that which is embodied in the law."[46]

This second sense of justice helps to shape the debate on Affirmative Action. The legal system and its interpretation of procedural justice sometimes baffle even the most highly trained jurists. But justice as an ideal higher than the law is even more complex. We often have a profound sense of indignation when we believe justice has been denied or violated by some outside force. Justice, as it pertains to Affirmative Action, is a moral issue and we must appeal to the higher ideal of morality.

The ideal of personal rights is central to debate over Affirmative Action. Those against Affirmative Action often argue on the basis of their individual right for justice. Conversely, those who support Affirmative Action argue the group's rights for justice. In a democratic society, justice is often assumed by the majority, while minorities are constantly struggling to achieve justice.

The objectives stated in the Constitution's Preamble include the establishment of justice and the promotion of the general welfare of its citizenry. The document further declares that it is "self-evident that all men are created equal and have as their inalienable rights life, liberty, and the pursuit of happiness." It is true that "men," at least in practice, was meant to refer to White males, excluding White women; Black men and women were later declared, in this same document, to be three-fifths of a person. Ironically, the truth of the statement "all men as equal" has always been evident to those procedurally excluded (Blacks and women) to in truth include them, although it then escaped the reasoning of the very framers of the documents themselves and continues to escape their progenitors. Blacks and women have always believed that they, having been created by the same deity, must be of equal value and were also vested with the same rights as White men, by virtue of the good and just nature of the Creator.

The seeds of Affirmative Action were planted in the late 1500s, when Europeans decided that Africa, its resources, and its people were to be exploited for their gain, as they wished, without serious regard for the will or design of the Creator. The whole idea of justice, as it applies to Affirmative Action or any other issue regarding God's creation, must be located not merely in the realm of political philosophy, law, or the Constitution that established our nation, but in the purposes, design, and standards of the Creator. Yet, in practice Affirmative Action boils down to a policy matter legislated by Congress and litigated by the courts. It is also a theological and a moral matter argued over by the masses, debated by scholars, and appealed to by those victims it seeks to aid.

Negley observes that Immanuel Kant's view was "that the ultimate purpose of legal justice is to make possible the realization of moral justice, but that legal justice cannot enforce moral justice."[47] Kant also argued for the "autonomy of human reason . . . what reason dictates to man becomes for him a commandment . . . the universality dictated by reason is not derivative from some supernatural source, for . . . any such source would be unknowable."[48]

The difficulty with Kant's argument is twofold. First, what reason dictates as moral to an individual is not accepted universally. The reasonableness of the morality of slavery, with all its indignities, certainly cannot and would not be argued as universally acceptable to the categorical imperative. Nevertheless, enlightened and reasonable people were the slave traders and masters who were able to see the universal principle of injustice and moral want of England's authority over themselves, but were unable to apply that same universal dictate to themselves and American slavery. Descartes's maxim, *Cogito ergo sum*, while understood by the framers of the American government and the plantation owners, from Jefferson and Madison to architects of Jim Crowism, still did not keep them from denying the ontology of African Americans. Moreover, reason has failed to create a truly just and moral society. America, often described as the land of liberty and justice, has not without the conscription to divine principles made successful appeals to its citizens to embrace justice for African Americans. The Civil Rights Movement is historical evidence enough. It was Martin Luther King's appeal to moral and civil justice, and the television camera's unique ability to expose, in glaring detail, the South's ugly resistance to equality and justice that ultimately made a difference. This exposure embarrassed the South and nagged at the conscience and hearts of well-meaning people from Washington to California and throughout the world. This embarrassment before the world also played an important role in changing unjust laws.

Kant is correct in asserting that the dictates of morality and justice should be seen through the eyes of reason; however, history has shown that man's free will has too often denied and ignored the dictates of reason and morality.

As it pertains to Affirmative Action, justice has the good fortune to be based on the very Constitution of this nation. When the framers penned that document, they made the error of using language that laid the framework for a modern society that indeed attempts, at least in rhetoric, the daunting task of promising justice. This reasoned and rational language granted inalienable rights given by our Creator and irrationally denied them to others, namely African Americans. Supreme Court Justice Thurgood Marshall wrote in response to the Allen Bakke court decision, " . . . it is more than a little ironic that after several hundred years of class-based discrimination against Negroes, the Court is unwilling to hold that a class-based remedy for that discrimination is permissible." Reason and morality seem to have escaped these men, and it is that same escape of reason that causes this generation of greedy and selfish men to launch the current assault upon Affirmative Action.

Inherent in the discussion of justice and equality is the consideration of race. Historically and contemporarily, Whites, particularly White males, have shown a total lack of willingness to concede their belief that, as a group, they often benefit above and beyond every other group of created beings, especially African Americans. Appeals to ideals of justice, morality, or Christian sensibilities have not yielded a genuine or enduring response from those set on avarice and self-aggrandizement. Affirmative Action, along with the Fourteenth, Fifteenth, and Sixteenth Amendments, seek by procedural justice to redress the effects of decades of unreasonable injustice. In a nation that prides itself in ethics and reason, it appalls some to know that injustice, which is inherently unreasonable to Christian men and women, is so endemic to the laws and policies constructed by those who argue the sacrosanctity of law and reason. In my view, only racism, racial supremacy, and abject hatred of those who hail from Africa can begin to explain the double standard embraced by so many of the architects of injustice. Curiously, Affirmative Action is based on the very principles contained therein and it is the only sane or plausible solution to the dilemma, particularly since morality and justice cannot be enforced. As Kant argued, the opportunity or the environment for justice is created through legislation.

Most arguments against Affirmative Action are based on the insidious belief that White males are deserving and entitled to 100 percent of everything. Simultaneously, the most vocal adversaries to the idea of entitlements for seniors and the children of single parents are these same Whites. Moreover, those who oppose Affirmative Action offer no solution to rectify or respond to the reality of race discrimination in this country that does not put the burden on the victims.

Recently, a CNN news town meeting on Affirmative Action policies in the state of California focused on contractors who do business with the state government. White contractors claimed to be victims of "reverse discrimination" over the loss of 3 percent of the state's contracts to minority businesses. What seemed incredulous was that Whites were indignant at the loss of any business to minority companies and were exposing their racism on national television. Many who oppose Affirmative Action are reasoning from the same set of beliefs as those that dare call "inferior" that which God created as good, "inferior" meaning less than human and destined forever to chattel status. C. Eric Lincoln, in his article, entitled, "Beyond Bakke, Weber and Fullilove: Peace from Our Sins," notes that, "It is one of those little ironies that taunt the record of human performance, that had not the statesmen who drafted the initial version of the Declaration of Independence yielded to bigotry in the interest of a political trade-off, the issue would have been dealt with summarily and American history might well have taken a different course."[49]

Arguments based on merit and qualifications are designed to disguise the belief that Whites are superior beings and entitled to all the goods and benefits of society by virtue of their perceived superiority. They believe that if by reason of good fortune some crumbs of opportunity are left over, after they have had their fill, then, and only then, may others partake.

White males have benefited from unofficial de facto Affirmative Action programs all along. The "old boy" network has operated successfully for many years. "Affirmative Action is necessary . . . to combat the expectations of assured success of the advantaged," writes Philip Green.[50] The small encroachment on that network by Affirmative Action is truly in question here. It is my belief that the concept of reverse discrimination is a misnomer at best, and at worst it is a vicious and wicked smokescreen designed to mask the subliminal desire to continue oppressing African Americans.

Many of the arguments are similar to that of Timothy Maguire's in his article, "My Bout with Affirmative Action." Describing himself as a victim, he complains about his "almost" expulsion from

Georgetown University Law School for writing an article entitled "Admissions Apartheid." In the article he compared the GPA and LSAT scores of Black students with those of the Whites in the law program. He quickly sweeps over the fact that his behavior was not only mean-spirited, which he admits, but also unethical, because it was based on private information from student records that he was hired to file. His behavior seriously questions whether he is morally qualified to take on the responsibility to uphold the law. His accusations that the school's practices were unethical and dishonest are incredible in the face of his own behavior.

More critical to the discussion is the fact that his points are purely based on White supremacist notions. Never in the article does he charge that the Black students who had not passed the LSAT were admitted. There is no indication that the numbers of Black students admitted differed greatly from those who actually graduated. His great expose of the disparity between the two groups amounted to .5 percent difference in GPA and an eight-point difference on the LSAT.

Where is it written that passing a culturally biased test with a higher score automatically makes one more qualified? Why do White males insist on this as a basis for arguments against Affirmative Action? The privilege and advantage of growing up White in America makes Affirmative Action necessary for Blacks. For example, if the passing score on an examination for employment is 80, and one applicant scores 82 and the other scores 88, is it necessarily true that the applicant with the higher score is more qualified? What if the applicant who scored higher had more experience, but was dishonest and disagreeable? If a person of a racial minority has passed the minimum requirements designated by the school or the business, that person should be deemed qualified. To argue that he or she is or is not qualified because someone else scored higher is patently unreasonable.

Writing about the concept of law, H. L. A. Hart says, "All theories of justice agree that to be just is to treat like cases alike . . . theories differ in determining which cases are deemed alike."[51] I suspect that Maguire has made the error of judging circumstances for Blacks in this country as being the same as they are for Whites. John Rawls held two basic principles of justice:

> First that equal right of the greatest liberty and fair opportunity, which regulates basic civil liberties and political rights. Second is

the difference principle, which regulates the distribution of wealth, income and status, allow inequalities only if they make the worst potential outcome as good as possible.[52]

Timothy Maguire fails to acknowledge the "difference principle" and completely ignores the reasons why African Americans may score a few percentage points lower on tests and have lower GPA scores. Variables such as inherent test bias, costly preparation courses, racist grading policies of White professors at the undergraduate and professional school level, and attendance at poorly staffed and ill-equipped urban public school systems can all put Black students at a disadvantage. Many White suburban schools, while funded with public money, are virtually private. They are well funded and endowed with state-of-the-art equipment and can attract a variety of educators capable of offering advanced courses in many disciplines. The only reason one would dismiss such differences as inconsequential would be to ensure that privilege continues to control opportunity. "To not oppress or to be just is not just to not act badly, but it is also to go further and do good."[53] The justification for maintaining race-based Affirmative Action policies is based on this principle. More than nondiscrimination legislation is needed; we must go further to restore or make restitution for what has been taken.

Racism and White privilege have not been sufficiently curtailed to warrant the elimination of Affirmative Action. To ensure that Blacks not be thrust into a state of overt oppression similar to the Jim Crow era, action must be taken. Black oppression is historically foundational, economically profitable, and irrationally upheld in the hearts and minds of Whites in this country. Affirmative Action laws and policies have been in existence for little over thirty years, and the Old Guard has not abandoned its philosophy of racial supremacy. We have not yet eradicated the affects of slavery or Jim Crow. African Americans are now beginning to develop some infrastructures that will serve as ramparts to tear down the wall of internalized racism. The Million Man March was just the first step. The strength of character needed to rebuild our own economies, communities, and educational system is making some small inroads, but the honeymoon of integration has begun to wear off, and more time and effort are needed.

There is, however, a more ancient rationale for Affirmative Action based on the biblical understanding of justice. Faith in the

God of justice on the one hand, and opposition to the justice of Affirmative Action on the other, is a non sequitur. Unfortunately, this seems to be very American and very Christian, albeit unjust and unbiblical.

The biblical idea of justice or the Hebrew's view of God as the source of justice and righteousness is the foundation of God's very nature. The psalmist states ". . . righteousness and justice are the foundation of His throne" (Ps. 97:2b). Biblical deity is regarded as the judge of the whole earth. Since God was the earth's creator, it followed that God established equity and justice (Gen. 18:25; Ps. 99:4). Further, the practice of justice was considered crucial to social relationships among themselves and other people. God was the judge in these matters, administering justice by punishing those whose conduct made the lives of others very difficult (Ps. 9:9). The people of God had very high expectations of justice, much like many of us who feel that justice is a highly valued birthright.

> It is key to note that massive amounts of material in the Old Testament are addressed to the rulers, men in positions of authority, kings, princesses, prophets and priests and the leading group in influence . . . the concern is with those wielding power over their subjects, and with the obligations of the strong toward the weak.[54]

Elements of biblical ethics, such as fairness, goodness, and justice, are integral to the Bible and its concern for the widows, fatherless, poor, and strangers (Exod. 22:21–27; Deut. 10:17–19; Ps. 16). "The ruler, person or group in authority though considered blessed by God to hold that position was also responsible and charged with carrying out the tasks demanded by the office."[55] Since judgment was thought to be issued from the throne of God, the rulers standing in God's stead were expected to reflect the holy and righteous nature of God.

As stated earlier, the arguments against Affirmative Action initiatives seem based on presuppositions. African Americans are viewed as criminal, shiftless, inferior beings undeserving of basic rights of justice. This view comes from Whites who disdain people of color, mainly African Americans, who are viewed as strangers, aliens, foreigners, and, according to Langston Hughes, are in fact "refugees in America." This attitude directly violates the biblical view of justice as seen in Exodus 23, Leviticus 19, and Deuteronomy 24, which all charge the strong to take an interest in favor of seeing justice done for the oppressed.

The Prophet Ezekiel says, "Again, though I say to the wicked, you shall surely die, yet if they turn from their sin and do what is lawful and right, if the wicked restore the pledge, give back what they have taken by robbery, and walk in the statutes of life, committing no iniquity, they shall surely live, they shall not die. None of the sins that they have committed shall be remembered against them; they have done what is lawful and right, they shall surely live" (Ezek. 33:14–16). This biblical statement strongly establishes the need for reparations for past sins. Because it was unconscionable to claim repentance and not make retribution to those victimized by one's evil, this is the most serious spiritual issue in the anti-Affirmative Action debate. The African American has been summarily denied human rights and civil rights for practically three centuries. This nation and Europe have made great economic gains, enabling those countries to lead the industrial world. Yet, they want to consider a few years of Affirmative Action as enough repentance and repayment—such that it should now be abolished.

The need for our nation to see itself as a just community is crucial to our survival. However, as a nation, we need to be unselfish and less egoistic; we must desire for others that which we ourselves possess. Clearly, positive steps, taken together, are still necessary to eradicate the affects of the evil of our legacy.

In the gospel of Luke, Zaccheus, when Jesus had eaten at his home, made the declaration that he would "give half my possessions to the poor; and if I have defrauded anyone of anything, I will pay back four times as much" (Luke 19:8). Race-based Affirmative Action gives this country the opportunity to make right the wrong on which it was established and sustained.

Another concept in Scripture that addresses the Affirmative Action argument is seen in the Old Testament injunction, "Do not muzzle the ox when he treadeth" (Deut. 25:4; also repeated in 1 Cor. 9:9 and 1 Tim. 5:18). In both instances in the New Testament, Paul uses this verse to argue for paying spiritual leaders for their ministry. His use, however, does not preclude the use for any people right for payment for services rendered. People, be they spiritual leaders or not, are more valuable than oxen. African Americans should also have the hope of sharing in this great crop being harvested, for it was planted by their ancestors in slavery.

How can it be rationally argued that we are undeserving of a rightful share? We are not asking to be repaid four times more than what was taken, nor are we asking to be repaid in full, but we are asking to be given free reign to eat from the fruit of the land (Deut. 24:17ff). In the concept of justice in Israel, the poor did not expect reward of material benefits beyond what was normally entitled for the average good life. They expected and had a right to expect fair dealings from rulers and the influential (cf. Amos 2:6:7).

Merit is not mentioned in any of the texts concerning justice for the oppressed. The qualifications of those advantaged by birth or robbery are not used as a measuring stick to justify beating the poor.

Unlike our system, there was no real machinery for changing the law. The law was considered immutable because it reflected the perfect will of the Deity. Most thinking people are no longer so idealistic as to think that our laws are divinely inspired. We are keenly aware that we have the privilege and responsibility to establish, rescind, and create legislation necessary to provide for what Kant calls the "freedom to act morally." As long as we continue to use the arguments that created the evil of racial supremacy of Whites, perpetuating a Black underclass in this nation, we will never really be a society of "liberty for all."

It is imperative that the Christian community, the moral right, and the family values proponents desist from the rhetoric that hides their sin and the sin of those with whom they have nothing in common other than their desire to see Affirmative Action abolished. Christians should no longer countenance as moral and ethical that which is immoral and irrational.

There may be a time in our country when Affirmative Action will not be needed to assuage the ravages of White supremacist idealism and practices; however, that time has not yet come! And until such a time, the African American church and pastor have to provide the leadership to keep the issue in the public's conscience.

PREFERENTIAL TREATMENT IS NO TREATMENT AT ALL

Legislation written by Republicans, eager to attract conservative and moderate White Democrats, essentially would eliminate all federal Affirmative Action programs. The version of that bill in the Senate bears the name of one primary sponsor—Dole.
—Richmond Times Dispatch, May 20, 1996, A3

The Film Industry says all the right things, but its continued exclusion
of African-Americans is a national disgrace.
—*People* magazine, March 18, 1996, cover

The industry is still a hotbed of racism; we're pretty much shut out.
—Frank Berry, quoted in *People* magazine, March 18, 1996

There is a lot of racism going on, and I'd be lying if I said there wasn't.
—Quincy Jones, *People* magazine, March 18, 1996, p. 45

I am even more convinced that the dismantling of Affirmative Action will do grave injustice to minorities and poor people. Affirmative Action, which some critics prefer to call preferential treatment, is based on several unsubstantiated premises. The first is the use of the term *preferential treatment*. Preferential treatment is a misnomer because minorities and Blacks are really not being given preferred treatment at all. Affirmative Action plans often afford victims of systematic racial prejudice the opportunity to achieve some semblance of fairness. The language of fair treatment or equal treatment would more accurately describe the purpose and intent of Affirmative Action. Moreover, to propose that Affirmative Action efforts provide an advantaged status to minorities is a fallacy. On the contrary, Affirmative Action initiatives at best institutionalize artificial parameters for the potential advancement of minorities. In other words, Affirmative Action goals and quotas discreetly project the most optimistic expectation regarding what a minority will be permitted to achieve or acquire regardless of his or her skills, talents, or abilities.

While conservative politicians, business leaders, and academicians are having us believe that compliance with Affirmative Action directives is tantamount to providing glorious opportunities to minorities, the subtle reality of how these directives actually limit possibilities for minorities is often overlooked. The application of Affirmative Action objectives in the practical world defines ultimate boundaries within which minorities must operate. Moreover, Affirmative Action efforts have been so maligned and demonized that the folk they were designed to help are often spiritually, socially, and economically harmed and demoralized by the process. Judge Clarence Thomas is a good example of the negative affects of Affirmative Action. A beneficiary of Affirmative Action during his education, he somehow now believes that self-help is a new phenomenon for Black folk. Affirmative Action does not obviate self-help.

Mainstream America's anti-Affirmative Action sentiment, led by political opportunists and fueled by those who believe and practice White supremacy, seeks to convince government leaders and popular culture that Affirmative Action is somehow a generous and benevolent endeavor. However, in order for this premise to be accurate, Affirmative Action would have to put minorities in a favorable position of some sort. Realistically, however, it affords minorities the potential to function at levels that would be considered only minimal or entry-level by Whites.

Government set-asides for minorities usually range from 20 to 25 percent in such awards as contracts, employment opportunities, scholarship monies, grants, etc. Rarely, however, do actual awards exceed the allocated numbers and amounts. It then seems peculiar and suspicious that minorities would consistently only be qualified at ironically the same percentage levels that have been designated by Affirmative Action initiatives. This normalization of minimalism is really an inherent form of regression toward an artificial norm.

Affirmative Action goals then tend to represent a best case scenario for the minority population. If such goals were identified and implemented in a similar fashion for American Whites, Whites would be enraged by the restrictions that these targets place on their ability to pursue careers, educational experiences, and economic development. Affirmative Action does not offer preferential treatment because it does not afford minorities the opportunity for a best case scenario or positions of power and influence. It merely addresses institutional imbalances that are perpetrated against Blacks and other minorities because of race. It addresses the a priori presumption of privilege that every White man in America possesses.

Much of the opposition to Affirmative Action is based on the fallacies and misconceptions that are either stated or implied in various arguments:

1. African Americans and women are less qualified than White males in the job market and workforce. There is a presumption of incompetence solely because of Affirmative Action.
2. White males do not discriminate and are not responsible for the maintenance of injustice.

3. When White males are not in superior positions of the greatest influence or power, it is because they have been mistreated and unfairly denied opportunities. White males *deserve* these positions; conversely, Blacks and minorities do not merit them because they are not as qualified as Whites.

4. Whites competed for the positions which they hold, notwithstanding the fact that they created the positions, the tests, and other requirements based on their inherent privilege, and because they are not White.

5. The traditions that have historically influenced employment practices, economic trends, and educational systems are to be regarded as canons by all. The canonization of the status quo is the essence of fairness and justice, and any deviation from this that seeks to balance tradition with innovation is construed as reverse discrimination.

These fallacious assumptions and beliefs are biased and bigoted. They are in opposition to those Scriptures that indicate that we were all created equal and in the image of God. However, we do know that the language of egalitarianism and equality did not include African Americans, so the architects of morality and ethics, from Plato to John Stuart Mill and Immanuel Kant, did not even consider the possibility that one day Black people would demand that they too were a part of the language of Holy Scripture and the United States Constitution. Biblically speaking then, no race or class of people is superior or inferior to another, and no race or class of people *deserves* to excel over and dominate all other races. Any tradition that perpetuates this perspective of pride and arrogance is sinful. Affirmative Action is only a modest effort to address this sin and inequity.

Moreover, it is naive to assume that White males do not discriminate. The lack of diversity in employment suggests that White males' positions of power are habitually used in an oppressive manner. These people have abused their power by advancing these self-serving policies and practices by routinely appointing other White males as successors in these positions. Often their appointment is the product of association. When Blacks are appointed, their behavior and personality must reflect the majority's ideological understanding and practice. These trends have then been institutionalized because of tradition and often without consideration of qualifications, merit, or the benefit of competition. As a result, positions of power and influence remain with White males and sustain the oppression of others, particularly African Americans. In my view, Whites have historically been both the architects and beneficiaries of preferential treatment.

Those who have a genuine concern for pursuing and upholding the biblical directives for equality, fairness, and mutual respect will carefully and objectively consider the following when evaluating the need for Affirmative Action.

1. Who defines and establishes qualifications and/or merit for educational, economic, or employment environments? Historically, the White males have held positions of power and influence. How can these people objectively represent all of the interests of our nation's diverse population? Moreover, what would motivate the oppressor to liberate the oppressed?
2. Why would the effects of Affirmative Action on White women, as opposed to African American women or women in general, be a factor in assessing its value? Does this not indicate an agenda to maintain a privileged race and class as opposed to an agenda of fairness and equality? Such an agenda identifies this group as superior and more worthy of concern in comparison than others.
3. How can color-blind and gender-blind criteria consistently produce results in favor of White males? There may be myriad reasons; however, intentional, subtle, insidious discrimination is also a viable explanation for an outcome that historically and consistently lacks racial diversity.

The Good Old Days—Romanticism at Its Worst

Finally, arguments of most equal justice and Affirmative Action critics are laden with faulty conclusions because they disregard many experiential truths. Critics seem oblivious to the fact that the traditions referred to as "canons of fair play" were not developed by a racially or culturally diverse group. Therefore, such traditions reflect the interests, biases, and experiences of those who have held positions of power and influence at the time they originated. This, too often in America and the world, means White men. Every major canon, from the books in the Bible to the constitutive elements of a liberal arts education, has been determined basically by White males. The tragedy is that they too often arrogantly believe that this is indeed the will of God. Additionally, there is no acknowledgment that minorities and women must often work twice as hard to achieve or acquire that which is a presumed right for White males. The fact that Whites inherit and pass along their positions of power and influence, as doctors and lawyers and CEOs, is ignored. Therefore, it must be recognized that Affirmative Action does not lower any standards for minorities, as some propose. In actuality, such actions would not be tolerated simply to benefit minorities. However, Affirmative Action does attempt to correct a system of bias by addressing cultural, racial, and gender imbalances and to remove barriers to positions of power and influence for minorities.

The dismantling of Affirmative Action initiatives is an effort to return to the "good old days" of absolute White supremacy and blatant and abject discrimination and racism. My hope and prayer is that enlightened policy makers and academicians, and church leaders, will not succumb to the lure to dominate and oppress those who are the poor, disenfranchised children of God.

As a Black person, I experience racism, both overt and covert, every single day. Sometimes I experience it in the bank while trying to cash a check or withdraw from my savings account when White high school graduates insist on seeing my driver's license for the umpteenth time. Sometimes I refuse to show it, saying in utter disgust, "Don't you know me? I come into this branch regularly. I have had an account here for over twenty years. I am tired of this harassment—this abject racism." At other times, I experience racism at McDonald's or Hardees or some other restaurant where the person seating guests or taking orders will simply assume that if two parties are at the counter or in a haphazard line, that the White person should be served first. I often have had to interrupt and assert that I was in line first and should be served. I am troubled by the assumption of privilege or the air of superiority displayed by the beneficiaries of benevolence, kindness, power, and money—these people are usually White.

In my view, the fact of race and racism is real—an existential reality, an inescapable fact of life. A society cannot be a color-blind society when it is diversely colored and the human mind and spirit are prone to recognize and advance that which is a reflection of itself. Affirmative Action is a necessary intervention that ultimately serves the public interest by forcing Whites to at least deal marginally and minimally with racism as a factor in politics, education, and employment.

RELIANCE ON CODE WORDS: PREFERENTIAL TREATMENT

Several philosophical assertions may suggest to some that I *beg* the question of the Bible's overall slant toward justice and fairness, and that God's interest in peoples' practice of justice and righteousness is itself a fallacy. In philosophy, "begging the question" is to assume the point in dispute; however, I make no such assumption. Instead, I suggest that certain biblical texts provide moral principles for Christians and Jews that will contribute to a more just and fair society. However, use of the term preferential treatment does indeed beg the question by assuming that remedies afforded minorities and the term preferential treatment are tautological. The truth is, "a word begs the question when its meaning conveys the assumption that some point in dispute has already been settled when there may still be some doubt or question about it" (S. Morris Engel, *The Study of Philosophy* 1981: 106). The term preferential treatment for Affirmative Action is an evaluative and judgmental description rather than a fact. To refer to Affirmative Action as preferential treatment is to convey the idea that it somehow does something wrong. The truth is that Affirmative Action attempts to remedy the pandemic and systemic presence of discrimination that has disproportionately affected Blacks and other minorities from slavery until the present. Without Affirmative Action, Whites will continue to enjoy preferential treatment, which in their view seems to be normative. Affirmative Action remedies a wrong rather than perpetuates one.

ARGUMENTUM AD POPULUM

Again, I am in the minority by making what is currently a politically incorrect and very unpopular argument for the continuation of a policy that I concede is flawed and inadequate. However, I do believe the policy is still needed because, as I suggested earlier, my existential situation is laden with the presence of racism, discrimination, and cavalier attitudes that presume the presence of justice and fairness. Many who oppose Affirmative Action do so by appealing to popular prejudice.

I cannot understand the argument that a White male who has enjoyed the benefits of ancestral domination and continued advantage can suggest that Affirmative Action, which is designed to bring about some semblance of parity, somehow unfairly penalizes Whites. Black people have been free for fewer years than they were slaves. For nearly 300 years, America's economy was sustained by the blood and sweat of a people whom Thomas Jefferson, the architect of America's freedom, held in bondage. Every White person in America is a beneficiary of this historic dehumanization. And, because Whites led by Jefferson, Washington, Monroe, etc., have an American heritage of domination and Orwellian double-talk, it seems difficult for them to now understand how they too benefited from this legacy. In my view, Black people continue to feel the effects of domination, the vestiges of slavery, and the double-talk of Jefferson: "All men are created equal" while Black men and women could be slaves. What a fallacy!

Finally, my interest in this subject is not limited simply to the theoretical or the logical. This is not an esoteric enterprise for me and I cannot afford to exclude my own moral selfhood from the debate. Before Affirmative Action, African Americans could not attend major southern public schools and universities. Images of dogs biting Black children, White sheriffs blocking doorways, and southern governors spewing out words of defiance and hate against Blacks cannot be erased from my memory, my experience. My passion for justice and fairness may sound inflammatory because the theme that runs through the arguments against Affirmative Action is that preferential treatment is unfair because it "penalizes someone, e.g., a White male . . ." and it "denies someone White what he deserves." Well, Black people deserve something too—at least the crumbs provided by Affirmative Action. Affirmative Action is not a panacea; it is an effort to help remedy historic unfair practices of insidious discrimination. And, the pastor as leader must provide the argument and the environment for keeping this and other issues of justice and fairness before the laity and in the public square. The pastoral leader is compelled to be a public intellectual, engaging society in some of the pressing issues of our day!

. 8 .

Toward a Constructive
Practical Theology

It is difficult to explain clearly the present critical age of Negro Religion.
First, we must remember that living as the blacks do in close contact with a
great modern nation, and sharing, although imperfectly, the soul-life of that
nation, they must necessarily be affected more or less directly by all the reli-
gious and ethical forces that are today moving the United States.
—W. E. B. Du Bois, *The Souls of Black Folk*

Community is a term that is so familiar to people
in the West and yet so hard to achieve.
—Malidoma Patrice Some, *The Healing Wisdom of Africa*

THE CHURCH AGAINST CHRIST—A CRITICAL NEED
FOR A NEW PRACTICE

One of my mentors and teachers, Samuel DeWitt Proctor, used to
say that "Jesus Christ is not very popular in the church." As a matter of fact, it seems that there is a significant element in the church
that is against Christ. What I mean is that the spirit of Christ as
manifested in love, peace, justice, and righteousness or "a new creation" seems to be absent from the actions and behaviors of persons in the organized church. Indeed Christ is the new creation or
the new order of being, as Paul argues in Galatians, and yet our
interest is in a new world order characterized by domination and
indifference.

Moreover, H. Richard Niebuhr argues that Christian theology and
Christian ethics can be summed up by two concise formulations:

163

God is love and love one another.[1] Unfortunately, there is both a lack of love for God and one another as evidenced by our mesmerization for the "things of the world." Even in the church, which at one time was a place characterized by the renewal of spirit or the embodiment of the kingdom of God, there now resides a discordant spirit and a reverence for that which is bureaucratic and "constitutional." The church's interest in Roberts Rules of Order or some other parliamentary document or legally binding agreement supercedes her interest in the moral or what Immanuel Kant called "the victory of the good over evil, and the founding of the kingdom of God on earth."[2]

Don S. Browning in his book *A Fundamental Practical Theology* seeks to introduce a new paradigm for the practice of ministry and theology—one that is theory laden, yet one that begins and ends in practice. He suggests that we begin with practice, move to theory, and return to practice! His scheme from practice to theory and back to practice is reminiscent of Donald A. Schon's book, *The Reflective Practitioner*, which suggests that practice should be grounded in reflection or reason. Unfortunately, reason also seems to have replaced God, and we can attribute this to persons like Immanuel Kant whom we shall discuss in detail later in this chapter.

Regardless of one's dominant leadership style, whether autocratic, bureaucratic, diplomatic, participative, or delegative—there must be time and opportunity to reflect in order to fully understand the dynamics of practice. The leader's style unfortunately is often dictated by the expectation of the organization. Traditional churches, particularly Baptists and Methodists, are bureaucratic in their structure and often force the leader or pastor to conform his or her leadership style to the preexisting organizational style. This is true especially in churches where federal, state,and local government workers tend to dominate and control the positions of leadership. Their mentality is often shaped by Big Brother, which is a metaphor for bureaucracy and constitutionality. This is an extension of the "this is business" phenomenon that I discussed in Chapter 1. Both phenomena are models that have corrupted and may eventually destroy the prophetic nature of the church. The African American church at one time, especially during its "invisible institution" days and throughout the nineteenth and early twentieth century, was perceived by its participants and adherents to its creeds as the "kingdom of God" or that place where renewal of spirit was evident or expected. Today, it is caricatured by comedians and forced to compete with the entertainment industry.

There is a mentality that suggests that the gospel should be packaged to "pack them in and keep them happy" in order that the bills can be paid. This means that if the preacher offends anyone, they will subsequently hold back their tithes and offering in an effort to "hit him where it hurts" until they can manipulate their way back into power or control.

This chapter will reflect the church's preoccupation with bureaucracy and laws as manifested in its practice of representative democracy which is thought to be more holy than any theocratic understanding of the church. God's rule is superceded by man's rule because our confidence is in constitutionality rather than Scripture, by-laws rather than the Bible, man rather than God.

These by-laws have been developed over many years of study and practice and belong as much to the committee as they do to me. I thank the unnamed church persons who have helped in this process.

In this chapter, I will set forth some policies, procedures, and/or by-laws that are designed to be Scripture-based and pastor friendly. However, I will first deal with two other areas: Anselm's "Faith Seeking Understanding" and Kant's "Reason over Christ." The final section will deal with the "Church for Christ."

Unlike Kant's ideal of the church as an ethical commonwealth, the local church is in fact a political commonwealth, structured and modeled after the entities of the world. The whole idea of an "official board" or "joint board" in the local church is based on an elitist model of democracy where a few people rule over the many. This is one of the first obstructionist entities that need to be extirpated from the structure of the church. It is designed to keep control of the church in the hands of tradition and to obviate any agogic or change elements in the church. It effectively turns the pastor into a politician and ensures that his or her prophetic role is kept in check. In some ways, this is an evil, i.e., demonic, structure that is gradually contributing to the death of the church. Many ministries and transforming programs and ideas are held hostage by the gatekeepers of the church's political structure.

THE RELATIONSHIP BETWEEN BELIEF AND UNDERSTANDING: ANSELM OF CANTERBURY

The cornerstone of Anselm's epistemology is expressed in the *Proslogion*. His most enduring words are:

But I do desire to understand your truth a little, that my heart believes and loves. For I do not seek to understand so that I may believe: but I believe so that I may understand. For I believe this also, that "unless I believe, I shall not understand." (Isa. 7:9)[3]

While I am in basic agreement with Anselm's claim that faith precedes understanding, the issue for me is whether belief or faith always needs cognitive approval. Anselm seems to imply that faith has no independent, "self-standing," i.e., inherent-virtue apart from its quest to know or to learn. Again, while I reiterate my veneration for the concept, I simultaneously question its accuracy. Does the leap of faith need necessarily a reason for its existence? The correlation between faith and reason is a noble one; however, does faith really need an epistemic grounding in order to be valid, or is faith itself a form of knowing, i.e., reason. It seems to me that Anselm equivocates on his own faith by according to reason, i.e., knowledge and understanding, a higher position than faith as he develops his argument.

Secondly, allow me to postulate that there are things that are believed and yet never fully understood, and there are things that are known prior to belief or apart from faith or belief. It is certainly not illogical to postulate that knowledge precedes belief. For example, if it were a fact that I knew or understood the essential and technical components of physics, I might believe something very different about the nature of God and the universe. In this case, it would be true that knowledge precedes belief rather than Anselm's postulate that belief precedes understanding. Moreover, faith as a precondition to understanding seems to obviate the apparent knowledge possessed by a potpourri of epistemologists. Anselm suggests that belief [in God] is necessary in order to understand or know. Yet, logic allows us to recognize that certain things can be known apart from belief. Moreover, it seems that the church is much less confident in her faith that she is in that which is visible and provable logically. As a matter of fact we often believe only that which we can justify with evidence that is concrete.

RELIGION AND THE CHURCH AS A POLITICAL COMMONWEALTH—IMMANUEL KANT

I want to engage Kant by providing an overview of his "Religion" and then to engage critically in some of his concepts. It seems to me that Kant's religion is reason and the superiority of the moral law. The moral law may not precede God, but it certainly supercedes God. As a matter of fact, the love of God is basically tantamount to respect for the moral law. Kant locates the highest good not in God per se but in the moral law. The only characterization we get of God is the moral law and the moral law, defined, is "right reason," which according to Kant is written in our hearts. Morality is the supreme hermeneutic in Kantian religion, and this is achieved through rationality rather than any empirical or experiential phenomena. Yet, it is fair to assert that Kant would indicate that to be moral, one has to also believe that the possibility of God exists. However, he asserts that one has to be moral on one's own. This seems to be a paradox if not a contradiction. While for Kant morality does not necessarily need or come from God, it leads inevitably to God via the highest good. However, in the preface to the first edition of "Religion," Kant asserts that man is self-sufficient and autonomous. He states:

> So, far as morality is based upon the conception of man as a free agent who, just because he is free, binds himself through his reason to unconditioned laws, it stands in need neither of the idea of another being over him, for him to apprehend his duty, nor of an incentive other than the law itself, for him to do his duty. At least it is man's own fault if he is subject to such a need; and if he is, this need can be relieved through nothing outside himself; for whatever does not originate in himself and in his own freedom in no way compensates for the deficiency of his morality. Hence for its own sake morality does not need religion at all (whether objectively, as regards willing or subjectively, as regards ability [to act]) by virtue of pure practical reason it is self-sufficient.[4]

While Kant is clear in his assertion that the autonomy of the will is the supreme principle of universality and that morality does not need religion at all, he does make it clear that "morality thus leads ineluctably to religion, through which it extends itself to the idea of a powerful moral lawgiver."[5] While he does not say so explicitly, he does imply that the moral law giver is God. I will return later to the issue of the autonomy of the will, or man's self-sufficiency.

The Practice of Good and Evil

Kant asserts that to be morally good one must actively battle or oppose the cause of evil.[6] The subordination of the moral law makes one evil. Moreover, Kant says, "But only what is opposed to the moral law is evil in itself, absolutely reprehensible, and must be completely eradicated; and that reason which teaches this truth, and more especially that which puts it into practice, alone deserves the name of wisdom."[7] Wisdom then is made manifest in practice, not in ideality, and like everything else, this wisdom is located in reason. Moreover, it seems that if man is by nature evil, as Kant asserts, and man is created in the imago dei, then evil is necessarily a positive attribute. Man's propensity to do evil does not mean that evil is sin, but rather it is an integral element in the nature of man. For Kant there are two basic principles: the positively good and the positively evil. The basis for evil does not lie in man's sensuality or sexuality but probably in our freedom, which harbors the possibility of putting the moral law at the bottom.[8] The son of God is the nonpersonified i.e., nonempirical idea of the good principle. "The archetype of the moral disposition in all its purity has come down to us from heaven and has assumed our humanity."[9] The Son of God is humiliated by this descent. The hope of man lies in his acceptability to God through a "practical faith in the son of God."[10] Yet, Kant says regarding the objective reality of this idea: "We need, therefore, no empirical example to make the idea of a person morally well-pleasing to God our archetype; this idea as an archetype is already present in our reason. According to the law, each man ought really to furnish an example of this idea in his own person; to this end does the archetype reside always in reason."[11] And, yet the limitations of reason or the very reason on which we depend will not allow us to conceive of moral worth and actions apart from some analogous relationship between the moral action and a human being.

Moral happiness for Kant is not contentment with one's physical state or physical happiness but "rather the reality and constancy of a disposition which ever progresses in goodness (and never falls away from it).[12] Moral happiness is a continuous process of migrating toward the good. Kant asserts that Freedom from the Sovereignty of evil means to be "freed from bondage under the law of sin, to live for righteous—this is the highest prize (man) he can win."[13]

Concerning the Ethical State of Nature, Kant argues that each individual is his or her own judge or each individual is autonomous. Nevertheless, men mutually corrupt each other. This means that association with other people becomes the occasion for corruption. Corruption cannot occur in a vacuum or in solitude, but in community with one's fellow citizens. The local church then becomes a perfect host for corruption inasmuch as it is a community.

Nature has an ethical state and a juridical state; one is political and the other is morally virtuous. The juridical state of nature "is one of war of every man against every other, so too is the ethical state of nature one in which the good principle, which resides in each man, is continually attacked by the evil which is found in him and in everyone else."[14]

The ethical state of man "is one of open conflict between principles of virtue and a state of inner immorality which the natural man ought to bestir himself to leave as soon as possible."[15]

Kant's definition of the church as an ethical commonwealth under divine moral legislation suggests both its invisible and visible nature. "The invisible church is the idea of the union of all the righteous under direct and moral divine world government. The visible church which is the actual union of men into a whole which harmonizes with that ideal."[16] The moral kingdom of God is manifested in the true visible church which must have universality, purity, freedom, and a priori settled principles. The church is an ethical commonwealth, i.e., a representative of the city of God. It is not a political commonwealth.[17] This is not the actual church I know because I find the local church to be overwhelmingly political—ruled not by an ethical ideal but by a pragmatic existentialism that often manifests itself in the immoral and the evil. This means that the church is indeed a political entity both in its organization and its ideology.

I turn now to Book Four, "Concerning service and pseudoservice under the sovereignty of the Good principle, or concerning religion and clericalism." The discussion is about the visible church ("which alone is here under discussion").[18] Kant states, "Now since a pure religion of reason, as public religious faith, permits only the bare idea of a church (that is, an invisible church) and since only the visible church, which is grounded, upon dogmas, needs and is susceptible of organization by men, it follows that service under the sovereignty of the good principle cannot, in the invisible church, be regarded as ecclesiastical service, and that this religion has no legal servants acting as officials of an ethical commonwealth."[19]

It seems that Kant is suggesting that the invisible church is in every man and that every right-thinking man can serve God via the "pure religion of reason." Moreover, he states that by pseudoservice (*cultis spurius*) is meant the persuasion that someone can be served by deeds which in fact frustrate the very ends of him who is being served.[20]

Moreover, it seems that even revelation, if it were possible, is a product of reason in Kant's understanding. He states, "Yet in part at least every religion, even if revealed, must contain certain principles of the natural religion. For only through reason can thought add revelation to the concept of a religion, since this very concept, as though deduced from an obligation to the will of moral legislation, is a pure concept of reason."[21] The pure religion of reason will have, as its servants (yet without there being officials) all right-thinking men, except that, so far, they cannot be called servants of a church (that is, of a visible church, which alone is here under discussion).[22]

CONCERNING THE SERVICE OF GOD IN RELIGION IN GENERAL

Revealed Religion vs. Natural Religion

Revealed religion is that religion in which I must know in advance that something is a divine command in order to recognize it as my duty. Natural religion is that religion in which I must first know that something is my duty before I can accept it as a divine injunction.[23]

The rationalist must on his own accord restrict himself within the limits of his own insight; moreover, the rationalist is he who interprets the natural religion alone as morally necessary, i.e., as duty in matters of belief. A pure rationalist is one who recognizes revelation, but asserts that to know and accept it as real is not a necessary requisite to religion. The naturalist denies the reality of all supernatural divine revelation.[24]

THE CHRISTIAN RELIGION AS A NATURAL RELIGION

It seems that Kant argues that Christian religion as a natural religion, morality united with the concept of God, possesses the prime essential of the true church, namely, the qualification for universality, so far as one understands by that a validity for everyone, i.e., universal unanimity.[25] Yet, this religion as a natural religion is individualistic and not universal. Inherent in its rationality is the un-actualized church. Kant says, "Because in the rational religion of every individual there does not yet exist a church as a universal union (*omnitudo collectiva*) nor is this really contemplated in the above idea."[26]

For Kant, there is a natural predisposition to goodness and a natural expectation of happiness proportional to moral conduct. However, duty should be performed because it is the right thing to do, not because of a promised or anticipated reward. Kant states:

> Perform your duty for no motive other than unconditioned esteem for duty itself, i.e., love God (the legislator of all duties) above all else; and love everyone as yourself, i.e., further his welfare from good—will that is immediate and not derived from motives of self-advantage. These commands are not mere laws of virtue but precepts of holiness which we ought to pursue, and the very pursuit of them is called virtue.[27]

In Book One of his "Religion," Kant maintained that the only way for man to be virtuous is on his own!

THE CHRISTIAN RELIGION AS A LEARNED RELIGION

Kant states, "The acceptance of the fundamental principles of a religion is faith par excellence (*fides sacra*). We shall therefore have to examine the Christian faith on the one hand as a pure rational faith, on the other, as a revealed faith (*fides statutaria*). The first may be regarded as a faith freely assented to by everyone (*fides elicita*), the second as a faith which is commanded (*fides imperata*)."[28]

For Kant religion is based on reason, but the Christian church is based on faith. He states, "The service of a church consecrated to such therefore is twofold: what, on the one hand, must be rendered the church according to the historical faith, and on the other what is due it in according with the practical and moral faith of reason. In the Christian church neither of these can be separated from the other as adequate in itself; the second is indispensable to the first because the Christian faith is a religious faith, and the first is indispensable to the second because it is a learned faith."[29]

THE AUTONOMY OF THE SELF—AN EXISTENTIAL PROBLEM

The issue of the autonomy of self is evident throughout Kant's work; however, this is the point where I'd like to critically engage him. Kant asserts categorically that man is an autonomous being subject to the need of nothing other than reason. He argues that nothing outside of the self is necessary to enhance or restrict man's freedom. Man "stands in the need neither of the idea of another being over him, for him to apprehend his duty, nor of an incentive other than the law itself, for him to do his duty. At least it is man's own fault if he is subject to such a need: and if he is, this need can be relieved through nothing outside himself. Hence for its own sake morality does not need religion at all."[30] The need for a higher authority or power over man is described by Kant as a "fault," i.e., a weakness, a flaw, a lack of something essential! I am troubled by this arrogant spirit and reasoning because the "self" to me is essentially a fictive structure "seeing through a glass darkly," i.e., formulating constructions and reconstructions of itself on a regular basis. The truth is that the self is more nonbeing than anything else because it is so elusive, here today and gone tomorrow. The self is often a manufactured product, a story developed by the creative mind of the subject. The local church's self-perception is often as flawed as the individual's. The church's self-description usually reads like a novel, laced with a few specific descriptions that could possibly be called facts; however, the essence of which is more honestly described as fiction. Kant's surety regarding the autonomy of the self is even more troubling given my hypothesis that the self is essentially an imagined entity. I am not talking about the body here, but the perceived self.

This is an extraordinarily egocentric, humanistic, and anthropocentric conclusion on Kant's part. It reminds me of William Ernest Henley's (1849–1903) poem "Invictus:"

Out of the night that covers me,
Black as the pit from pole to pole,
I thank whatever gods may be
For my unconquerable soul.

In the fell clutch of circumstance
I have not winced nor cried aloud.
Under the bludgeoning of chance
My head is bloody, but unbowed.

Beyond this place of wrath and tears
Looms but the horror of the shade,
And yet the menace of the years
Finds, and shall find, me unafraid.
It matters not how strait the gate,

How charged with punishments the scroll,
I am the master of my fate:
I am the captain of my soul.

This autonomy of the will or finding comfort only in the self seems to suggest that Kant was a different kind of Christian, if a Christian at all! (I know of his church affiliation.) Similarly, Alfred Lloyd Tennyson in his poem "Idylls of the King" makes an identical point when he writes that "For man is man and master of his fate." The spirit of Kant, Henley, and Tennyson contrasts vividly with African American poet laureate Langston Hughes when he writes in his poem "Prayer":

I ask you this:
which way to go?
I ask you this:
Which sin to bear?
Which crown to put
Upon my hair
I do not know,
Lord God
I do not know.

The destiny of man is not determined by his own reason or his own will but by a higher power, as Langston Hughes suggests. Man is not an autonomous being as Kant vehemently asserts, and as the church seems to have come to believe and practice. While reason is a critical component of the nature of man, it is not to be deified as Kant does. It seems to me that he postulates throughout his "Religion" that reason is the highest authority. The concept of reason permeates his philosophy to the extent that it [all but] replaces God. Inasmuch as Jesus is an archetype or a construct of reason, likewise God or the moral lawgiver occupies an ideational position in Kant's theology of reason. For Kant, not even God can be put above the moral law. Again, for him and for others such as Henley and Alfred Lord Tennyson, it is what we as rational human beings do, not what God can do for us, that is critical to Kant's philosophy. This perspective is contrary to slave religion and Black church theology, which are heavily dependent on the power of God to transform evil individuals and structures and turn the world upside down and inside out as God did when he freed the children of Israel and led Moses across the Red Sea.

And yet the church has indeed replaced God. It has to a great extent become a god, an idol developed and sustained by its own nature and kingdoms. I am more and more aware of so much that the church does that is unrelated to the will of God. Too often even its worship is paganistic and self-absorbing and exalting of its own hegemonic nature. Much of the pomp and circumstance of the church is grounded in a worldly desire to conquer and control and hold hostage the prophetic utterances of the church and the people of God.

In the following section, I outline the architectonic that characterizes the local church. Churches tend to think that their salvation and efficiency are intimately tied to a constitution and by-laws. Accordingly, I present the following structure to satisfy the church's need to mimic the government's structure. This is why I believe that it is fair to say that the church is more of a political entity than she is willing to admit.

THE POLITICAL STRUCTURE OF THE LOCAL CHURCH[31]

General Provision

The following are the By-Laws of the local church.

These By-Laws may be amended, revised, or otherwise changed in the same manner as they were adopted. They shall complement and supplement the church constitution. No By-Laws herein may be in conflict with the mission of local church.

Nominating Committee

The Nominating Committee shall be appointed by the Pastor of the church when deemed necessary in order that the vision and mission of the church can be carried out smoothly.

Church Historian

This person should be someone who knows and understands the methods of history and the history of the church. The Historian should serve at the request of the Pastor.

Personnel Committee

The Personnel Committee is headed by the Pastor of the church and consists of the following: Chair of Diaconate, Chair of Trustees, Chair of Missions, and anyone else deemed necessary by the Pastor on an ad hoc basis.

Ministry Development

The Pastor is encouraged to allow himself or herself to be used by God in formulating a vision for Ministry for the church. The development of new ministries is expected and encouraged. The Pastor's leadership in this area is supported by the congregation.

The Stewardship Committee

The Stewardship Committee should be appointed annually by the Pastor in order to implement a Stewardship plan for the congregation. These persons should be good stewards and tithers and are expected to help foster a good stewardship atmosphere and practice throughout the congregation.

Strategic Planning Committee

This is an ad hoc group whose goal is to help plan for the future growth and development of the church. The group is appointed by the Pastor with the understanding that they are to develop a three- to five-year plan for the church's physical, economic, and spiritual development.

Sabbatical Leave

The Pastor is entitled to a sabbatical leave of six months after the first seven (7) years. At the end of ten (10) years, he/she should receive a nine (9)-month sabbatical and a one-year sabbatical after twenty years of service. Sabbaticals are intended to help the Pastor renew his/her spiritual commitment. Full compensation is provided during sabbaticals.

CHURCH MEMBERSHIP

General

This is a Christian church under the Lordship of Jesus Christ. The membership retains unto itself the right of self-government in all phases of the life of this church. The Bible and its teachings shall supercede all other authorities.

The membership reserves the right to determine who shall be members of this church and the condition of such membership.

Pastor

The Pastor is responsible to God through the congregation under the auspices of the Holy Spirit. The Pastor serves as the leader and undershepherd for the congregation. The Pastor shall be the leader of the church in all its activities and administration and shall preach the gospel, administer the ordinances, watch over the membership, and have charge of the welfare of the congregation and the stated services of public worship. In addition, the Pastor shall have supervisory authority over all paid and volunteer staff of the church and shall be a member of all committees and auxiliaries of the church. As administrative leader, the Pastor shall have authority to negotiate contracts and agreements that are commensurate with administering the approved budget. The Pastor shall have a minimum education that includes the Master of Divinity with three years of pastoral experience. The degree must be from a fully accredited (ATS) seminary or graduate theological school. The earned doctorate is preferred.

It is imperative that the Pastor's chief concern be the visionary equipping of the congregation for wholistic growth through meaningful worship, educational and outreach experiences that will lead the congregation into an encounter with the Almighty.

Diaconate

The Diaconate Ministry is responsible to the Pastor of the church. The Diaconate and the Pastor are the only two biblical offices mentioned in the Bible. The Diaconate is composed of persons who serve as the spiritual leaders of the church and community. They function as armor bearers of the Pastor in carrying out the church's mission mandate and enabling the pastoral vision for ministry. Though many churches separate the deacons and the deaconesses, the inclusive term Diaconate is clearly the most biblically accurate. Men and women full of the Holy Spirit may serve in the Diaconate Ministry.

Trustee Ministry

The Trustee Ministry is responsible to the church and Pastor. Though Trustees are necessary for the effective and efficient maintenance of the church, it is not a biblical office. Trustees are state, mandated in Virginia and some other states whose responsibility is to the physical property of the church. The Trustees shall hold in trust all property belonging to the church and shall take all necessary measures for its maintenance. They shall keep the building in working order, but they shall have no power to buy, mortgage, lease, or transfer any real property without the specific vote of the church authorizing such action. The Trustees' role is limited to the building and its maintenance. Trustees are recommended by the Pastor to the congregation for confirmation. Authority: Virginia code 57–2:1 through 57–21

Christian Education

Responsible to the Pastor through Minister of Christian Education. The Ministry of Christian Education shall provide an ongoing wholistic educational ministry which will equip the congregation for growth and maturity. The ministry shall be responsible for the organizing, administration, and supervision of the entire education program of the church including Sunday School, Vacation Bible School, Youth and Children's Ministry, etc.

Treasurer

Responsible to the church and Pastor. Working with the Pastor, Trustee Ministry, and Financial Secretary, the church Treasurer is the custodian of the church finances. The Treasurer shall have custody of all funds of the church and all deposits made in the name of the church and its auxiliaries. The Treasurer is appointed by the Pastor for confirmation by the church and serves a two-year term. He/She is eligible for a second term, but can only serve two consecutive two-year terms.

Assistant Church Treasurer

Also appointed by the Pastor, the Assistant Treasurers have the same responsibilities as the Treasurer.

Church School Superintendent

Church School Superintendent is responsible to the Pastor through the Minister of Christian Education. The primary task of the Church School Superintendent is to administer the Church School, operating under the guidance of Christian Education. The Superintendent leads in organizing and staffing its church school in order that the church's mission is fulfilled. The Church School Superintendent shall assist with the leadership of the church school, exercising the authority and performing the duties pertaining to that office, in accordance with the general policies and procedures of the Christian Education Ministry. The Superintendent shall serve a one-year term and is eligible for two consecutive one-year terms. Afterwards, he/she shall step down and will only be eligible to serve after the lapse of one term. The Superintendent shall be appointed by the pastor in consultation with the Minister of Christian Education.

Vacation

The Pastor is entitled to a one-month paid vacation annually to be taken at his/her discretion and in whatever increments that are desirable.

Other Leave

The Pastor can be out of the pulpit no more than eight (8) Sundays thru the year for other evangelistic services. If the Pastor becomes sick or incapacitated for a period of more than six months, then the Diaconate in consultation with the Pastor must determine a return date or mutually decide on a course of action.

The Pastor is entitled to determine the most feasible methods and persons for implementing his/her vision and the church's mission. The Pastor is entitled to veto any person or recommendation emanating from any group, committee, or ministry in the church.

Staffing

This is a direct responsibility of the Minister of the church. The Minister may consult with other church leaders as needed in order to facilitate the needs of the ministry and to foster smooth transitions.

Pastor

A. The Pastor is the spiritual and administrative head of the church; is an ex-officio member and chairman of all boards and committees; shall preside at all meetings of the church. The Pastor shall hold the aforementioned offices until resignation, retirement, permanent disability, death, or termination, whichever comes first.

B. It shall be the Pastor's responsibility to preach the Word, to care for the stated services of public worship, to administer the ordinances, and to promote the spiritual welfare of the church and those whom it serves.

C. The Pastor shall oversee the business, civic, and social concerns of the church on a day-to-day basis and shall use the power of his/her executive office to implement the ongoing programmatic goals of the congregation and its duly constituted ministries.

D. The Pastor shall set short and long-range goals for the church and make a report of the year's work at the annual meeting; establish and enforce appropriate administrative procedures for effective and efficient operation; and initiate such rules as may be necessary to advance the work of the church.

E. The Pastor, in consultation with the appropriate ministry(ies) or committee(s), shall have the responsibility of calling such Associate or Assistant Pastors and Ministers as may be necessary to carry out the ministries of the church.

F. The Pastor shall be responsible for the staff development, assigning of duties, the supervision, and formal evaluation of the church ministerial staff.

G. The Pastor, or the Pastoral Relations Committee upon request of the Pastor, may elect to counsel, advise, mediate, arbitrate, reconcile, place on probation, suspend and/or terminate members of the ministerial staff whose performance, interpersonal relationships, or conduct at or away from the church is unsatisfactory and/or contrary to the written and implied ordinances of the church.

H. Within thirty (30) days upon confirmed notification that a vacancy in the pastorate will occur or has occurred, the church shall formulate a Pulpit Search Committee with the specific task of recommending to the church a candidate for Pastor.

I. The calling of a Pastor shall be done upon the recommendation of the Pulpit Search Committee. The church shall elect a new Pastor by two-thirds (⅔) vote of the members present at a special meeting called for that purpose.

J. The Pastor shall be responsible for training all church officers and members through annual evaluations and personnel conferences with church officers.

K. The Pastor shall have veto power over any church group or organization decision that is not in keeping with the vision and mission of the church.

Youth Minister

The Youth Minister is responsible to the Pastor. To provide ongoing wholistic ministry to young people between the ages of 13 and 18 that will enable them to live as productive Christians.

Goals

1. To minister to the various needs of young people in the church and community.
2. To develop well-rounded young people—intellectually, socially, emotionally, physically as well as spiritually.
3. To make spiritual growth a priority by being an active participant in the teaching and worship ministries.
4. To possess the ability to lead young people to Christ.
5. To remain proficient, consistent, and organized in the execution of all responsibilities.

Responsibilities

1. Enable youth to learn biblical content and to interpret its relevance to personal and corporate experiences.
2. Prepare youth for involvement in various aspects of leadership.
3. Train youth in all aspects of church life.
4. Maintain good rapport with youth, parents, and school.
5. Organize, plan, and implement a yearly wholistic program for youth to include Bible Study, creative expression, youth issues, vocation, preparation for life, fellowship, etc.
6. Maintain accurate records of all youth.
7. Maintain confidentially in counseling, except when situation dictates otherwise.
8. Take seriously the need to maximize all opportunities that will assist teens in the development of their spiritual life.

Missions and Social Concerns

The church should allocate a minimum of 10% of its budget for the church's missions and outreach programs. Tithing is for the church organizations as well as the people.

Currently, several organizations get donations from the church budget such as the Lott Carey Convention, Baptist General Convention, etc. We should continue these contributions as a worldwide missionary ministry. There may be local organizations that could be added such as the Baptist Children's Home. We need to support foreign missions in Africa and other parts of the world.

Basic help programs such as food and clothing programs, referrals, visitations, calls, etc., need people more than money to be successful. The following structure is proposed to provide an organizational nucleus for programs that depend on volunteer effort.

Church Missionary Society

Ten (10) missionary circles comprise the current Missionary Society. These circles provide various help-related services. The circles are unified in their purpose but each functions autonomously; therefore, some duplication will occur. The circles have no church funding. They depend on membership dues and programs held to raise supplemental funds to carry out their missions.

The missionary circle can function more efficiently with focus, structure, and funding from the church. They can be the nucleus for the church's local mission and outreach programs. The current Missionary Society could be combined with other church organizations, such as the Pastor's aid, helping hands, etc., and be given responsibility for specified programs such as the food and clothing programs.

Each organization would have specific responsibilities. Two or more groups may be jointly responsible for a program. This structure would focus the Missionary Society to a local Help Ministry. They would be encouraged to support church outreach instead of expending their valuable time and effort to raise money for these programs. Part of the function of the Missionary Society would be to organize additional volunteer support from the general congregation to support the church's Help Ministry.

The direction and focus would come from a coordinating group under the direction of the Pastor and/or his designated representative.

Administrative Council

The Administrative Council is responsible to the Pastor. The Administrative Council leads the Church in carrying out its (the church's) mission statement in conjunction with the pastoral vision for ministry. The council provides harmony as it seeks to offer direction in developing goals, objectives, and long-range planning. Through the work of the council, the congregation is unified, supported, and encouraged to strengthen their relationship with God as they seek to grow spiritually under the Lordship of Christ.

Goals

1. To make spiritual growth a priority by being an active participant in the Ministry of Teaching (attendance in Church School, Bible Study, and other teaching/learning opportunities) and worship.
2. To lead persons to Christ.
3. To maintain an open and honest communication with co-partners in ministry—pastor, staff, leaders, ministries, and congregation.

Leadership Qualities

1. Ability to effectively listen and communicate well with others.
2. Ability to work well with others.
3. Openness to various opinions.
4. Skills in researching issues and information related to the church's mission and ministry.
5. A genuine love and interest in responding to concerns of congregation and community.

6. Regular attendance in Church School, Bible Study, and other teaching/training events.

Responsibilities

1. To serve as a vehicle for refining, clarifying, and communicating the church's vision for ministry.
2. To organize and implement a process for short- and long-range ministry planning.
3. To establish goals and objectives and evaluate the mission and ministry of the church on a regular basis.
4. To keep congregation informed of actions, resource opportunities, and needs of local association, state convention, and national conventions.
5. To encourage commitment and inclusiveness in the life of the church.
6. To lead congregation in support of local association, state convention, and national conventions.
7. To take advantage of available training opportunities.

Responsible to the Pastor

The records of a church are its autobiography. They mark the historical pathway along which the church has come in its spiritual and ministerial growth and developmentation. For this reason it is imperative that the Church Clerk work closely with the Church Secretary and Pastor to ensure that accurate membership records and church actions are preserved in a most efficient manner.

Goals

1. To make spiritual growth a priority by being an active participant in the ministry of teaching and worship.
2. To possess the ability to lead persons to Christ.
3. To remain proficient and organized in the execution of all responsibilities.

Responsibilities

1. Ensure that all church records are best accurately, efficiently secure and accessible.
2. Prepare reports of all essential business matters of the church.
3. Maintain accurate records that cite motives and intentions of every decision made by the church and its leaders.
4. Prepare reports of all essential business matters of the church for distribution to membership.
5. Maintain an accurate account of church membership.

6. Mark an up-to-date account of church history.
7. Maintain and exhibit effective written and oral communication skills.
8. Master the English language.
9. To train and be trained in the effective and efficient execution of assigned tasks.
10. Computerize membership roll and church actions.

Church Secretary

The Church Secretary is responsible to the Pastor. As the church seeks to fulfill its mission and ministry, it is imperative that there be a chief center for the organization of clerical functions. The Church Secretary works closely with the Pastor as the church's chief clerical personnel. He/she possesses a mastery of office skills, demonstrates the ability to assume responsibility, exercises initiative and sound judgment in making decisions within the scope of assigned authority.

Goals

1. To develop a well-organized and accurate clerical system.
2. To make spiritual growth a priority by being an active participant in the Teaching Ministry and worship.
3. To remain loyal to the task.
4. To possess the ability to lead persons to Christ.
5. To be a competent people person who has the ability to relate to persons on various levels and in a variety of situations.

Responsibilities

1. Develop an organized correspondence and filing system.
2. Serve as an information and referral bank.
3. Take seriously the need for accuracy, task completion, and confidentiality.
4. Possess a working knowledge of the leadership roles and function of all ministries.
5. Work closely with the Pastor in all endeavors.
6. Maintain a spiritual, warm, and friendly disposition.
7. Keep abreast of new technology and procedures in office management.
8. Master correct usage of the English language.
9. Maintain and exhibit effective written and oral communication skills.
10. To train and be trained in the effective and efficient execution of office management skills.

11. Develop and utilize an accurate system of computerization.

Financial Secretary

The Financial Secretary is responsible to the Pastor. Accountability of the liquid assets of a church is extremely necessary for effective missions and ministry. The Financial Secretary serves as an integral part of the church's financial team.

Goals

1. To make spiritual growth a priority by being an active participant in the ministry of teaching and worship.
2. To possess the ability to lead persons to Christ.
3. To remain proficient and organized in the execution of all responsibilities.
4. To work as a member of the financial team along with the Treasurer and Finance Committee.

Responsibilities

1. Maintain accurate and up-to-date records of the financial situation of the church.
2. To maintain and report an accurate account of all income and expediters.
3. Gather complete financial information for periodic congregational review.
4. Develop an accurate up-to-date system of record-keeping.
5. Computerize financial records.
6. Keep congregation abreast of financial standing.
7. Maintain and exhibit effective written and oral communication skills.
8. Serve as member of Stewardship Committee.
9. Train and be trained in the effective and efficient execution of assigned tasks.
10. Keep abreast of regulations and opportunities in the financial arena.
11. Maintain an accurate account of all check vouchers.

CHURCH FACILITIES

Guidelines

1. Permission to use the church facilities must be given by the Pastor or Trustee Ministry. All dates must be cleared by the Church Secretary. A Facilities Use Form must be completed. This form can be

obtained from the church office or the custodial staff and signed by the aforementioned persons.

2. Any nonchurch member using the church facilities will be requested to give a specific donation to the church fund.

3. Members using the Sanctuary for weddings are requested to use wax protectors for lighted candles. See details on wedding policies and procedures.

4. No food or drinks beyond the dining area. Absolutely no eating in the Sanctuary.

5. The lending of tables and chairs is discouraged; however, the Pastor under certain circumstances may decide to lend tables and chairs.

6. Persons who set up decorations should remove decorations after each affair.

7. Space for placing signs limited to the bulletin boards. No signs are to be attached to painted walls or glass cases. Before placing any notice, please check with the church office.

8. If you have requested the use of the dining and kitchen areas, and a death of a member occurs, serving the member's family will be first priority. Also, funerals will take priority over other activities, including weddings.

9. Funerals for nonmembers of the church can only be approved by the Pastor and officers.

10. Persons using the kitchen are responsible for the cleaning after the affair. The stoves, refrigerators, sinks need to be thoroughly cleaned and sanitized. Chlorox Bleach should be an active cleaning ingredient.

11. An advance donation is requested in the amount of Fifty Dollars ($50.00) to be held until the inspection of the kitchen and dining area is made. If the area is not cleaned, the donation is forfeited to pay for cleanup.

CHURCH DISCIPLINE

Church Discipline in this context is the means and process of enforcing the rules and guidelines set by the church body according to Scripture to help monitor and control the conduct of her members. Discipline must not be exercised in a spirit of arrogance for effectiveness and justice. It must be done with gentleness and love (Gal. 6:1).

The church is responsible for exerting its observant supervision over its members. Therefore, there are definite and positive purposes for church discipline. Objectives and purposes for church discipline can be stated in definite terms:

- To encourage and protect the Right.
- To cherish and promote the Good.
- To edify the Body of Christ as we worship.
- To unify and strengthen the Body of Christ as we conduct the church's business.
- To restrain and remove any inappropriate behaviors.
- To maintain order and to provide a uniform way to deal with offenses within the body of the church

There are three laws of Christ's church (Prov. 6:16, 19; Rom. 16:17).

1. The law of love—John 13:34
2. The law of confession—Matt. 5:23, 24
3. The law of forgiveness—Luke 17:3, 4

Offenses: Private/Public

There are two classes of offenses requiring discipline referred to as private and public. A private offense means something personal, between two persons, although it could have been committed in public. A public offense is something committed against a group— the church in its collected body, the membership.

We could call these offenses private and general which are sufficiently descriptive for all practical purposes.

A. Private offense: A private offense is an offense against an individual. "If thy brother shall trespass against thee" (Matt. 6:14).
B. Public or General Offense: A public or general offense is one claimed to be a breach of Christian morals or a violation of covenant, faith, or duty.

TERMINATION OF MEMBERSHIP

Members may be dismissed from our membership by:

1. Uniting with some other Baptist Church requesting a letter of recommendation. A letter will be sent to the Church Clerk.
2. By notification by some congregation other than Baptist that the member has united with them.

3. The unexplained absence of a member from all the meetings of the church for six (6) months shall be considered sufficient reason for termination.

4. Nonresident members. Members who move away shall, as soon as possible, furnish the church office or the Church Clerk their new address. If, for any good reason, they desire to retain their membership in this church, they shall communicate by letter to the church, through either the Pastor or the Church Clerk, or give satisfactory reason why they cannot do so.

5. When a member requests that his or her name be erased from the church roll and no charges have been prepared against them. The officers shall investigate and if they have ascertained that the member cannot be reclaimed, they shall present to the church a recommendation that at the request of said member, the name be erased from the membership roll. The church may immediately act on such recommendation. Upon granting the request, the member ceases to be a member of this church.

6. In case of habitual violation of covenant obligations or non-Christian conduct, it shall be the duty of the officers or a designated committee to counsel and admonish. If this proves ineffectual, the committee may report the case to the church for dismissal or other action.

7. Should a member become an offense to the church and to its good name by reason of immoral or non-Christian conduct, or by persistent breach of his/her covenant vows, or nonsupport of the church, the church may terminate his/her membership by a majority vote, but only after due notice and a hearing, and after faithful efforts have been made to bring such member to repentance and restoration of membership.

ADMINISTRATION AND FINANCE

We are charged to work toward making the church a reflection of the mind of Jesus Christ through establishing in a Christian manner the importance of order and discipline in the church through good, up-to-date administrative practices. We have to meet the needs of the whole person, and all of us must be accountable in our practice of Christian faith. We are called to be Christians in whatever situations and places we find ourselves—not just on Sunday mornings, but every day of the week. As we work together toward the goal of church unity and spiritual renewal, let us resolve to be guided by the spirit of Jesus Christ—a spirit of Jesus Christ—a spirit of love and peace.

Membership

Complete annual registration to update church records each year.

Staff

A. Minister of Music is responsible for the music of the church to carry out the church's mission and the Pastor's vision. The Minister of Music will report directly to the Pastor.

B. The Financial Secretary handles the financial reporting and record keeping concerning the church and its membership. Reports directly to Pastor and Treasurer. Performs financially-related duties as assigned by the Treasurer and Pastor.

C. Volunteer Coordinator—works with Pastor, staff to advise the church membership of assistance needed by the church staff for tasks which are outside the norm.

D. Administrative Assistant—completely responsible for Pastor's and church's administrative needs. Reports directly to the Pastor.

E. A Treasurer and two (2) Assistant Treasurers to be responsible for the financial accounting of the church's income, receipts, disbursements, etc. Reports directly to the Pastor.

Leadership

A. Membership to the Diaconate Ministry (deacons, deaconesses) Trustees and Finance Committees comes by recommendation of the Pastor. Approval comes by vote of the congregation in a church meeting. Diaconate members will serve as active for a three (3)-year term. Those who have served with distinction for a long period of time will be elevated to the status of emeritus. Recommendations concerning status of membership as it pertains to breach of confidentiality, nonparticipation, noncooperation which cause division among board and/or church will be evaluated by the Pastor and board and recommendation made to the congregation when necessary.

B. New members of the Diaconate (Deacons, Deaconesses) and Trustee Ministry are to serve for a three (3)-year term. Afterwards they will rotate off the board for one (1) year in order to be eligible to serve again. In order to serve again, the person will have to have a record of faithful support of the mission and ministry of the church.

C. Use of additional young deacons and deaconesses
    1. Identify qualifications for becoming deacons and deaconesses.
    2. Recruit women deacons.

3. Recruit junior deacons (under 18).
4. Should be investigated as a potential leader.
5. Traditional male boards/committees should not be restricted to men, but open to women.
6. Should support all church activities (Bible Study, prayer meeting, Church School, etc.).
7. Should attend training workshops and seminars.
8. Should be honest and committed to stewardship goals.
9. Should address parliamentary procedures for conducting church meetings.
10. Should possess leadership ability, understanding, caring, and a serious attitude.
11. Should hold office for a two-year term with the possibility for one two-year reelection; afterwards, the chairperson must rotate out of the position for at least one year.

D. The Pastor in consultation with chairpersons of the Diaconate and Trustee Ministry shall be responsible for staff as it relates to hiring, supervision, evaluation, and termination. All employees and ministers are subject to supervision of the Senior Pastor directly or indirectly.

E. The pastor's Advisory Council will consist of the chairpersons of the Diaconate, Trustees, Ushers, Ladies' Fellowship, Men's Fellowship, Youth Fellowship, Missionary Society, Board of Christian Education, and Treasurers.

F. The Joint Ministry (Diaconate, Clerk, Trustees, and Finance) shall be called together at the discretion of the pastor for purposes of church leadership and development.

Organizations/Committees

A. Should elect their own officers.
1. Should be trained by the pastor.
2. Must elect qualified officers, i.e. born-again, spirit-filled individuals.
3. Should attend training workshops/seminars on an annual basis.
4. Should hold office for a one-year term with the possibility for an additional one-year reelection; afterwards, the chairperson/president must rotate out of the position for at least one year.

B. Overlapping groups should be combined in order to be more effective.

Other Leaders (Christian Education, Church School Superintendent, Treasurer, Church Clerk)

A. Will be appointed by the Pastor: The Church Clerk will be a volunteer position which is responsible for recording, processing, and maintaining records of all church business meeting transactions. The Church Clerk is also responsible for all official church membership records and communications. The Church Clerk works closely with the Pastor and the Administrative Assistant.

B. Sunday School Superintendent shall be appointed by the Pastor and work under the direct supervision of the Minister of Christian Education.

C. Should be trained by the Pastor.

The Broadcast Ministry

A. Secure improved service to broadcast worship service.
B. Develop tape library. Record each worship service.
C. Extend outreach ministries. Focus on local area.

Policy

A. This church will be guided by the Holy Spirit, the teaching of Scripture, and the Pastor.

B. A central church treasury established whereby all organizations' funds are included as part of the overall church funds to be used for the programs of the church.

C. There will be no church user fees for members in good financial standing.

D. All officers and members are encouraged to tithe and give offerings either weekly, bi-weekly, or monthly.

E. Celebrate the church's and the Pastor's anniversary annually.

CHURCH FINANCE

Stewardship and Tithes

The Pastor of the church, in conjunction with the Minister of Christian Education/Stewardship, must educate the congregation on the meaning and purpose of stewardship.

1. Programs should be developed to encourage individual tithing in order to phase out group fund-raisers.

2. Special churchwide projects should be developed to support various church Stewardship goals.

    a. Mortgage burning

    b. Giving for years of membership

    c. Sacrificial offerings

    d. Pledges

  3. The Stewardship Committee shall teach the members about the need to support the ministries of the church.

Annual Pledges and Regular Offerings

A. All groups are to submit annual budgets based on program planning consistent with the mission of the church and the vision of the church.

  1. The annual church budget should be available for each member to see the church's proposed programs and the finances needed to obtain the goals.

CHURCH WEDDINGS

All church weddings are subject to the direction of the Pastoral and Ministerial staff and if possible should be held during the regular morning worship service.

Christian marriage between a man and a woman is a very important and sacred fellowship. "It is ordained of God and divinely established as the only approved way of replenishing the earth" (McNeil, 1961:43).

Marriages shall be performed at the altar. The altar is a sacred place in the church used for special events such as marriages and prayer. In the Old Testament, the altar has great significance (cf. Ex. 29:36, 37, 44; 30:26-28; Lev. 8:10; Num. 7, see Ex. 43:18–28). The pulpit furniture will not be moved for weddings.

Your desire to have a church wedding is indicative of the fact that you want to ask God's blessing upon your marriage. God will not withhold his blessing from you if you will earnestly seek to accept the blessing he offers.

The purpose of a church wedding is to share your joy with the congregation and to enable the congregation to join you in invoking God's blessing upon your marriage. The purpose is not to put on a show for your friends. Following this idea does not prevent you from having a beautiful wedding, but it does set certain limitations on what may properly be done.

All marriages in the church will be performed by the Senior Pastor or his/her designee. Persons cannot bring in an outside minister to perform weddings. However, if the couple wants a minister to assist the Pastor, they must seek permission from the Pastor. The Pastor is the final authority on the etiquette of marriages in the church and the procedure that the wedding party is to follow. Church weddings are religious and sacred services that need not be exercises in secular creativity, nor expressions of individuality. They are subject to the rules of the church interpreted by the Bible and the Pastor, undershepherd of the church. The altar, i.e., the area in front of the pulpit will be used for performing weddings. The directress and the bride should address responsible questions to the Pastor who is the final authority in the appropriate use of the church.

There may be more than one wedding on the same day, so please try to be as cooperative as possible.

Decorations

Decorations in the sanctuary should be modest and in keeping with the architecture and present decorum of the building. Usually a lightly (modestly) decorated sanctuary will reflect the seriousness of the wedding vows and simultaneously reduce costs. The throwing of rice and other confetti is not allowed in the sanctuary. When the church fellowship hall is used for receptions, modest decorations are also recommended. The pulpit furniture cannot be moved for weddings, nor should the church's normal decorations be altered.

Photographs

The marriage service is a sacred service, which should have no intrusions such as those that come from the taking of pictures, particularly flash pictures. Therefore, we request that no pictures be taken after members of the bridal party have entered the vestibule of the church and are proceeding to the altar. Nor are pictures to be taken during the ceremony unless it be a time exposure from the balcony. Pictures may be taken at the rear of the vestibule as the bride enters and as the bridal couple recesses. After the service is concluded, pictures may be taken at the altar. Friends and relatives of the couple should be informed about these rules and requested to observe them.

In order to expedite the taking of pictures after the ceremony, it is advised to give the photographer a list of the groups or persons you wish photographed. By planning to take the first pictures of the group involving the largest number of persons, some of the bridal party can be dismissed to attend to other things.

Wedding Receptions at the Church

The church encourages its members to use the church's facilities for wedding receptions. However, caterers and others need to be advised by the church and the President of the Hostess Committee regarding the care and operation of kitchen facilities.

Any person using the church for such activities is responsible for his/her own physical safety; however, the church encourages all parties to be safety and health conscious at all times.

Each wedding party is responsible for securing its own catering service, and making arrangements for food service and decorations.

Also, in the Protestant church, and especially the Baptist Church, alcohol is not allowed in the sanctuary or the fellowship hall. The use of alcoholic beverages is not allowed on church premises. Receptions are to be terminated no later than 10:00 p.m. except on Saturdays when they are to be terminated no later than 9:00 p.m.

Details concerning the reception may be discussed with the church secretary to be passed on to the Pastor.

Wedding Music

The music for weddings should be sacred and in keeping with the spirit of worship in the church. The wedding ceremony is a worship service and should be approached accordingly. Popular, non-religious love songs are not appropriate and cannot be used in church weddings unless the Pastor specifically approves.

Music speaks for its age and reflects its age. Couples considering particular pieces of music should be encouraged to ask: Is this music raising up the life-style and values which I want to emphasize? Each couple has to reach their own answer, but they should do it with integrity (Biddle 1974:84).

Because the wedding is a worship service as well as a time of witness, it is a religious and spiritual occasion that should be approached with reverence.

The church wedding service is the church at worship and the church in witness. Music in the wedding should contribute to Christian worship and witness. Some people come to weddings who seldom, if ever, attend regular church services. The entire wedding service, but especially the choice and performance of music, can be credited to the church's worship and witness (Biddle 1974:85).

The church is a sacred place and any music used should reflect an appreciation and understanding of the power of the Almighty God. The words to the music used in a Christian church wedding should be appropriate to praise God. The church wedding is an occasion for corporate worship and is not the same as a civil wedding or a private ceremony. "There is a trend away from vocal soloists in church weddings" (Biddle, 1970). However, they are still used and can enhance the service if properly prepared and grounded in understanding the meaning of a church wedding. Any questionable music should be first discussed with the Minister of Music, who will resolve it or take it up with the Senior Pastor. Please try to comply with the purposes of the church wedding.

Wedding Rehearsals

Wedding rehearsals should be determined in conjunction with the Pastor. Persons who are in the wedding party and all others present are expected to be sober and alert during the rehearsal and the actual wedding. The Pastor or a staff minister will attend the rehearsal.

Fees

It is suggested that the custodian be given $50.00 for the church cleaning and that the church be given $200.00 for the church maintenance. The clergy gift should be discussed with the Minister. The groom is generally responsible for taking care of this.

Miscellany

The marriage license is to be delivered to the church office in the week prior to the wedding ceremony or given to the Pastor on the day of the wedding.

No wedding or receptions will be scheduled during Holy Week.

All arrangements for dressing room areas, setting up of the reception area, and opening of the building are to be made with the custodian and church secretary.

The Pastor will assist in arranging the program material, inasmuch as the church wedding is a worship service.

If an aisle runner is desired, it must be provided by the florist or caterer.

The florist and/or caterer should be instructed, when employed, to remove all equipment immediately after the wedding is concluded. Flowers and decorations must be in place no later than one hour preceding the wedding. Please check with the church office to schedule a time for decorating the church.

Sources

Hiscox, Edward T. *The Star Book for Ministers*. (Valley Forge: Judson Press), 1968

McNeil, Jesse Jai. *Minister's Service Book for Pulpit and Parish*. (Grand Rapids, Michigan: William B. Eerdmans Publishing Company), 1985

Biddle, Perry H. Jr. *Abingdon Marriage Manual* (Nashville: Abingdon Press), 1974

OFFICE PROCEDURES AND POLICIES

Attendance

Your acceptance of any position at the church requires you to make a commitment to fulfill your duties and responsibilities in a professional manner. To do so requires daily attendance and continuous punctuality. There will be times when you are required to be absent; however, these times should be on an exception basis only. If you will be late arriving or must leave early, it is your responsibility to properly notify your supervisor as soon as the requirement becomes known. You are required to notify your supervisor as soon as possible if you will be absent to allow for proper coverage of your duties while you are away. Failure to properly notify the proper person of your absence on three consecutive occasions will result in a loss of pay and possible disciplinary actions.

Salary Administration

A. An annual performance appraisal will be provided for all personnel. The employee will be specifically informed as to their performance of all duties assigned. The employees will be advised of the areas where the goal is being met and the areas where improvement is needed. Interim counseling sessions will be held with an employee who is not meeting the basic requirements of the assigned job.

B. Salary increases will be determined based on recommendations form the Pastor and the financial status of the church.

C. Upon resignation an employee will be paid for any unused vacation time if appropriate notice (two weeks) has been given to the Senior Minister.

D. Upon termination the employee will be paid for any unused accrued vacation time. Unless the employee has been involved in an incident which is unethical, fraudulent, breach of confidentiality, there should be a two-week notice of intent to terminate.

E. Employees are paid weekly on Thursday. If payday falls on a holiday, the payday is moved back one day.
F. All staff will have deductions for social security, Medicare, federal and state tax. The employee's share of health, etc., will be deducted at employee's request.

Employment Benefits

A. The church provides either a health or death and retirement policy for full-time employees. The staff is normally covered by the Minister and Missionaries benefit board (M&M), which provides health, disability, retirement, and death coverage.
B. All nonordained staff are required to participate in the social security program. The church is required to deduct social security contributions and Medicare contributions from all payments and to provide a matching share from the church. Auxiliary personnel are required to pay their own social security.
C. Vacation
   1. Pastor shall be allowed a minimum of four weeks of vacation per year.
   2. Leadership staff (Minister of Christian Education and Minister of Music), secretarial and custodial staff—shall begin to accrue vacation leave employment which may not be taken until after six months of employment. Leave shall be earned at the following rate:
   a. Less than ten (10) years = 1 day per month
   b. Ten (10) to fifteen (15) years = 1 ½ days per month
   c. Greater than fifteen (15) years = 2 days per month
D. Compensatory Time
   1. Salaried personnel are considered exempted, therefore, they will not be allowed overtime compensation. They may, however, be granted compensatory time and one half based on the Senior Pastor's approval.
   2. Part-time personnel are considered nonexempt; therefore they may be paid overtime at the rate of time and one half based upon the Senior Minister's approval.
   3. Accrual of compensatory time is limited to one day per quarter and must be taken within a year. Use of compensatory time must be coordinated with the Senior Minister and taken at a time when it will not adversely affect the support to the church.
E. Bereavement Leave
   1. Five days of leave with pay will be granted to employees for the death of any member of their immediate family. The imme-

diate family consists of mother, father, sister, brother, husband, wife, child, grandparent.

Membership Contributions

All member contributions will be recorded to the member's account when reported in the appropriate envelope assigned to the member. Monies not reported in the assigned envelope cannot be properly credited and will be counted as general church income. Members will be furnished a statement of their contributions quarterly.

Members will be notified by letter of the following:

A. Returned check for insufficient funds.
B. Discrepancies in money actually in the envelope versus the amount written on the envelope.

Church Bulletin

All notices and musical selections for the bulletin must be in the church office no later than Wednesday. Input received after Wednesday will not appear in the bulletin for that week. If the input is needed earlier, a notice will be run in the bulletin the week before. No changes will be made to the bulletin without the Senior Minister's approval.

Church Calendar Maintenance

An up-to-date calendar of events must be maintained on the computer with a master copy maintained in the lower lobby on the bulletin board.

A. All requests for use of the church sanctuary or fellowship hall must be requested on the appropriate form and scheduled only after approval by the Pastor/Trustees.
1. Request must be dated upon receipt, for priority purposes, and approved within two (2) working days.
2. The requester must be notified of decision within three (3) working days.

Conduct

The image of the church should be upheld at all times. You are expected to conduct yourself at all times in a Christian and professional manner. To ensure you promote the image conducive to that of a church, it is required that the following rules be adhered to:

A. Confidentiality is critical. You must never divulge any information relative to the operations of the church to anyone other than those authorized by the church. At no time should such information be divulged outside of the church. To specifically identify some of the information considered confidential:

1. Personnel data
2. Financial data
3. Pastoral letters, memos, and records of counseling sessions.
4. Organizational data.
5. Pastoral staff or other employee, home phone, itinerary, phone log.
6. Conversations or comments overheard.

Remember: This is not all inclusive.

B. Your personal business must be conducted to preclude embarrassment to the church. All financial obligations must be properly handled.
C. You must always use your time appropriately, never neglecting to fulfill the responsibilities and duties of your position.
D. Your dress and attire should always be professional and appropriate for a church.
E. Personal work or chores can only be done during your lunch period. Doing so at other times is fraudulent.
F. You must always follow the instructions of your superiors. Problems in this area should be directed to the Senior Minister.

Personnel Files

Personnel files will be maintained for all employees. The files will contain the following:

A. The original application for employment and resume.
B. A file card to show the employee name, address, telephone number, social security number, marital status, date of employment, number of dependents, person to call in case of emergency (name and number), insurance beneficiary, date of birth.
C. Pre-employment physical clearance.
D. Form W-4.
E. Bereavement Leave
    1. Five (5) days of leave with pay will be granted to employees for the death of any member of their immediate family. The immediate family consists of mother, sister, brother, husband,

wife, child grandmother, grandfather, mother-in-law, father-in-law.

F. Sick Leave

1. Full time employees will accrue one day of sick leave per month. Part-time employees will accrue one hour of sick leave for every 20 hours worked. Sick leave is to be used for all illnesses to include disability, nonwork-related, maternity, pregnancy complications. After one year of employment, advance leave may be approved by the Senior Minister up to one week. Prior to granting this leave, the employee must use all except one week of the accrued vacation time to cover the illness. An employee may request up to six weeks of leave without pay for extended illness or maternity leave.

G. Holidays—there will be eight paid holidays granted to all employees. The holidays are as follows:

1. New Year's Day
2. Martin Luther King's Birthday
3. Memorial Day
4. Independence Day
5. Labor Day
6. Thanksgiving
7. Christmas Day
8. Easter Sunday

Any holidays falling on a scheduled day off will be observed as followed: Saturday Holiday = Friday; Sunday Holiday = Monday; Monday Holiday = Tuesday.

H. Jury duty will be considered a paid day.

I. Training-paid training time will be allowed when required and approved by the Senior Minister.

Classification of Personnel

All employees classified as staff will be considered as either full-time or part-time. The office personnel and custodial personnel will be classified as staff.

1. Full-time employees will work a minimum 40 hours a week.
2. Part-time employees will work less than 20 hours a week.

All other employees will be considered auxiliary support (other than staff).

EMPLOYMENT POLICIES

General

1. Precise job description shall be developed for each staff position of the church and approved by the Personnel Committee.
2. All salaries will be determined by the Budget Committee and Pastor based on comparable salaries in the general area for comparable job classifications.
3. All employees will serve under a 90-day probationary period to determine their ability to fulfill the requirements of the position. At the end of the ninety days, the first-line supervisor and the Senior Minister will discuss the employee's performance and determine if the employee will be retained.

Recruitment

1. Recruitment of ministerial staff, office staff, custodial staff, and musical staff will be done by a committee that is chaired by the Pastor. Selection of appropriate candidate will be accomplished through the following process:
   a. Establish an interview panel to consist of the committee and a technical expert for the position to be filled.
   b. Conduct the actual interview and rate and rank the top three candidates.
   c. Make offer to top candidate.
2. All new employees must have a physical which will be paid for by the church. The church will designate the doctor.
3. All persons responsible for the funds of the church will be bonded.
4. The following paperwork must be completed in the church office:
   a. W-4 form.
   b. Retirement enrollment forms, if needed.
   c. Insurance forms, if needed.
   d. I-9 Immigration form.

CHURCH BUDGET PHILOSOPHY

The church is a nonprofit religious organization that is at its best when members and officers function in a supportive role to the Pastor who is the undershepherd, the leader, and Chief Executive Officer. When the Pastor's vision is allowed to flourish and take root in the congregation, the church becomes the predominant beneficiary. Moreover, the Finance Ministry, like all other church groups and auxiliaries, endeavors to embody the mission of the church as an integral part of its practice of Christianity. The mission statement is as follows:

In a nonprofit entity, the Pastor manages the budget. This means that once the church approves the budget, it is not necessary to go through a re-approval process at any time unless there is a need to augment or supplement the budget in some way. The Pastor is accountable for the budget and has to make adjustments according to the income and expenditures of the church. Budgeting is a tool or guide. It is like a road map which provides parameters for the leader of the church to operate. It has some built-in fluidity which allows for and encourages managerial discretion.

Once the budget is approved by the church after much prayer and analysis, as the leader of the church, the Pastor is responsible for implementing and managing the actual budget. The use of administrative discretion is inherent to the budget management process and is correlated with the Pastor's ability to discern the best use of resources within the confines of the budget.

In the church, the ultimate responsibility for giving toward the budget rests with the membership; however, as leader, the membership has entrusted the Pastor with the responsibility of managing the budget with the advice of the Finance Ministry or usually the Trustees.

One of the responsibilities of the Finance Ministry is to serve as an advisory group to the Pastor. Accordingly, the Finance Ministry generally advises the Pastor and helps in any way possible to ensure the success of meeting the demands of the budget. This means that they support tithing, offerings, and other agreed methods of making sure that the church members fulfill their responsibility as Christians. The Finance Ministry understands that God has blessed them with wisdom and faith and they are to share these gifts with others.

The Pastor should determine the honorarium, or pay, for the guest minister based on the budget. This responsibility should not be delegated to anyone else. No group, treasurer, or committee should micromanage the budget. The budget should be managed by the Pastor and his or her staff.

Director/Minister of Christian Education

The Director/Minister of Christian Education is responsible to the Pastor. Teaching is fundamental in helping persons understand their role and responsibility in the community of faith. The Director/Minister of Christian Education provides an ongoing holistic educational ministry will equip the congregation for spiritual growth and maturity.

Goals

1. Provide learning experiences for persons of all ages which will enable them to grow in their understanding of the gospel and how it relates to their daily living.
2. Lead in recruiting, selecting, and training persons for various responsibilities.
3. Work with the Superintendent in organizing an effective Church School.
4. To be literate in the Bible and in theology.
5. Be a resource person who provides counsel, advice, and direction in curriculum selection and design.
6. Work with various ministries and committees in setting goals, planning, designing, and implementing programs.
7. Coordinate educational activities for all ministries.
8. Work closely with the Pastor to interpret and implement his/her vision for the Educational Ministry in light of the church's mission statement.
9. Work closely with the chairperson of the Educational Ministry and the Pastor to implement a holistic Educational Ministry.
10. Assist ministries to remain balanced in meeting needs of the congregation and community.
11. Develop ministry and program designs that are doctrinally, theologically, and biblically sound, and are relevant to the needs of all age groups.
12. Maintain updated inventory skills and resources available within the congregation.
13. Assist in the recruiting and training of potential leaders.
14. Inspire and support the work of the various ministries through attending their meetings and offering constructive input.
15. Create new avenues for reaching people.
16. Work closely with the Pastor and the chairperson of the Educational Ministry to develop and implement long-range plans.
17. Design and implement a Disciplining Ministry.
18. Promote good public relations within the congregation and community.
19. Keep abreast of new trends in Christian Education.
20. Maintain up-to-date information on available Christian Education resources.
21. Supervise educational staff.

22. Work as team member with paid and unpaid staff.
23. Serve as teacher of teachers and trainer of trainers.
24. Secure teaching equipment and resources.
2 5. Maintain current library resources and media equipment.
26. Counsel with Ministry leaders and others with special problems, needs, or concerns.
27. Be available for confidential consultations, the sharing of successes, and the offering of encouragement.
28. Committed and dedicated to personal spiritual growth as well as the spiritual growth of others.

Disciplining Ministry

Scriptural Basis: Matt. 28:16–20

In the Great Commission, Jesus commands us to GO, TEACH, BAPTIZE. When new members are added to the church, it is imperative that we be faithful to this community by integrating them into the Body of Christ so that spiritual growth can take place. To give the new Christian, new member, restored member, or any member the best possible start as they begin and/or continue in their faith journey toward spiritual maturity. The sessions are intended to assist persons in becoming integrated into their new life in Christ and the local church body. Thus, through the discipline process, the new member is moved from membership to disciple to discipline.

Goals

1. To provide support and encouragement to each new member.
2. To integrate new members into the total life of the church.

Objectives

1. Identify and apply what it means to be a disciple of Jesus Christ.
2. Execute their privileges and responsibilities as a church member.
3. Participate fully in Church School, Bible Study, and other church ministries.
4. Exhibit holistic spiritual growth in every aspect of their lives.
5. Move from membership to disciple to discipline.

Leadership Qualities

1. Make spiritual growth a priority by being an active participant in the Church School, Bible Study, other teaching/training opportunities, worship, etc.

2. Remain faithful to God and the assigned task.
3. Maintain and exhibit effective listening and communication skills.
4. Ability to organize.
5. Ability to lead others to Christ.
6. Competent people person who has the ability to relate to persons on various levels and in a variety of situations.

Leadership Responsibilities

1. Work in conjunction with the Pastor, Director/Minister of Christian Education, and the chairperson of Christian Education to organize and implement an effective and holistic discipline process.
2. Coordinate all class sessions and fellowship opportunities.

Media Ministry

Scriptural Basis: Matt. 28:18–20

It is imperative that the church use all available avenues in order to communicate the mind, message, mission, and ministry of Jesus Christ to its congregation and the community.

Goals

1. To make spiritual growth a priority through attendance in Church School, Bible Study, other teaching and training events, worship, etc.
2. To provide media resources and taping, for ministries within the church.

Objectives

1. To provide consultations and taping for other ministries.
2. To distribute tapes to the sick and shut-in, persons living out of town, the unchurched, etc., and to tape worship experiences.
3. To train others how to use media equipment.
4. To work in conjunction with other ministries to carry out the church's mission and ministry.

Leadership Qualities

1. Make spiritual growth a priority by being an active participant in Church School, Bible Study, other teaching and training opportunities, worship, etc.
2. Remain faithful to God and assigned task.
3. Ability to work well with others.

4. Research and organizational skills for coordinating an effective ministry.

Leadership Responsibilities

1. Develop and produce video and audio resources for church ministries.
2. Coordinate taping of services with the Pastor and other ministries.
3. Distribute tapes in a timely fashion.
4. Train persons of all ages to operate media equipment.
5. Purchase and maintain adequate equipment.
6. Become familiar with the overall mission and ministry of the church and how these impact the direction of media ministry.

THE CHURCH FOR CHRIST

"I appeal to you, brethren, by the name of our Lord Jesus Christ, that all of you agree and that there be no dissensions among you, but that you be united in the same mind and the same judgment" (1 Cori. 1:10).

Paul's letter to the Corinthians puts us in touch with the actual life of a particular local church around the middle of the first century. We get a sense of history—a sense of understanding the Christian church over the years. And we get a better understanding of the preacher's response to their words and actions. I am also drawn to this letter because it is so point-blank, straight-up, and so straight-forward, so descriptive, and down to earth in its focus. This letter deals with Christian doctrine and Christian ethics. It sets forth how we ought to live and how we ought to act as Christians. A lot of us probably don't really know how we should live on a day-to-day basis, and maybe the reason some of us act the way we do is because we don't know the difference between "is" and "ought." You see, Paul knew what was going on in the Corinthian Church. He knew what the deal was. But the difference between what it was (or what it is) and what it ought to have been was like the difference between night and day.

It had been reported to Paul that in this church there was a great deal of quarreling among the people. They were a church, but there was little understanding of Christian teaching because somehow they didn't relate being a Christian to being kind and honest; they, by some strange understanding or lack of understanding, didn't relate being a church and practicing Christianity to actually loving one another and doing the right thing.

Paul was concerned about the church at Corinth because the people didn't really love one another which manifested itself in too much dissension, too much discord, too much disunity. They didn't know to whom they belonged. Some folk were saying that they belonged to Paul, others said they belonged to Apollos, others said they belonged to Cephas, and others said they belonged to Jesus Christ. Paul is disturbed—so much so that he says in essence, "You don't belong to me!" As a matter of fact, I am glad I didn't baptize of you except Crispus and Gaius. So you don't belong to me, and even if I would have baptized you, it would not have been in my own name! Certainly, this is no way for Christians to act. The church is not supposed to be a place of quarreling, division and dissension. I appeal to you brethren—in other words, I urgently request of you, I plead with you, I petition you, I pray by the name of our Lord Jesus Christ, that all of you agree and that there be no dissensions among you, but that you be united in the same mind and the same judgment.

What does church unity mean? How do we bring about unity in the church of Jesus Christ? How do we overcome dissension to create a bond of unity in the church, the ecclesia, the called-out people of God?

First, we have to learn to love one another. Love is the unifying principle, the glue that created the bond between people of different experiences and backgrounds. We are not talking about confusing love with sex as so many folk in the church have done. We're not talking about friendship which could be another form of love, because we have some folk in church who are friendly with only a few folk, who usually think and act just like they do. But we are talking about the love of God, the love that crosses social class and educational boundaries. This love is not going to be persuaded to follow the crowd in its wrongness, but will stand up for right regardless. There are some people in the church who are active in organizations and on boards who display the most vicious and mean behaviors that one would ever witness. Folk have even cursed or used the name of God in vain against another brother or sister, and others have gotten so angry as to provoke a fight even in the church. Is this love? This is certainly no way for Christians to act. This is no way for the church, the called-out people of God to be acting. Jesus says when someone slaps you on the one side, turn the other cheek, or if someone takes your shirt, give them your coat also. This is the ethics of Jesus Christ, not all this foolishness, this quarreling as was taking place in Corinth. But we are to love each other as Christ loved the church. This is what church unity is all about.

If we are to have unity in the church, we need to know to whom we belong. Paul was faced with a church, a local congregation, that was messed up and mixed up, so much so that they were all going in different directions. Some folk were over here in their little group. They were folk who said they belonged to Paul. Let's call them the "Paulites." They were intrigued by Paul. They liked him; he had really turned them on and they were not going to support or work with anyone else because they belonged to Paul. Maybe they had been in the crowed when he first preached at Corinth, or maybe some of their relatives liked him or they just felt loyal to him because they knew of his past life or were impressed with his transformation. For some strange reason, this group of folk said they belonged to Paul. Maybe they were the folk who had also gone to the University of Tarsus and this was like the alumni club—whatever the situation, they belonged to Paul.

Now we also have another group. The folk in this group said they belonged to Apollos. He was probably drawn into Paul's presence "through the good offices of Prisca." In the Book of Acts 18:24, he is described as an Alexandrian Jew. He was eloquent and well versed in the Scriptures; he was fervent in spirit, an accurate speaker and teacher on the things concerning Jesus. Apollos. They liked the way he talked—the way the words flowed fluently and flawlessly from his lips. They belonged to him because he was smooth and smart, eloquent, and erudite. So this group formed as loyalists to Apollos.

There was yet another group that belonged to Cephas or Petros, or Peter, the one whom Jesus called Simon Barjona or Simon, the son of John (cf. Matt. 16:17). Some folk said they belonged to him maybe because he was bold and strong, or maybe because he was outspoken or they knew that he was close to Jesus—whatever the reason, there were those who pledged allegiance to Cephas.

In addition to these groups, there was still another who said they belonged to Jesus Christ. Out of the entire church, there was just a small number that claimed Christ as the focus of their devotion. Jesus Christ, the very foundation of the church, had the allegiance of only a small percentage of the people in this Corinthian Church. The majority of them belonged to everybody else except Jesus. This divided loyalty upset Paul and he asked, "Is Christ divided? Was Paul crucified for you? Or were you baptized in the name of Paul?"

Today, we ask the same thing. To whom do you belong? We are not first a member of any board, or auxiliary. How can one belong to the choir, usher board or anything else and not belong first of all to Jesus Christ? One can't be in the local church and belong to Paul or Apollos or Cephas. One can't be divided in one's faith and loyalty. No! One must know to whom one belongs! We have to first belong to Jesus Christ if there is going to be unity in the church.

Jesus Christ is the unifying force within the Christian church because He didn't die for one. He died for all, and through Him we are saved.

Notes

CHAPTER 1

1. Carter G. Woodson, *The Mis-education of the Negro*.

CHAPTER 2

1. Albert M. Wells Jr., ed., *Inspiring Quotations: Contemporary and Classical* (Nashville: Thomas Nelson, 1988), p. 50.
2. Karl Barth, *Church Dogmatics: The Doctrine of God*, Vol. II, Part 2 (Edinburgh: T&T Clark, 1957), p. 306.
3. Ibid., p. 347.
4. Ibid., p. 351.
5. Plato, *Five Dialogues,* The Euthyphro, p. 22.
6. Ibid., p. 9.
7. Aristotle, *The Metaphysics,* Book Alpha 1 (New York: Penguin, 1998), p. 5.
8. Ibid., p. 3.
9. Ibid., p. 5.
10. Paul Tillich, *The Courage to Be* (New Haven: Yale University Press), p. 4.
11. Ibid., p. 32.
12. Ibid., p. 165.
13. Riggins R. Earl Jr., *Dark Symbols, Obscure Signs: God, Self, and Community in the Slave Mind* (Maryknoll, NY: Orbis Books, 1993), p. 169.
14. Ibid., p. 170.
15. John F. Kennedy, *Profiles in Courage* (New York: Harper & Brothers, 1956), pp. ix–x.
16. J. Philip Wogaman, *Christian Moral Judgement* (Louisville, KY: Westminster/John Knox Press, 1989), p. 29.

17. Ibid., pp. 29–30.

18. Samuel K. Roberts, *In the Path of Virtue: The African American Moral Tradition* (Cleveland, OH: Pilgrim Press, 1999), p. 41.

19. Ibid., p. 65.

20. Ibid., p. 66

21. Kennedy, *Profiles in Courage,* p. 36.

22. Ibid., p. 46.

23. Ibid., p. 48

24. Ibid., p. 51

25. Allan A. Hunter, *Courage in Both Hands* (Los Angeles: New Century Foundation Press, n.d.), p. 5.

26. Ibid., p. 7.

27. Mark Hyman, *Blacks Who Died for Jesus: A History Book* (Nashville: Winston-Derek Publishers, 1988), p. 8.

28. Ibid., p. 10.

29. Ibid., p. 50.

30. Ibid.

31. Ibid.

32. Quinton Hosford Dixie and Cornell West, eds., *The Courage to Hope: From Black Suffering to Human Redemption* (Boston: Beacon Press, 1999), p. 9.

33. Kwame Ture and Charles V. Hamilton, *Black Power: The Politics of Liberation in America* (New York: Vintage Books, 1992), p. 139.

34. David J. Garrow, ed., *The Montgomery Bus Boycott and the Woman Who Started It: The Memoir of Jo Ann Gibson Robinson* (Knoxville: The University of Tennessee Press, 1987), p. 43.

35. Ibid., p. 168.

36. Adam Fairclough, *Martin Luther King Jr.* (Athens: University of Georgia Press, 1995), p. 1.

37. Ibid., p. 20.

38. Ibid., p. 24.

39. Ibid., p. 25.

40. Ibid., p. 33.

41. Ibid., p. 54.

42. Ibid., p. 72.

43. Ibid.

44. Ibid., pp. 85–86.

45. Ibid., p. sg.

46. Ibid., p. 122.

47. Kareem Abdul-Jabbar and Alan Steinberg, *Black Profiles in Courage* (New York: William Morrow and Company, 1996), p. 73.

48. Ibid., p. 77.

49. Ibid., p. 78.

50. Ibid., p. 82.

51. Ibid.

52. Ibid., p. 86.

53. Ibid., p. 90.

54. Sarah H. Bradford, *Scenes in the Life of Harriet Tubman* (New York: Books for Libraries Press, 1971), p. 1.

55. Ibid., p. 7.

56. Ibid., p. 22.

57. Ibid., pp. 22–23.

58. Ibid., p. 38.

59. Carleton Mabee with Susan Mabee Newhouse, *Sojourner Truth: Slave, Prophet, Legend* (New York: New York University Press, 1993), p. 12.

60. Ibid., p. 44.

61. Ibid., p. 51.

62. Ibid., p. 55.

63. Bruce M. Metzger and Roland E. Murphy, eds., *The New Oxford Annotated Bible with the Apocryphal/Deuterocanonical Books* (New York: Oxford University Press, 1994), p. 271–OT.

64. Ibid., pp. 274–OT.

65. Ibid., pp. 617–OT.

CHAPTER 3

1. Carter G. Woodson, *The History of the Negro Church* (Washington, D.C., The Associated Publishers, 1945), pp. 14–15.

2. Ibid., p. 15.

3. Albert J. Raboteau, *Slave Religion: The Invisible Institution in the Antebellum South* (New York: Oxford University Press, 1978), p. 290.

4. Leroy Fitts, *A History of Black Baptists* (Nashville: Broadman Press, 1985), p. 222.

5. Ibid., p. 226.

6. Francis M. Dubose, *How Churches Grow in an Urban World* (Nashville: Broadman Press, 1978), p. 81.

7. Gayraud S. Wilmore, *Black Religion and Black Radicalism* (New York: Doubleday, 1973), p. 89.

8. Milo Brekke, Merton Strommen, and Dorothy Williams, *Ten Faces of Ministry* (Minneapolis: Augsburg Publishing House, 1979), p. 9.

9. E. Franklin Frazier, *The Negro Church in America* (New York: Schoken Books, 1974), p. 36

10. Ibid., p. 36

11. Ibid., p. 45

12. Ibid., p. 48

13. Ibid., p. 86

14. C. Eric Lincoln, *The Black Church Since Frazier* (New York: Schoken Books, 1974), p. 113

CHAPTER 4

1. Council on Interracial Books for Children, *Fact Sheets on Institutional Racism* (New York: Council on Interracial Books for Children, 1984), p. 27.

2. Ibid.

3. Steve Suitts, *Patterns of Poverty: A Special Report of the Southern Regional Council* (Atlanta: Southern Regional Council, 1984), p. 7.

4. Cf. *Ministry in America*, David Schuller, Merton Strommen, Milo Brekke, eds. Chapter 5 lists the sixty-four core clusters and their profiles. The present writer draws extensively from these data and uses the same clusters in an effort to contrast the political and the religious. Also, descriptions of the core clusters are extracted from the book. Because these authors have already done the statistical tests that resulted in the core clusters, the present writer did not have to repeat that process.

5. Ibid., p. 104f.

6. The original survey asked respondents to rate the items using the following seven-item scale: Highly Important, Quite Important, Somewhat Important, Undesirable, Detrimental, Reject Item, and Does Not Apply. For purposes of explanation, the writer has combined the seven categories to form three new categories: Important, Undesirable, and No Opinion.

7. Lawrence J. Peter and Raymond Hull, *The Peter Principle* (New York: William Morrow and Company, 1969), pp. 2, 4.

8. Richard J. Stillman II, *Public Administration: Concepts and Cases* (Boston: Houghton Mifflin Company, 1980), p. 112.

9. Martin Luther King Jr., *Why We Can't Wait* (New York: Harper and Row, 1964), pp. 78–79.

10. Katherine Bradbury et al., *Urban Decline and the Future of American Cities* (Washington, D.C.: Brookings Institution, 1982), p. 22.

11. Jill Nelson, "Out of Work: The People Behind the Statistics," *Black Enterprise* (May 1982), p. 64.

12. Aaron Wildavsky, *Speak the Truth to Power: The Art and Craft of Policy Analysis* (Boston: Little, Brown, 1979), p. 254.

13. Ibid., p. 258.

14. Alan Pifer, *Black Progress: Achievement, Failure and an Uncertain Future* (New York: Carnegie Corporation, 1977), p. 9.

15. Ibid., p. 11.

16. Sar A. Levitan and Isaac Shapiro, *Working But Poor* (Baltimore: The Johns Hopkins University Press, 1987) p. 3

17. George Gilder, *Wealth and Poverty* (New York: Basic Books, 1981) p. 128

18. Luke 4:18f

19. See for example, Bertrand Russell, *A History of Western Philosphy* (New York: Simon and Schuster, 1972).

CHAPTER 5

1. Gayraud Wilmore's *Black Religion and Black Radicalism* explains the African and American connections that influenced Black religious practices in America. The melding of the two traditions has contributed to the uniqueness of the Black church experience. For a more detailed analysis, see the first three chapters.

2. *New American Standard Bible,* 1 Cor. 14:5–6.

3. Duncan Timms, *The Urban Mosaic: Towards a Theory of Residential Differentiation* (Cambridge: The University Press, 1971), p. 211.

4. Christopher Lasch, *The Culture of Narcissism: American Life in an Age of Diminishing Expectations* (New York: W. W. Norton, 1979), p. 29.

5. Ibid., p. 22.

6. Reinhold Niebuhr, *The Nature and Destiny of Man*, vol. I (New York: Charles Scribner's Sons, 1941), p. 182.

7. Ibid., p. 182.

8. Paul Tillich, *The Courage to Be* (New Haven: Yale University Press, 1952), p. 32.

9. Ibid., p. 36.

10. For a more comprehensive view, see Ira Glasser's article, "Racism Is Alive and Well and Living in Disguise," *Christianity and Crisis* (March 31, 1981).

11. Lenneal Henderson Jr., "Beyond Equity: The Future of Minorities in Urban Management," *Public Management* (June 1982), p. 2.

12. Ibid., p. 2.

13. Peter Paris, *The Social Teaching of the Black Church* (Philadelphia: Fortress Press, 1985), p. 28.

CHAPTER 6

1. Suitts, *Patterns of Poverty: A Special Report of the Southern Regional Council,* p. 12.

2. Hart M. Nelson, Raytha L. Yokley, and Anne K. Nelson, eds., *The Black Church in America* (New York: Basic Books, 1971), p. 303.

3. Ibid., p. 307.

4. David R. Morgan, *Managing Urban America* (North Scituate, MA: Duxbury Press, 1979), p. 12.

5. Ibid., p. 15.

CHAPTER 7

1. Poem written for the NAACP by Langston Hughes (April 1, 1964). unpublished.

2. Affirmative Action for the purpose of this paper is defined as "public or private policies or programs that seek to provide opportunities or other benefits to people on the basis of, among other things, their membership in a specified group or groups." See Jones, James Jr., *The Origins of Affirmative Action* (Davis, CA: University of California at Davis, 1988), pp. 383, 388.

3. Harry Edwards, "The Annual John Randolph Tucker Lecture: The Future of Affirmative Action in Employment," *Washington & Lee Law Review* 44 (1987), pp. 763, 763–764.

4. Ibid, p. 764.

5. *Good News Bible* (New York, American Bible Society: 1993), p. 1093.

6. Hugo Zorrilla, *The Good News of Justice: Share the Gospel: Live Justly,* (Scottsdale, PA.: Herald Press, 1988), p. 11–13

7. *Good News Bible*, p. 1362–63.

8. Ibid.

9. *Good News Bible*, p. 1872.

10. Ibid, p. 974.

11. Ibid, pp. 958–59.

12. Ibid, pp. 2109–10.

13. Paul Spickard, "Why I Believe in Affirmative Action," in *Racial Preference and Racial Justice: The New Affirmative Action Controversy,* Russell Neieli, ed. (Washington, D.C.: Ethics and Public Policy Center, 1991), pp. 105–6.

14. W. E. B. Du Bois, *The Suppression of the African Slave Trade in the United States of America: 1638–1870* (Baton Rouge: Louisiana State University Press, 1965), pp. 48–49; United States Commission on Civil Rights, "Civil Rights: A National, Not a Special Interest. A Statement of the United States Commission on Civil Rights" (Washington, D.C.: United States Commission on Civil Rights, June 25, 1981), p. 1.

15. Lerone Bennet Jr., *The Shaping of Black America: The Struggles and Triumphs of African Americans, 1619 to the 1900s* (New York: Penguin Books, 1993) pp. 63, 65–202.

16. "Civil Rights: A National, Not a Special Interest," p. 2.

17. Jones, "The Origins of Affirmative Action," p. 388.

18. Ibid, p. 383.

19. Pub. L. No. 89–110, 79 Stat. 437 (1965) as amended by Pub. L.

20. "Civil Rights: A National, Not a Special Interest," pp. 3–8.

21. Ibid., pp. 7–9, 120–122.

22. Bennet, *The Shaping of Black America,* pp. 248–68.

23. U.S. 537 (1896); "Civil Rights: A National, Not a Special Interest," pp. 10–11.

24. Bennet, *The Shaping of Black America*, pp. 248–268.

25. 163 U.S. 537 (1896); "Civil Rights: A National, Not A Special Interest," pp. 10–11.

26. Merrick T. Rossein. *Employment Discrimination: Law and Litigation*, Vol. 1. (Deerfield, IL: Clark, Boardman, Callaghan, 1995), pp. 1–18.

27. U.S. 483 (1954); "Civil Rights: A National, Not A Special Interest," p. 11.

28. Congressional Record 6547–50 (1964); "Remarks of Senator Hubert Humphrey," *110 Congressional Record* (1964), pp. 6547–50; Rossein, *Employment Discrimination*, footnote 55, pp. 1–23.

29. Lyndon B. Johnson, "To Fulfill These Rights," commencement address at Howard University (Public Papers 635, 638, June 4, 1964).

30. Ibid, p. 638; *The Shaping of Black America*, p. 278.

31. Charles D. Lowery and John Marszalek, eds., *Encyclopedia of African American Rights: From Emancipation to Present* (New York: Greenwood Press, 1992) p. 4.

32. Rossein, *Employment Discrimination*, pp. 1–18.

33. Pub. L. No. 88–352, 78 Stat. 241 (codified as amended at 42 U.S.C. Section 2000a—2000b (1982)).

34. Code of Federal Regulations 339 (1964–comp.), p. 54.

35. E. D. R. 358 (March 22, 1995).

36. James P. Smith and Finis R. Welch, "Closing the Gap: Forty Years of Economic Progress for Blacks" in *Racial Preference and Justice: The New Affirmative Action Controversy*, pp. 499, 500–01.

37. U.S. 395–97 (1978); "Civil Rights, A National, Not a Special Interest," p. 91.

38. John Jacobs, "Black America, 1989: An Overview," in *The State of Black America* (Washington, D.C.: National Urban League 1990), pp. 1, 5–6.

39. E. D. R. 336 (22 March 1995); 4 E. D. R. 365 (29 March 1995).

40. E. D. R. 365 (29 March 1995).

41. "Civil Rights: A National, Not a Special Interest," 1, pp. 121–122.

42. E. D. R. 325 (29 March 1995).

43. E. D. R. 284 (8 March 1995).

44. Cornel West, Preface to *Race Matters* (Boston: Beacon Press, 1993).

45. Glenn R. Negley, "Justice," in *Collier's Encyclopedia*, Vol. 13 (New York: PF. Collier Inc., 1993).

46. Ibid.

47. Ibid.

48. Ibid.

49. C. Eric Lincoln, "Beyond Bakke, Weber, and Fullilove: Peace from Our Sins—A Commentary on Affirmative Action," *Soundings* (Winter 1980), p. 361–380.

50. Philip Green, "Guarding the Ramparts of Privilege: The New Individualism, Christianity, and Crisis (30 March 1981), pp. 74–81.

51. D. J. Richards, ed., *Seminar Reading on Justice and Society* (New York: Aspen Institute of Humanistic Studies 1980); also see H. L. A. Hart's book *The Concept of Law* and John Rawls's book, *A Theory of Justice* for more details.

52. Ibid., p. 2.

53. Ibid., p. 37.

54. Birger Gerhardssno, *The Ethics of the Bible* (Philadelphia: Fortress Press, 1981).

55. Ibid., p. 12.

CHAPTER 8

1. H. Richard Niebuhr, *Christ and Culture* (New York: Harper and Row Publisher, 1951) p. 46

2. See Immanuel Kant, *Religion Within the Limits of Reason*

3. Anselm of Canterbury, The Major Work ( ) p. 87

4. Ibid., p. 3

5. Ibid., p. 5

6. Ibid., p. 50

7. Kant, p. 51

8. Cf. Reinhold Niebuhr, *The Nature and Destiny of Man* and Paul Ricouer, *The Symbolism of Evil*.

9. Ibid., p. 54

10. Ibid., p. 55

11. Ibid., p. 56

12. Ibid., p. 61

13. Ibid., p. 85

14. Ibid., p. 88

15. Ibid., p. 89

16. Ibid., p. 92

17. Ibid., p. 93
18. Ibid., p. 140
19. Ibid.
20. Ibid., p. 141
21. Ibid., p. 144
22. Ibid., p. 140
23. Ibid., pp. 142–143
24. Ibid., p. 143
25. Ibid., p. 145
26. Ibid.
27. Ibid., p. 148
28. Ibid., p. 151
29. Ibid., p. 152
30. Ibid., p. 3
31. This entire section is the result of collaboration with a committee of members of the Second Baptist Church, Richmond, VA. The individuals shall remain nameless; however, I extend to them thanks for their input. Moreover, some of this information may have been obtained from unknown sources.

Index

About the Author

James Henry Harris is professor of pastoral theology and homiletics in the Graduate School of Theology, Virginia Union University, and Senior Pastor at Second Baptist Church, both in Richmond, Virginia. He is the author of *Black Ministers and Laity in the Urban Church* (1987), *Pastoral Theology* (1991), and *Preaching Liberation* (1996). He was a 1996 Henry Luce III fellow in theology and recently a Citizen Scholar in theology, ethics, and culture at the University of Virginia.